VOLUME 1

CRITICAL REFLECTIONS ON WOMEN, FAMILY, CRIME AND JUSTICE

Edited by
Isla Masson, Lucy Baldwin and Natalie Booth

P

First published in Great Britain in 2021 by

Policy Press, an imprint of
Bristol University Press
University of Bristol
1-9 Old Park Hill
Bristol
BS2 8BB
UK
t: +44 (0)117 954 5940
e: bup-info@bristol.ac.uk

Details of international sales and distribution partners are available at
policy.bristoluniversitypress.co.uk

British Library Cataloguing in Publication Data
A catalogue record for this book is available from the British Library

ISBN 978-1-4473-5868-8 hardcover
ISBN 978-1-4473-5869-5 paperback
ISBN 978-1-4473-5867-1 ePub
ISBN 978-1-4473-5870-1 ePdf

Cover design: Clifford Hayes
Front cover image: Ed Barrett

Contents

List of figures

Notes on the contributors

Alexandria Bradley is a former prison addiction practitioner, who specialises in trauma-responsive practice. She is currently undertaking an examination of the implementation of trauma-informed practice across the UK prison service. Her research explores the impact of trauma-responsive working within the criminal justice system. Alexandria is a lecturer at Leeds Beckett University and co-leader of an innovative prison–university partnership to support higher education within a long term and high security male prison.

Anna Jones is a senior lecturer in Education at London South Bank University (LSBU), where she is the Course Director for the BA (Hons) Education Studies degree and teaches and supervises trainee teachers on the PGCE primary course. Anna is also a co-convenor of the LSBU Education for Social Justice Research Group and was a co-facilitator in two Learning Together projects, which brought together students from LSBU, HMP Pentonville and HMP Brixton. Her research interests focus on the educational experiences of vulnerable pupils, including looked after children, children who have been excluded from mainstream schools and/or those at risk of exclusion and children who experience poor mental health and trauma.

Anna Kotova is a lecturer in Criminology at the University of Birmingham. Her work focuses on the experiences of families of people in prison and the interpersonal relationships of men and women in prison. She has conducted research on the experiences of partners of men serving long sentences and the experiences of men with sexual offences and histories of sexual abuse serving their sentences in a therapeutic community. She has been the recipient of the British Academy's Rising Star Engagement Award.

Erin Power is a PhD candidate and graduate teaching assistant at Edge Hill University, where she teaches on BSc and MSc modules including: Women, Girls and Offending; and the Social and Economic Contexts of Crime. Her PhD research is concerned with experiences of care during prison theatre in a neoliberal context. Erin also works as a freelance prison theatre facilitator and as has previously held roles including Groupwork Quality and Development Officer and Women's Groupwork Coordinator for the Prison Advice and Care Trust (Pact).

Her research interests include theatre and practice, care and care aesthetics, neoliberalism and feminism.

Isla Masson is a lecturer in Criminology at the University of Leicester, where she is also MSc Course Convenor. Her research interests predominantly lie in women in the criminal justice system, motherhood, incarceration and restorative justice. Her book *Incarcerating Motherhood* (Routledge, 2019) was based on her doctoral research, which explored the longevity of short terms of incarceration on mothers. She currently volunteers with the Independent Monitoring Board at HMP Onley and is a Trustee at The Boaz Project, which is a therapeutic work environment for adults with learning difficulties.

Jenny Earle previously led the Prison Reform Trust's Transforming Lives programme, UK, to reduce women's imprisonment. Among other roles, prior to that Jenny was a senior legal policy analyst at the Equality and Human Rights Commission.

Kirsty Day is Head of Recovery Services at the Nelson Trust. She is a fellow of the Griffins Society and, in 2015, she conducted a nuanced research project to investigate the barriers or facilitators of disclosure for sex working women in residential drug treatment. Her research findings and commitment led to the creation of the trauma-specific intervention The Griffin Programme. Kirsty is a trauma-responsive practitioner, who also specialises in developing and facilitating inspiring and bespoke training programmes for practitioners within the criminal justice system.

Lucy Baldwin is a senior lecturer at De Montfort University. She is a qualified social worker and probation officer with over 30 years' experience in criminal and social justice. Her doctoral and additional research focuses on maternal imprisonment and its impact on mothers and their children. Her edited collection *Mothering Justice* (Waterside Press, 2015) was the first whole book in the UK to take motherhood and criminal justice as its focus. She is a passionate advocate for penal and sentencing reform. She is also an active trustee for Children Heard and Seen, a national charity supporting children with a parent in prison.

Michaela Booth is a Longford Trust scholar with research interests in lived experience leadership, attribution and human capital. Since leaving prison herself, Michaela has received a first class degree in applied criminology, is currently studying for her Masters, and is leading user involvement across Care UK's Health in Justice division. Michaela is dedicated to enhancing the efficiency and effectiveness of utilising lived experience in research and across the criminal justice sector, as well as ensuring that reciprocity, equity and inclusion underpin the frameworks driving the lived experience movement forward.

Natalie Booth is a senior lecturer at Bath Spa University. Her research seeks to understand how prison is experienced by family and friends of people incarcerated in England and Wales. Having explored 'maternal imprisonment and family life' during her doctorate, she authored a book revealing the previously untold experiences of those charged with the responsibility of looking after children of female prisoners 'from the caregivers' perspectives'. Her written work also contributes to our understanding about the maintenance of relationships and family contact during imprisonment, mothers and women in prison, and developments in penal policy relating to women and families.

Nicola Harding is a lecturer in Criminology at Lancaster University. She has previously worked at Leeds Trinity University and Manchester Metropolitan University, where she completed her PhD. Her PhD examined women's experiences of punishment, with subsequent research projects focusing on innovation in the criminal justice system and security sector. Nicola's broad research interests include women and social control, critical approaches to community punishment, understanding lived experiences of the criminal justice system, alongside creative forms of qualitative research.

Paula Harriott is a former prisoner and social change activist. Reflecting on lived experience, power, privilege and knowledge equity, she leads the Prisoner Policy Network at the Prison Reform Trust in her role as Head of Prisoner Engagement. Since her release from prison in 2008, she has dedicated her professional working life to creating space and opportunity for prisoners and those in contact with the criminal justice system to play a leadership role in creating innovative solutions to entrenched social issues, both in prison and beyond the walls. Recent publications are *Voicelessness: A Call to Action* (University of Ottawa Press, 2019) and *All our Justice* (Routledge, 2020).

Rose Mahon is Head of Excellence and Development at the Nelson Trust and a nationally recognised practitioner for her inspirational work. Rose has over two decades of experience working within residential services and community services for women. In 2017, she was named Criminal Justice Champion at the prestigious Howard League for Penal Reform's Community Awards, to recognise her dedication to supporting women to recover. She is passionate about embedding trauma-responsive approaches within women's rehabilitation.

Zinthiya Ganeshpanchan is Founder and CEO of the award-winning Zinthiya Trust, a charity supporting women and girls to be free from violence and poverty. She has over 15 years of experience working with women and girls fleeing gender-based violence, including in conflict settings. She is a current fellow of the Winston Churchill Memorial Trust carrying out research on community intervention models to prevent violence against women and girls in Nepal and Sri Lanka. She is also a Fellow (Gender) of the Clore Social Leadership Foundation.

Acknowledgements

To those that we love, including early arrivals, know that we love and appreciate you more than anything! On this occasion we'd like to thank the contributors to this edited collection, their participants, their service-users/clients, and their supporters for helping us to draw attention to their work, research, ideas, and experiences. Without them, this book would not be possible.

Isla, Lucy and Natalie

Foreword: critical reflections from the Women, Family, Crime and Justice network

I was privileged to participate in the inaugural conference that launched the Women, Family, Crime, and Justice network. It was a dynamic and diverse gathering, determined not only to share knowledge and insights in an inclusive way, but also to provide opportunities for cross-fertilisation between research, personal experience, policy and practice.

Mainstream discussions of crime and punishment rarely distinguish between women and men. This renders women invisible, marginalised as a small minority within a heavily male-dominated justice system. It has taken a long time for the criminal justice system in particular to understand that relationships are a significant 'criminogenic risk factor' for women, because they are such a strong protective factor for men. When men are sent to prison, women keep the home fires burning, visit them in prison, care for their children and provide essential support. The reverse is not true. Meanwhile, women with criminal convictions are regarded as doubly deviant – not only have they broken the law, but they have also offended against feminine stereotypes, especially if they are mothers.

This is an important book, contributing to an important project – a growing body of literature by, for and about women whose circumstances and constrained choices have conspired to make them 'a female offender'. I especially welcome the thematic focus on stigma and shame, as that is an under-researched dimension of the gendered impacts of punishment, one that needs greater recognition.

Despite growing political consensus about the futility of short-term imprisonment, it remains the case that nearly three quarters of women sentenced to prison are given sentences of less than 12 months, overwhelmingly for non-violent offences. The disregard for children when a mother is imprisoned (despite government claims that children's best interests are at the heart of all decision making) is matched by institutional disregard for the impacts on women themselves of forcible separation from their children.

The UK has one of the highest rates of women's imprisonment in Western Europe. It is well evidenced that high rates of imprisonment are closely associated with high levels of inequality, and it is salutary to note that in 2019 the UK fell six places in the global rankings of gender inequality, from an ignoble 15th place to 21st place (Global Gender Gap Report, 2020).

During my years at the Prison Reform Trust leading the Transforming Lives programme to reduce women's imprisonment, I have been steeped in the travesties of justice that too many women experience. While the statistical data tells a story – about the disproportionate punishment routinely meted out to women for minor offences – it certainly does not tell the *whole* story. Without the work of feminist researchers, practitioners, activists and criminologists, as represented in this collection, we could not make sense of it. Through their critical reflections, these contributors help us understand the many layers of systems failure, double standards and disadvantage that result in women's criminalisation, while being clear that the point is to achieve change.

This is not only an insightful book, but also a rallying cry – a call to action to transform the justice system, so that it delivers for all women.

Jenny Earle
Transforming Lives Programme Director,
Prison Reform Trust (2012–20)

1

Starting the conversation: an introduction to the Women, Family, Crime and Justice network

Isla Masson, Natalie Booth and Lucy Baldwin

Introduction

> 'There can be few topics that have been so exhaustively researched to such little practical effect as the plight of women in the criminal justice system.' (Corston, 2007, p 16)

A significant amount of attention has been paid to the challenges facing women in the criminal justice system (CJS) and, more recently, towards families affected by imprisonment. While research and policy interest in these overlapping areas is evident, it is disheartening to say that much-needed change has been slow to be actualised. It often feels as if we are going round in circles.

The three editors of this collection have aired concerns about the ineffectual 'promise' of change following the publication of the Female Offender Strategy by the Ministry of Justice (MoJ) in England and Wales in 2018 (Booth et al, 2018). While our concerns remain as strong today as they did at the time of writing that piece, it is clear to us that many of the problems lie with the social injustices that comprise our neoliberal[1] and patriarchal[2] society. Repeatedly, issues pertaining to housing, education, poverty, mental health, addiction and abuse are identified as factors constituting the inadequate social circumstances that women and families in contact with the CJS have had to negotiate, often throughout their lives. Therefore, in spite of the ever-growing body of evidence within these areas, sadly significant social injustices persist.

Fortunately, continually challenging these injustices is the vital work of researchers, academics, activists and practitioners. Their strong commitment for change intends to illuminate, respond and reduce, and ideally remove, damaging issues for women and families affected by the CJS. Acknowledging this, the Women, Family, Crime and Justice (WFCJ) research network was launched by the editors in April 2018 to provide a collaborative space to bring together like-minded people from research, practice and academia, to critically discuss, disseminate and address some of these injustices.

Convening the WFCJ network

Prior to our initial meeting, the three editors were each working in related fields, and were pleased to realise the overlap in research interests; bonding over a passion to make a difference. Due to structural pressures in higher education prioritising competition and novelty over collaboration, we recognised that often those with similar research interests feel they must compete with each other, and sometimes tread on each other, rather than working together for the benefit of WFCJ-related areas. Our hope for the network, and for this edited collection, is to provide opportunities that allow for a louder conversation and critical reflections that bring about meaningful change. The network's primary objectives are to facilitate and support staff, students, policy makers, external agencies and the public, in addressing issues relating to women, families, crime and social justice. We seek to achieve this via four core areas of activity:

- research and policy impact;
- knowledge transfer;
- interdisciplinary teaching and programme development;
- dissemination and publication.

Research and policy impact

We feel very strongly about the importance of the relationship between research, practice and policy development. Through the network, it is our intention to conduct, facilitate and discuss research and practice that make a real difference to the lived experiences of women and families in contact with the CJS. For us, this network is about providing a platform for a variety of speakers to share their experiences and research. In doing so, we encourage an open dialogue about challenges faced by women and families affected by the CJS. This can sometimes include more uncomfortable discussions about the way in which 'evidence' is collected, disseminated and/or used in policy making. For example, several of the chapters in this edited collection explore the importance of 'voice', encouraging researchers and practitioners to consider the impact of research, such as who benefits from their research. It is important that these discussions are not held in an academic bubble, as for meaningful change to be achieved at policy level, the inclusion of a variety of experience and viewpoints is necessary.

Knowledge transfer

Since the network was established, the WFCJ convenors have delivered regular seminars with a variety of informative and passionate speakers from research, academia and practice, including those with first-hand experience of their CJS. Each of these events has been well attended by a diverse audience, which has encouraged open dialogue and reflections that have had far-reaching consequences for people living, working and studying in related areas of social and criminal justice. In order for us to achieve change, we must build upon each other's work and navigate together the ongoing obstacles faced by women and families affected by the CJS.

The chapters in this edited collection were written as a result of these conversations and reflections, and are authored by people with lived experience, academics, researchers, practitioners and activists. The overarching aim of this book is to enable a wider audience to engage further with these critical reflections, and while we do not necessarily agree on everything, as feminists it is important to listen to all voices and experiences. While our own experiences bring us to different positions on certain WFCJ subjects and the content of individual chapters may not resonate with every reader, it is important that we champion the significant insights produced, and allow a space for varied critical reflections from those working in this field. It is not about having a single voice or opinion, but about listening to and considering the multiplicity of voices.

Interdisciplinary teaching and programme development

We are confident that the network, and this collection, will be of interest to those developing or running programmes in a range of interrelated fields, including (but not limited to) criminology, sociology, social work and social policy. There is relevance for vocational professional qualification courses, to both undergraduate and postgraduate courses, and to practitioners working within and around social and criminal justice areas.

As already mentioned, WFCJ-related areas have been vastly explored in recent years. However, the issues constituting this field require ongoing critical discussion to capture the emerging and ingrained issues that endure owing to lack of positive or actual change. Therefore, the new insights and critical reflections that comprise this edited collection will have synergy with interdisciplinary teaching and learning programmes in England and Wales, and further afield. We hope the reflection points, or questions, at the end of each chapter will aid further critical thinking for teaching and learning purposes as well as self-reflection.

Dissemination and publication

As the WFCJ network seeks to question current, oppressive social and criminal justice approaches, encouraging a questioning of why, as well as how, things require change in order to achieve justice, the work presented is relevant to a wide international audience. It is our aim that the critical reflections that comprise this edited collection are disseminated in a sensitive, accessible and progressive way. Those who have presented thus far at the seminars include early-career researchers, established researchers, academics and practitioners. This, therefore, brings together diverse bodies of evidence and experience, invigorated by new and emerging knowledge and understanding surrounding women, children and families affected by social and criminal justice.

The current collection

This book showcases a variety of research on women, family, crime and social justice, critically examining different experiences and outcomes of our current CJS, mostly in the context of England and Wales. As a whole, the book explores different aspects of the CJS, examining how these vulnerable groups are often ignored, oppressed and repeatedly victimised. Each chapter challenges different aspects of policy and/ or practice, and each contributor tackles a different issue faced by women and/or families, exploring original research and/or their direct engagement with these groups in their frontline work. However, it is important to note that this collection only captures some elements of women, family, crime and social justice; it is not intended to be a comprehensive handbook, but a platform for critical discussions that can be used to inform research activism and positive change.

The editors and many of the contributors are feminist researchers who, by definition, are exploring issues related to women to bring action and change to a very vulnerable and often overlooked population. The contributors are united by a passion to support and cultivate change, and so much of the work undertaken to inform each chapter is bottom-up, service-user led or service-user oriented, and policy driven or policy relevant, with tangible and practical recommendations being offered. We think that each chapter provides a fascinating insight into a gendered aspect of harm within our CJS and wider society, be that relating to, for example, pre-existing trauma, schools and education, or user voice. We invited the chapter contributors to build upon their initial seminar presentation, keeping the conversation current and relevant to the readers. As part of this, authors were asked to include some reflection points, or questions, at the end of their chapter, to encourage the reader to reflect upon their own practice, as well as encouraging the reader to challenge the status quo and taken-for-granted assumptions. Although each chapter can be appreciated as a standalone contribution, there are overarching issues and themes throughout, which have been highlighted when appropriate.

Chapter overview

In Chapter 2, Nicola Harding, an academic, researcher and activist whose research broadly focuses on critical perspectives of crime, deviance and social control, discusses the way in which women who serve a community sentence in a women's centre must successfully navigate a game in order to be deemed a 'success story' by criminal justice practitioners. Harding outlines how 'playing the game' involves women managing their trauma in acceptable ways, as well as displaying appropriate gendered characteristics of desistance. Towards the end of the chapter, Harding demonstrates the feasibility of playing the game through three different experiences, including her own. The combination of lived experience and research makes this chapter an essential read for those interested in the power and gendered dynamics constituting community punishments for women.

Another group of socially and culturally disadvantaged women in the UK are discussed in Chapter 3. Zinthiya Ganeshpanchan, a researcher-practitioner who works to alleviate poverty and abuse with often hard-to-reach groups in Leicester and Leicestershire, along with Isla Masson, articulates the variety of embedded practices that affect women from South Asian communities, and the ways in which women are not able to access appropriate support networks due to this ongoing marginalisation. By including the voices of many affected by these practices, the chapter articulates the harrowing and distressing experiences of people for whom these structural and cultural oppressions are a reality. The chapter provides an important opportunity to better comprehend these lived experiences, although sadly it is clear that despite the tireless work of Ganeshpanchan, and others, we have a long way to go before this oppression is eradicated.

Drawing on a trauma-specific intervention pilot with women with sex-working histories, Chapter 4 highlights the necessary trauma-informed foundations, practices and staff to support healing in this context. Through research with participants and facilitators of the Griffin Programme, Alexandria Bradley (a former Her Majesty's Prison and Probation Service practitioner, who specialises in trauma-informed, responsive and specific practice), Kirsty Day (the Learning and Development Lead at the Nelson Trust, delivering trauma training nationally) and Rose Mahon (a leading national trauma responsive practitioner and the Head of Excellence and Development at the Nelson Trust) articulate the significant transformative experiences and journey that can be achieved. Contributing to our understanding of the necessary context for trauma-informed programmes to thrive, the chapter makes important recommendations, so that lessons can be learned from the good practice captured in this pilot.

In a slightly different way, Chapter 5 provides a comprehensive set of practical recommendations that require action in order to respond to enduring harms that mothers experience as a result of short custodial punishments. Isla Masson, an academic whose research focuses primarily on women's experiences of incarceration, draws on research directly undertaken with mothers for whom these punishments brought about severe and disproportionate personal, psychological, physical and familial disadvantages. There is a strong need for these proposed interventions to be implemented, if we are to have a genuine chance of responding to the considerable failings found in both social and criminal justice practices and policies.

Chapter 6 provides new insights about family engagement services in prisons, in which the reader is invited to think critically about the purpose, positionality and problems that surround its current operations. Erin Power illuminates the complexities and contradictions of this work within the current neoliberal social context, drawing on research, policy, theory and personal experience of being a family worker in a female prison in England. The detailed analysis demonstrates the precarity of this work, despite it being vital to many affected by imprisonment, which makes it an important contribution to our understanding of the constrained ways in which prison-based family work can operate.

Reviewing the operations of a different social institution, Chapter 7 critically explores the challenges and opportunities of schools in supporting children affected by imprisonment. Anna Jones, an education academic and teaching practitioner, draws on primary research with school leaders from a variety of school settings. The chapter highlights areas of good (and poor) practice, while hammering home some of the local and national barriers to ensuring that all children and families are appropriately supported during these often difficult circumstances. As the reader is encouraged to think critically about the role that schools can perform, important lessons can be learned from the findings of this research.

Chapter 8 proposes practical and innovative ways that researchers working with families (and other stigmatised groups) in contact with the CJS might work collaboratively with organisations and service users to produce ethical and impactful outcomes. Anna Kotova, an academic conducting research with prisoners and their loved ones, draws on findings from her recent policy engagement and impact project to demonstrate the importance of a joined-up approach, if we are to respond effectively to issues of social and criminal justice. As part of this, she critically considers the benefits of utilising creative and non-traditional academic routes to generate and disseminate knowledge, and encourages the reader to also think outside the box.

This argument is similarly found in Chapter 9. Lucy Baldwin, a matricentric feminist criminologist with a social worker and probation officer background, explores how feminist research should – and can – be approached within WFCJ-related areas, and how she has accomplished this in her own work. Through reflexive and candid discussions about her own personal and professional background, she invites the reader to remain critically aware of the relationship between the researcher and the researched, and to thoroughly consider how this intersects with theoretical, methodological and epistemological components of research. It is an excellent example of how in-depth reflexive practices can enhance and aid the research process.

Chapter 10 also invites the reader to reflect critically on research approaches, purposes and practices with women with lived experience of the criminal justice system. Authored by Michaela Booth and Paula Harriott, two user-focused practitioners and activists, the contribution takes the form of a letter to the research community to ask for deeper reflection on the mechanisms of conducting research in related fields. The innovative contents of this final chapter promise to stimulate new thoughts and considerations for readers' own future practices.

Concluding thoughts

We, the editors, feel that important works such as those found in this edited collection deserve to be celebrated as they reflect a number of voices and perspectives, and speak to a diverse audience by shedding light on new developments and new ideas. In doing so, they have far-reaching implications for research, policy and practice. Indeed, the aim of the WFCJ network is to drive change, to prevent us from going round in circles, and it is hoped that this will be both a long-term change and a collaborative endeavour. Therefore, if anyone would like to join the network mailing list for announcements about seminars and future projects, or indeed would like to present their work or ideas at a seminar, please do contact the editors, or follow us on Twitter (@WomenCri1).

Before we hand over to our contributors, we would like to identify one final point. Each of the authors self-identifies as a woman, and has written their chapter in incredibly challenging times. Coronavirus disease (COVID-19) has changed the world and created unprecedented anxiety and grief for many people and communities internationally. We already know that women often carry out the bulk of unpaid labour within the home, even when they are externally employed (Office for National Statistics, 2016), and it would seem that this pandemic has further skewed women's demands and created a further divide (for example, Blundell et al, 2020), and has particularly 'held back' female academics (Matthews, 2020). Many of the contributors, as practitioners and researchers, have continued working with and for vulnerable and often invisible women and families during this time. We are, therefore, even more grateful to these amazing women for honouring their commitment to this project, and hope that you, the reader, enjoy their chapters as much as we enjoyed editing them.

Notes

[1]   And therefore privatisation and reduced public expenditure on social services.
[2]   Where men hold the majority of power.

References

Blundell, R., Joyce, R., Costas Dias, M. and Xu, X. (2020) 'COVID-19 and inequalities'. Available at: https://www.ifs.org.uk/inequality/covid-19-and-inequalities/. Accessed: 12 June 2020.

Booth, N., Masson, I. and Baldwin, L. (2018) 'Promises, promises: can the Female Offender Strategy deliver?', *Probation Journal*, 65(4): 429–38.

Corston, Baroness J. (2007) *The Corston Report: A Review of Women with Particular Vulnerabilities in the Criminal Justice System*, London: Home Office.

Matthews, D. (2020) 'Pandemic lockdown holding back female academics, data show'. Available at: https://www.timeshighereducation. com/news/pandemic-lockdown-holding-back-female-academics-data-show#. Accessed: 29 June 2020.

Office for National Statistics (2016) 'Women shoulder the responsibility of "unpaid work"'. Available at: https://www. ons.gov.uk/employmentandlabourmarket/peopleinwork/ earningsandworkinghours/articles/womenshouldertheresponsibilit yofunpaidwork/2016-11-10. Accessed: 20 June 2020.

2

Playing the game: women and community punishment

Nicola Harding

Introduction

It perhaps seems frivolous to consider the serious subject of how women experience punishment as simply 'playing a game'. The experiences of criminalised women are varied and complex, often dictated by a woman's intersectional position within society (Clarke and Chadwick, 2017). Yet by grouping together those aspects of criminalised women's experiences that are shared, we can begin to understand how criminalised women's lives are shaped by institutions of social control and structures of punishment. Conceptualising these shared experiences through a boardgame, allows the subjugated experience of navigating community punishment as a criminalised woman to be conveyed to academic researchers, criminal justice practitioners, policy makers and students in ways that are easily understood. By placing knowledge of experiences that are far outside our own realm of understanding into the simplistic framework of a boardgame, we can make what is hidden, visible.

This chapter narrates the findings of a piece of feminist participatory action research (Harding, 2018; Harding, 2020b) completed with criminalised women in the North West of England. Using creative methods such as creative writing, photography (photo voice and photo elicitation) and narrative map making, this research aimed to capture the way in which punishment intersects with women's daily lives. In order to communicate the findings of this research to multiple audiences, a research-informed boardgame was produced that was later used as a tool to communicate women's lived experiences of community punishment to probation practitioners at the 'Women in NAPO conference' in 2018. While the simplicity of a boardgame contrasts with the complexity of criminalised women's experiences, its accessibility can act as a starting point to consider how these experiences can challenge, unsettle and disrupt existing understandings of how criminal justice punishes women and how criminological researchers theorise those at the margins of the criminal justice system – understanding women's navigation of community punishment as playing a rigged game.

Examining criminalised women is not a new endeavour. Heidensohn (1968; 1985; 2012) has highlighted the importance of understanding criminalised women across her long career, while Smart (1977) first called for more attention to be paid to the female experience in the late 1970s. Since then, the multiple works of Carlen (1983; 1985; 1989; 1998) and Carlen and Worrall (2004) have led the way in critically understanding women in prison. Worrall (2008), Worrall and Gelsthorpe (2009), Gelsthorpe and Hedderman (2012) and Gelsthorpe et al (2007) have examined how criminal justice responds to the needs of women both in prison and in the community, while Chadwick and Little (1987), and Clarke and Chadwick (2017) have offered critical understandings of the criminalisation of women. Booth et al (2018) unpicked the 'Female Offender Strategy' (MoJ, 2018). Masson and Österman (2017; and Österman and Masson, 2018) examined alternatives to imprisonment, such as restorative justice and criminalised women, before joining Epstein (2014) and Baldwin and Epstein (2017) in bringing much-needed attention to mothers in the CJS (Masson, 2019). Minson et al (2015) and Minson and Condry (2015) highlighted legal arguments around the sentencing of mothers and the rights of their children.

While this is not a comprehensive review of the contribution of feminist scholars to the understanding of women's experiences of criminalisation, these scholars have produced the corpus of work that critical scholars like myself, Barr (2019), Greenwood (2019) and Elfleet (2018) have then built upon, when examining criminalised women's experiences of community punishment and gender-specific provision. The body of existing work by feminist criminologists underpins this research, by understanding the way in which policy, practice and criminological theory intersect with criminalised women's experiences of simply navigating the world as a woman, such as motherhood, poverty and victimisation.

Methodology

This study brings together feminist and participatory action research to examine the experiences of women subject to community punishment and probation supervision. Thirty-two women took part, with four of the women considered to be criminal justice practitioners (working in various third-sector positions, often within a women's centre), and 28 of the women either currently experiencing community punishment and probation supervision or having experienced this in the previous two years. The women in this study were all based in the North West of England, were all white British, and were aged between 20 and 67 years old.

Ethical approval was granted for a wider range of creative methods, yet the women selected photo voice, creative writing and map making to collect the research data within a participatory action research framework. In two groups (made up of peer mentors and women completing an unpaid work order), 27 criminalised women and one criminal justice practitioner produced 25 narrative maps, 18 letters titled 'Dear future me …', and 220 photographs. These were then used to perform six separate thematic analysis sessions, where group photo elicitation was then audio recorded in most cases. Most of the women selected their own pseudonyms, yet the peer mentors organised and ran their own networking lunch, where they presented the findings of this research to local politicians and criminal justice workers and openly discussed the narratives as their own.

This creative data, and the co-produced analysis that followed, offered rich narratives that brought to life the everyday experiences of criminalised women in the North West of England (further explanation of this methodology and research design can be viewed in Harding, 2020b). It is from this data and co-produced analysis that the 'rules of the game' emerged.

The rules of the game

This chapter demonstrates how a new theory of navigating criminalisation can be understood dynamically and in practical terms through the help of a boardgame. As shown in Figure 2.1, this boardgame was designed to demonstrate processes of navigating risk management highlighted through women's lived experiences of community punishment and probation supervision. Designed to disseminate the research findings to probation practitioners, the game shows the steps that women sentenced to community punishment have to progress through, in order to navigate criminalisation and formal structures of punishment in the community.

When criminalisation occurs, there is a period of learning. This is where criminalised women enter the penal field, whether for the first time or not, and become subject to new rules, regulations and restrictions specific to their sentence and the space within which

Figure 2.1: Navigating criminalisation board game (based on Harding, 2020a)

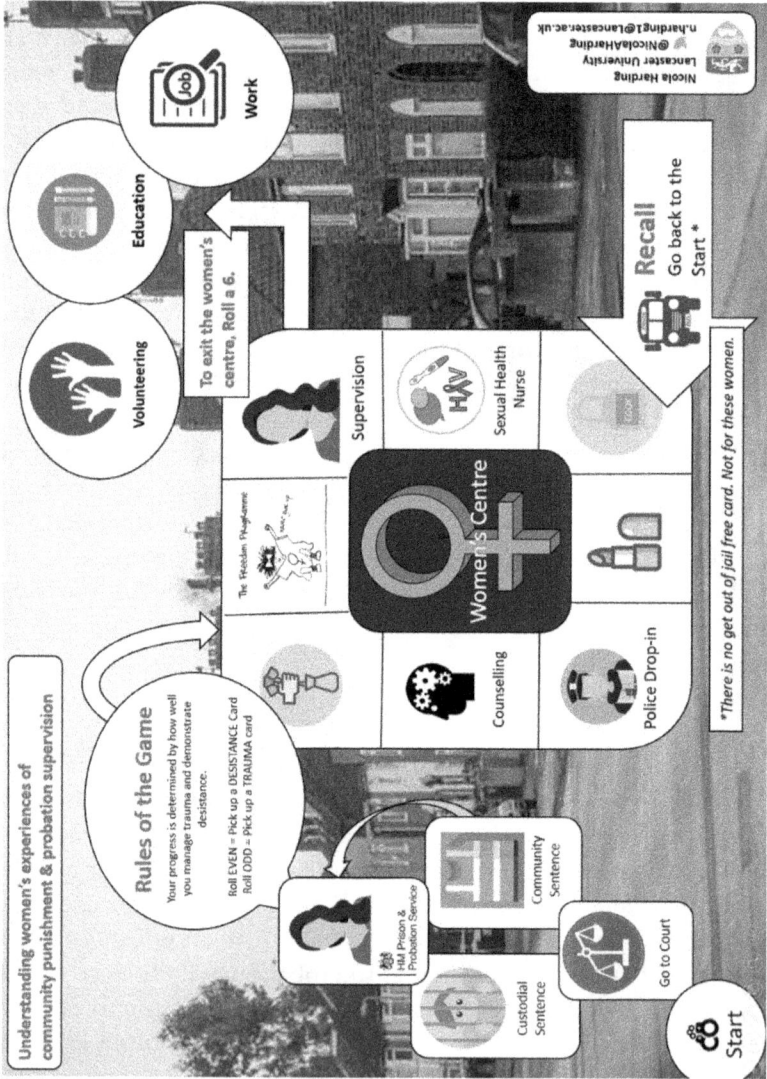

their punishment will take place. The women in this study had either finished their orders or were currently completing unpaid work orders within the women's centre.

The women's centre is a liminal space (Shields, 1991; Baldry, 2010), where women are thought to be transformed through empowerment (Daly and Maher, 1998). However, this research found that the inclusion of punishment activities in the women's centre directly conflicted with notions of transformation through empowerment, substituting the transformative potential of these community interventions with a focus on 'reform' and female respectability in its place (Clarke and Chadwick, 2017). As such, the women in this study learned from the other women around them, the peer mentors, and the female criminal justice practitioners, that in order to be viewed as 'reformed', they needed to minimise the 'troubled' or 'mad' construction of the female criminalised self (Worrall, 1990). The women were managing (but not treating) the trauma they had been experiencing over their life course and during criminalisation (Herman, 1992), while also rejecting the 'bad' criminal woman label by offering up demonstrations of desistance that focused on positive, feminising activities that demonstrate respectability – namely mothering, health and wellbeing (slimming), and homemaking.

Criminalisation begins the moment a woman is labelled as deviant, which also begins a process of navigating institutional structures within the criminal justice system. Where women come into conflict with the law, this conflict becomes the property of the legal system and is then passed on to the criminal justice system to resolve through punishment (Christie, 1977). The conflict no longer belongs to the woman and the party she has 'offended' against; she is now just a pawn in the criminal justice game. Once she is in the punishment arena, in this case the women's centre, the game is played by women being assessed on their ability to manage trauma and demonstrate desistance.

In this game, the trauma card represents how the women in this study visibly managed – or not – the trauma they had experienced, and the desistance card shows how gendered characteristics of a 'respectable' woman were demonstrated, in order to show themselves as reformed.

The trauma card

In order to play this boardgame, women need to manage the trauma they have experienced across their life course, but also the trauma of criminalisation itself (Harding, 2020a). This is denoted in the game by pulling a trauma card. These cards offer examples of how women managed trauma, successfully or unsuccessfully, with an instruction to move either backwards or forwards, depending on how the action was perceived by criminal justice practitioners.

Within this study, the women managed trauma in two very distinct ways: through laughter and imagination. While both mechanisms acted as the visible social manifestation of managing trauma, or at least demonstrated whether a woman was managing trauma, laughter was generally viewed poorly by outsiders, while imaginary narratives were viewed more positively as aspiration. Although these external perceptions are significant to how a woman 'plays the game', whether they are viewed positively or negatively, both demonstrate that trauma is being managed to different extents.

In one session, while drawing maps together on a warm and sunny day, the windows were open wide to cool the room, and a busker from the busy shopping street three storeys below could be heard belting out love songs through a hi-fi system:

Busker: "Goodbye my lover, goodbye friend... You have been the one... You have been the one for me" [Sniffs]

Christine: Did you f****** pay him or what? [Everyone laughs]

The practitioners peered through adjoining windows with puzzled expressions as laughter punctuated the otherwise sombre and tear-filled sessions. To an outsider, this laughter may have seemed crass, proof enough to question the authenticity that the various trauma-filled narratives offered as descriptions of the women's everyday lives subject to community punishment. Surely laughter means that the tears she is still wiping away are just 'crocodile tears', an act for the others in the room? However, laughter was a way in which the women managed their own experiences of trauma. Prior to the busker's interruption, Christine had been discussing years of domestic abuse as we made maps of our lives together. Her story was moving and relatable for many of the women; we all had tears in our eyes and the room was thick with emotion. By making that joke, and causing laughter, Christine was able to talk about and manage her trauma, using laughter as a mechanism to defuse and make sense of the trauma in a safe way for her and for the group.

Bussie (2015) discusses laughter as 'ethical and theological resistance' in the face of oppression and dehumanisation. Drawing on excerpts from Leymah Gbowee's memoir, *Mighty Be Our Powers* (Gbowee and

Mithers, 2011), Bussie (2015) highlights how, when laughter is used as a coping mechanism in response to a traumatic event, others label it, and those who are laughing, as 'sick' or immoral (see also Garrick, 2006):

> 'We all howled and choked. A Swedish boy who was working with the Manchester researchers looked at us in horror. "You people are sick!" he shouted and ran off. We almost killed ourselves laughing. You laugh instead of cry. You laugh because you survived and, in an hour, something else might threaten your life. What else can you do?' (Gbowee and Mithers, 2011, p 213)

There were many times when the women in this study said, "if we don't laugh, we will cry". They realised they were breaking the roles expected of them, where this laughing could be perceived as mocking the justice system, their punishment or their victims. However, all of the laughter that occurred within the sessions was used to break the tension in the room and make the unspeakable trauma that they had experienced in their own lives more bearable.

Herman (1992, p 133) suggests that 'the core experiences of psychological trauma are disempowerment and disconnection from others'. Therefore, it is understandable how the collective activity of laughing during times of acute hardship, oppression and psychological pain, may provide a way of resisting the trauma imposed by oppressive structures. Laughter can empower the survivor of trauma to recount the experience, re-narrating it in a way that makes sense of the trauma experienced (Herman, 1992).

Helen shared an image of her car parked up and subject to a confiscation order. The image is symbolic of Helen's loss of freedom due to her conviction, as she had lost the ability to return to her life in America, and she had lost her car and her independence through losing her driving licence. This had made her more dependent on her friends and family, something she discussed with discomfort and sadness. It was a significant part of the trauma of criminalisation for her. However, Helen and the whole group then made the sale of Helen's car to each other a running joke of the session, with Helen herself offering me "a lift home" with her (on the bus) as we got up to leave:

Helen: This is a very definite punishment for me, yeah.
Abbey: Whereas for me, I'm learning to drive, so I just look at that picture and only see a positive.
Helen: Do you want to buy a car?

Abbey: [laughing] Depends how much!
Shannon: Will you do her a good deal?
Rachel: Will you do it for her on the weekly?
                  [all laughing]

While this may have appeared to be a big joke, it had been looked upon distastefully by the unpaid work practitioner, who pulled a disapproving face and quickly sought to calm the women, by uttering, "Come on now". The 'joke' was a way of processing the trauma that Helen had felt throughout her previous traumatic relationships and the 'justice' process. It was not really about the car, but about defusing the other aspects of her narrative that she found difficult to talk about. Independence was extremely important to her, and she described how she had prided herself on the ability to get away from the abusive relationships and protect her daughter. Walking past her car that she could no longer drive each day was not traumatic because she had to take the bus, but because it was a symbolic representation of all that she had been through. Helen expressed that losing her independence felt like failure.

Herman (1992) describes reconnecting with oneself as a key stage in recovery from traumatic events, recognising that imagination plays a key part in this process. Imagination was also used by the women in different ways to diffuse the pain of trauma. They talked about the photographs as belonging to an imaginary other, with phrases such as "well she may have felt this …" or "that might mean this … to her", even if they were images that they had taken or letters that they had written. When the women themselves interpreted the images, it was easier to manage their trauma, by dislocating their own experiences from the outputs they had contributed. In contrast, the peer mentors who were further away from punishment took ownership of their own narratives and felt more able to discuss painful experiences as their own.

Imagination was also used as a way of making sense of the future, and to ease the pains of the day, by imagining a better future untouched by the stigma of the criminal label in order to negotiate their 'haunted future' (Morriss, 2018). We can see this here in Amy's 'Dear future me …' letter, where she revisits happier times from her past without stigma and transfers this to her future in the form of an imaginative dream, in order to escape the pains and stigma of criminalisation of the present:

> 'Dear future me … Being able to drive and live in the countryside / by the seaside.' (Amy, unpaid work)

Amy identified in her letter that the seaside is somewhere they would rather be, and she links this back to the place where she had lived before becoming criminalised:

> 'I've drawn a house with me myself, my house, and my kids. With North, East, South, West. We moved south. I've drawn a beach and beach huts, because that's where we were happy.' (Amy, unpaid work)

In revisiting old desires and happier times, Amy constructed a fantasy of how life can be in the future, based on her life before the traumatic event(s). A therapeutic environment can make the link between fantasy and actions towards that goal (Herman, 1992). These depictions of an imaginary elsewhere can serve a dual purpose: managing trauma, but also demonstrating an imaginary 'reformed' future identity (Healy, 2014). As such, despite the simplicity of presenting the findings through a 'trauma card' and a 'desistance card' within this game, the reality is that of a more dynamic and synthesised relationship between managing trauma and demonstrating desistance. This relationship is not always synchronous with ways of managing trauma, often acting in opposition to positive appraisals of demonstrations of desistance, or vice versa. Therefore, the way in which the trauma card is played can only be understood when accompanied by a desistance card.

The desistance card

Put most simply, desistance is ceasing from committing crime (Laub and Sampson, 2001). Desistance theory is not one agreed theory of how lawbreakers stop committing offences, but rather a collection of theories that seek to understand why those with a past history of criminal behaviour no longer commit criminal acts. Despite multiple theories in existence, very little research has included or focused on female desistance, with studies either focusing entirely on male samples or including a small number of women. There are a few exceptions to this, examining female desistance explicitly (Stone, 2016; Österman, 2017). Yet there is little consensus among these studies, as they have produced contradictory findings (Sommers et al, 1994; Giordano et al, 2002; Broidy and Cauffman, 2006; Kreager et al, 2010).

Laub and Sampson (2001) propose that desistance occurs through specific turning points in individuals' lives as they transition to adulthood and beyond. Examples of such turning points are often considered as gaining employment or getting married. Here 'the love of a good woman' is often stated as the point at which men begin to desist; interpersonal relationships and the formation of meaningful bonds promote informal social controls that reduce reoffending (Laub and Sampson, 2001). Broidy and Cauffman (2006), using a historic sample similar to Laub and Sampson (2001), also concluded that social capital such as that found in marriage or motherhood is a key determining factor in desistance for women with convictions, whereas Kreager et al (2010) found that motherhood, rather than marriage, led to desistance among a sample of high-risk women from Denver. Feminist criminologists are highly critical of the usefulness of desistance theory, with an overemphasis being placed upon the individual, rather than acknowledging structural influences that are unique to criminalised women's lives (Farrall et al, 2007; Baldry, 2010; Gelsthorpe and Wright, 2015).

Here, the desistance card represents the way in which women demonstrate a 'reformed' feminine character, and not desistance itself. Desistance, the absence of further criminal behaviour, cannot be accurately measured or observed (Farrington, 1986; Barnett et al, 1989; Baskin and Sommers, 1998; Laub and Sampson, 2001), yet criminal justice practitioners are constantly assessing a woman's risk of reoffending based on a wide variety of dynamic measurements (MacKeith, 2011). As such, the desistance card describes behaviours and aspects of their lives and experiences that they show in order to demonstrate themselves as 'reformed' and 'respectable' women. This research shows, through the desistance card, representations of gendered characteristics that focus around women's respectable demonstrations of motherhood, homemaking and reworking their bodies to meet this imagined feminine ideal.

Motherhood

Motherhood is an area of criminalised women's lives that has been examined in depth by feminist criminologists, particularly as it relates to the practicalities and emotional aspects of punishment of mothers in the criminal justice system (for example, Baldwin, 2015; Booth, 2021; Masson, 2019; Minson, 2020). The women in this study demonstrated that they understood from a very early stage in their criminalisation the importance that their role of being a mother has to their punishment. Sophie recalled the attention paid by the sentencing judge to her status as a mother:

> 'I got asked if I was on my own and if I was a mother. Now, I don't feel that if I was a man he would ask if he was on his

own and if he was a father. I felt that it was very important to my sentencing that I was on my own and I was a mother.' (Sophie, community sanction)

Even before her probation supervision had begun, Sophie was aware that her role as a single mother would come under scrutiny as, in her mind, it was that role that had led to her receiving her sentence (see Chapter 9 for further discussion of single mothers). She thought that she may have received more unpaid work hours or additional punishment if she had not been a single mother; therefore she knew that her mothering activities were significant to her punishment. However, she also commented on the strain she felt at having to ask her ex-partner or mother to help with childcare so that she could complete her order, as the women's centre did not offer childcare and children were not permitted in the building.

Jessica and Sarah shared many photos of themselves doing healthy activities with their children, such as walking them to school and taking them on hikes. However, those who were beyond child-rearing age, such as Frances, used their position as grandmother or aunt to demonstrate traditional norms of motherhood. Frances reflected on her earlier experiences as a mother in comparison to her current experiences as a grandmother. For her, becoming a grandmother has given her an opportunity to be the 'mother' that she felt unable to be when she was a single mother to her three children – a 'good' mother:

'I didn't miss out on anything with my kids because it is what you do when you have … are a parent and you're on your own, you have got so much going on and you're like … and then you do have grandkids and it is a cliché but it is a totally different experience being a grandparent than it is being a parent, brilliant, absolutely.' (Frances, peer mentor)

Frances felt overwhelmed by motherhood when her children were younger, and included the pressure of being a single parent as one of the contributing factors that led to her criminalisation. It was only now, as a grandparent, that she felt able to perform a nurturing and caring role.

Motherhood was such a significant theme within the women's narratives that all women found a way to connect themselves to mothering roles. The few women who had had children removed from their care declined to share their stories of past motherhood as part of this study, particularly during audio recording. However, they still discussed themselves as mothers in the present and future, with detailed visions of futures within which they would be reunited with their children.

Homemaking

The domestic sphere has always been considered a traditionally feminine space (Mallett, 2004), a value reflected by the women in this research. The 'home', through depictions of various forms of houses, was the most frequently produced image within this research and was always the first coded and analysed. The women in this study viewed home as so intrinsically linked to themselves, that their house embodied their own emotions, behaviours, and mental state:

Frances: As a woman, the home is supposed to be our pride and joy. It's our home, our kids [home].

Jessica: It's a reflection on you, if you're feeling down. If you're not doing well and you're feeling down, you lose interest in your house. I have neglected other houses in the past.

Frances: Yeah, so have I. So, when you get better, you're house proud.

Frances and Jessica identify their connection to home and talked in depth about it. Frances admitted that as part of her order she could not live at her home address for a duration, so she had moved into her father's property. Yet, she would sneak into the back of her house, so she could not be seen, and clean the house while the children were at school. Such was her need to ensure that her home was kept well, she could have been recalled back to prison if caught.

It is here that we can begin to see how demonstrating transformation of the home as an extension of herself can come into conflict with the responsibilities of punishment:

'Every other house I had was never finished. It was never fully decorated; it was never homely. It didn't feel comfortable. It was a house – this one feels like a home. Especially when people come in now and say, "oh haven't you got a lovely home?" – I never had that. It was, well cos my house was just chaotic constantly. With [ex-partner] in, there was no routine, there was, just nothing was ever done or anything.' (Jessica, peer mentor)

Jessica states the importance of her home now – in contrast to the other properties she had lived at prior to and during criminalisation. She is able to demonstrate how she has transformed her home environment from chaotic to a space that others find aesthetically pleasing, a space she can feel proud of – ultimately, a space that represents her well as a respectable and reformed woman.

Women's bodies

If we triangulate traditional ideas of the 'respectable feminine women', we envisage a nurturing mother, who keeps an immaculate house and takes pride in her appearance, striving to make her body smaller (Friedan, 1963). As this chapter has shown so far, the key to demonstrating desistance is to try to emulate these ideals, the third of which is a focus on their body. For women under surveillance, joining a weight-loss programme that includes weight-loss surveillance through recording meals and weekly weigh-ins, extends and internalises the institutional surveillance experienced through punishment.

Claire took a photograph of her weight record book and shared other images of healthy homemade cooking. She discussed needing help and support to fully commit to losing weight and how this can only be achieved by being measured by an external party. Claire demonstrates how, through the process of punishment and probation supervision, she learned that to conform to the ideals of wider society, negative behaviours should be subject to surveillance and recording to facilitate change. Therefore, this is how the women demonstrated power over areas of their lives that deviated from societal values, such as their size and weight:

Researcher: Why go to Slimming World?
Shannon: Because you're getting monitored, aren't you?
Abbey: Yes, because otherwise you are like shame on this now, I have got to go in here today, I better lose today. So, you make sure you are going to lose, don't you?

The women also displayed images of hairbrushes on dressing tables and make-up, to show that they were trying to improve their outward presentations of self as a more socially acceptable woman.

The key to demonstrating desistance is not simply that the women show and voice their experiences as mothers or homemakers, or even that they are practising healthy wellbeing that includes taking care of their bodies. It is that these activities are positioned as demonstrating a transformative process. For example, where Sarah's son was not really attending school or was always attending late, she is now not only prioritising getting him there on time, but they are practising organised and healthier ways of travelling to school by walking together. Through offering one image of the back of her son in his school coat as she walked him to school, Sarah can convey that shift in maternal practice to the criminal justice practitioner observing the study. Where Jessica had previously moved home many times, she could now share with others feedback on how she had transformed her home. And where Claire pictured her weight-loss booklet, she could quantitively prove her success at transforming herself through the amount of weight she had lost.

Therefore, the most important aspect of demonstrating desistance in this setting is about how well the women can demonstrate transformation of the self and their surroundings in a convincing enough way to signal that they have reformed and are now respectable.

Ending a rigged game

When playing the game, the trauma and desistance cards dictate the speed and direction to which a criminalised woman will move around the board, or through the system. On the board, the system is conceptualised as a loop, with no clear way to exit the board and become a success. This very much mirrors the experiences of the women in this study. There was no real conception of what success looked like, as there were no clear instructions or 'rule book', with peer mentors being held as role models still within the system themselves but no longer being subject to punishment.

Two significant issues became apparent during analysis and observation. First, that three specific outcomes could be enacted at any point, not simply at the end of a woman's sentence of punishment. These are: recriminalisation; institutional warehousing; or 'success'.

Second, success story narratives were dependent upon women exiting the penal field. They did this by engaging in mainstream activities such as employment, volunteering (outside of the women's centre), engaging in training (outside of the women's centre), or taking part in further or higher educational opportunities (again, outside of the women's centre). In other words, success meant moving on from sites of punishment, including the women's centre, and only returning occasionally to share the story of how you did it, in order to inspire others.

This is significant, because the actions that determine how well a woman can navigate community punishment – by demonstrating desistance and managing trauma – offer no real roadmap for achieving the goals of finding a job, obtaining a volunteer opportunity, or engaging in education or training beyond the penal field. As such, not everyone can easily navigate their way to success. However, how well an individual can manage trauma and demonstrate desistence will dictate whether she is recriminalised, institutionally warehoused or goes on to become a success. These outcomes can be demonstrated within three narratives: Shannon's, Rachel's and my own.

Shannon

Shannon is one of the women completing an unpaid work (community service) order at the women's centre. With her order coming to an end, Shannon did not have any form of exit plan from the penal field of the women's centre beyond her order ending. At the end of the research, her order had ended, and she signed up to repeat a course at the women's centre that she had already completed. Shannon struggled to visibly manage her trauma; although she made attempts to do so, these were not viewed favourably by the criminal justice practitioner.

Shannon talks about her life in self-depreciating and derogatory terms, visibly labelling her and her family 'The Clampets' on her map. This refers to a television family who are poor, uneducated and viewed negatively or as a point of ridicule. By labelling herself in this way, it shows that she has experienced and internalised negative stigma across her life course for experiencing poverty and for not necessarily fitting in with normative societal demands. By ridiculing herself, she is using humour as a defence mechanism and as a way of processing the hurt and trauma she experienced as a result of that stigmatisation. Criminalisation and the labelling processes involved are just another point at which the negative labels – applied to her and to her family from her early childhood – become reinforced. All of Shannon's contributions to the photo elicitation and data analysis involve her offering detached opinions about what the photograph could mean and making jokes about the situations depicted in the photographs, rather than connecting the images to aspects of her own experience and narrative, as most of the peer mentors have done.

The lack of narrative in Shannon's contributions to the research show that she has yet to rebuild a consistent narrative about her own life experiences. Yet, the use of humour suggests that she is making early attempts to manage traumas through humour. The trauma of criminalisation, of domestic abuse and poverty (both past and present) interrupts her ability to reflect on experience and offer a consistent narrative about her life. This is an observable undoing of the self that is caused by trauma. Shannon's inability to offer a clear, consistent narrative about her life, including how her life relates to law breaking and punishment, influences her interactions with the criminal justice worker and her probation officer, as she reports that they "don't understand" her. As such, Shannon remains within the women's centre, as she fails to fully manage the trauma experienced across the life course in a way that prompts the criminal justice worker to see her potential as a success story – so she is not offered an opportunity to exit the penal field. She becomes institutionally warehoused.

Rachel

Rachel was halfway through her unpaid work hours at the beginning of the research, and frequent absences from unpaid work meant that she did not progress through her order much during the research period. She had received community payback/unpaid hours after a drink driving offence, and she had also lost her driving licence and her car. She had an allocated probation officer, who Rachel said she did not see much of. She agreed that the main point of contact in the women's centre was Nat, who facilitated her unpaid work.

When Nat introduced me to Rachel, she identified her as a "PPO", a persistent prolific offender (Farrall et al, 2007). However, this was Rachel's first offence and her first time at the women's centre. The negative perception of her behaviour, and the mislabelling of her as PPO, was a form of recriminalisation; a penalty for not demonstrating the desistance characteristics needed to be considered by the practitioner as a woman on the pathway to reform.

Rachel's inability to offer a consistent or believable demonstration of desistance can be seen through observations as she drew her map. In it, she depicted her home, going to court, losing her car, going to the shops to buy alcohol, herself being "very drunk", and the disapproval of her family. It was only through discussions around the table with other women, examining what they had put on their maps, that she added her nephew "keeping her good". The map follows the other women's style of map, but rather than placing more positive aspects of their lives, such as children, as her focus, she concentrated on her own negative behaviour when drunk. While she does represent a desire to become a mother, this is only done begrudgingly, when prompted by Nat.

This activity demonstrated that Rachel was not permitted to display a true representation of her life experiences or feelings; rather, she was pressured into demonstrating a desisting narrative through motherhood (via her nephew) or potential motherhood (trying for a baby). However, as she had to be prompted to add these things to her map, they were not convincing displays to the other women or to the practitioner. As such, nobody sought to correct the practitioner as she recriminalised Rachel through her stigmatised labelling of her as a PPO.

Nicola

If Shannon is an example of what happens when a woman struggles to visibly manage trauma (she becomes institutionally warehoused), and Rachel is an example of what happens when a woman cannot convincingly demonstrate desistance (she becomes recriminalised), I felt necessary to reflect on my own experiences of community punishment and the position I am in now to consider the outcomes for women who are considered a 'success story'.

I completed a two-year probation supervision order, after receiving a nine-month suspended prison sentence in February 2008. After six months' attendance at the probation offices, I was referred to the women's centre, where I spent the remainder of my sentence completing courses and being monitored by my probation officer, very much like the women in this study. I attended daily during this period and quickly completed all of the available courses, repeating some of them two or three times.

I exited the women's centre after being offered a place on a selective drugs and alcohol awareness course that was being run by an organisation with a further education college in my local city. Not all the women were offered this opportunity, just one other woman and myself. We were given help in applying, interview preparation and support when accessing the course via the in-house childcare. This was my route out of the penal sector into further education and volunteering as a peer mentor; it was how I exited the penal field.

I have taken lots of time to reflect about why it was that the practitioners helped my friend and I to get onto the course, and why it was not an opportunity offered to all. Through this research, I have been able to make sense of my own experiences through those of the women in this study. I now understand that the practitioners saw more of themselves in me than they did in some of the other women. I feel they wanted me to succeed, because I reminded them of themselves and, therefore, they believed I could do it. I had accrued more situational, social and cultural capital prior to punishment than most of the other women. This enabled me to quickly observe and assess what was required of me, to navigate this period of punishment in ways that made sense to me. In this case, taking the practitioners' help to exit the penal field was the most desirable way to use my agency in order to reduce my level of risk and the control that the practitioners had over my life.

I am now introduced as a 'success story' at the project where I used to volunteer, but this is not because I had any additional skills or talent than the women around me who did not go on to be considered as such. It is due to my ability to manage trauma and to demonstrate desistance in ways that mirrored the criminal justice practitioners enough to prompt them to invest in me.

Conclusion

This study started with the broad aim of capturing the experiences of women subject to punishment outside the prison gates. By collaborating with criminalised women in a participatory action research project, where creative methods were used to perform a collaborative analysis, an emerging theory of navigating gendered criminalisation offered the opportunity to understand the role of institutions of social control, their agents, and the structures of community punishment imposed upon criminalised women's lives. From this, a boardgame was developed, to better share these experiences with a wider audience than simply those who may read an academic research paper.

The boardgame has since been used with probation practitioners, to help them understand the experiences of those with whom they work, and their own role within a system that sees punishment as a gateway to rehabilitation and reform. By conceptualising this research as a boardgame, 'rules of the game' emerged, whereby women must demonstrate gendered characteristics of desistance; namely, visible motherhood (but not too visible, children are not allowed in the women's centre), homemaking, and the transformation of our bodies. They must also simultaneously manage their trauma in acceptable ways, so that the risks associated with not managing trauma are visibly reduced. This does not necessarily mean that trauma has been managed; in fact, there were many barriers, such as long waiting lists for cognitive behavioural therapy (CBT), that meant trauma was unlikely to be dealt with in any meaningful way during the period of punishment. There also needs to be a recognition of the trauma of criminalisation itself, where the women are having to simultaneously bear the weight of this new traumatic experience of punishment while minimising and projecting a managed face of trauma to the criminal justice practitioner.

The final outcomes of the boardgame are representations of the overall outcomes for the women in this study and women in gender-specific community punishment provision across England and Wales – institutional warehousing, recriminalisation, or a 'success'. To demonstrate the significance of these outcomes for the women in this study, I reflected on Shannon's experience of institutional warehousing. She displayed adequate enough demonstrations of desistance, but these were compromised by her current inability to manage trauma in a way that identified her to the practitioners as someone in whom to invest the additional resources needed in order to exit the penal field. As such, she remained within the women's centre beyond punishment.

Rachel did not demonstrate desistance in ways that the practitioner deemed appropriate, causing her to be labelled as a persistent and prolific offender, despite this punishment being her first offence. By being labelled in such a way, Rachel was denied opportunities given to some others that may assist her in exiting the penal field, like access to education or volunteering opportunities; she was being recriminalised without any further criminal offence.

Finally, I reflected on my own experiences of community punishment, in order to think critically about what it is about certain individuals that are held up as an example of what a 'success story' should look like. Importantly, it was my likeness to the female practitioners and my level of situational social and cultural capital accrued prior to entering the penal field that allowed me agency to demonstrate desistance and to manage trauma in ways that prompted the practitioners to invest additional time and resources in helping me to exit the penal field and move into mainstream education, employment and training opportunities. I was quickly able to understand the rules of the game and therefore use them to my own advantage.

This demonstrates that the necessary opportunities to exit the penal field – and to move on from punishment contexts – are not embedded within the activities of the women's centre. Rather, they are reliant upon the goodwill and motivation of the female practitioners to seek out criminalised women to invest in. In a time of increased pressure and withdrawal of resources from the third sector, this reliance upon staff members to go the additional mile to support a few chosen women means that, ultimately, when being sentenced to community punishment, women are entering a rigged game.

Reflection points

- Is it possible to punish women with community punishments within a women's centre space? Think about how the functions of punishment may conflict with the women's centre's aims of female empowerment.

- What does managing trauma, rather than dealing with trauma, mean for a criminalised woman's long-term desistance journey? Think about the difference between dealing with trauma, perhaps through official interventions such as cognitive behavioural therapy, and managing trauma, which is more about appearing to others as not being affected by trauma.
- Can you locate the woman's agency when 'playing the game'? Is she passive in this process, or can understanding the rules of the game quickly be an advantage to women navigating punishment? Can she play the game to her own aims and advantage?

References

Baldry, E. (2010) 'Women in transition: from prison to ...', *Current Issues in Criminal Justice*, 22(2): 253–67.

Baldwin, L. (2015) *Mothering Justice: Working with Mothers in Criminal and Social Justice Settings*, East Sussex: Waterside Press.

Baldwin, L. and Epstein, R. (2017) *Short But Not Sweet: A Study of the Impact of Short Custodial Sentences on Mothers & Their Children.* Available at: https://www.dora.dmu.ac.uk/bitstream/handle/2086/14301. Accessed: 11 December 2020.

Barnett, A., Blumstein, A. and Farrington, D. P. (1989) 'A prospective test of a criminal career model', *Criminology*, 27: 373–85.

Barr, Ú. (2019) *Desisting Sisters: Gender, Power and Desistance in the Criminal (In)Justice System*, London: Palgrave Macmillan.

Baskin, D. R. and Sommers, I. B. (1998) *Casualties of Community Disorder: Women's Careers in Violent Crime*, Boulder, CA: Westview Press.

Booth, N. (2021) 'Gendered prisons, relationships and resettlement policies; three reasons for caution for imprisoned mothers', British Journal of Criminology. Advance online access. https://doi.org/10.1093/bjc/azab018.

Booth, N., Masson, I. and Baldwin, L. (2018) 'Promises, promises: can the Female Offender Strategy deliver?', *Probation Journal*, 65(4): 429–38.

Broidy, L. M. and Cauffman, E. E. (2006) *Understanding the Female Offender*, US Department of Justice.

Bussie, J. A. (2015) 'Laughter as ethical and theological resistance: Leymah Gbowee, Sarah, and the hidden transcript', *Interpretation: A Journal of Bible and Theology*, 69(2): 169–82.

Carlen, P. (1983) *Women's Imprisonment: A Study in Social Control*, London: Routledge and Kegan Paul.

Carlen, P. (1985) *Criminal Women*, Oxford: Polity Press.

Carlen, P. (1989) 'Feminist jurisprudence or women-wise penology', *Probation Journal*, 36(3): 110–14.

Carlen, P. (1998) *Sledgehammer: Women's Imprisonment at the Millennium*, London: Palgrave Macmillan.

Carlen, P. and Worrall, A. (2004) *Analysing Women's Imprisonment*, Devon: Willan Publishing.

Chadwick, K. and Little, C. (1987) 'The criminalization of women', in P. Scraton (ed) *Law, Order, and the Authoritarian State*, Milton Keynes: Open University Press, pp 254–78.

Christie, N. (1977) 'Conflicts as property', *The British Journal of Criminology*, 17(1): 1–15.

Clarke, B. and Chadwick, K. (2017) 'From "troubled" women to failing institutions: the necessary narrative shift for the decarceration of women post-Corston', in L. Moore, P. Scraton and A. Wahidin (eds) *Women's Imprisonment and the Case for Abolition*, London: Routledge, pp 31–51.

Daly, K. and Maher, L. (1998) *Criminology at the Crossroads: Feminist Readings in Crime and Justice*, Oxford: Oxford University Press.

Elfleet, H. (2018) *Gender Responsivity in a Women's Centre: Post-Release Experiences after the Corston Report (2007)*, Ormskirk: Edge Hill University.

Epstein, R. (2014) *Mothers in Prison: The Sentencing of Mothers and the Rights of the Child*, What Is Justice, working paper, Howard League.

Farrall, S., Mawby, R. C. and Worrall, A. (2007) 'Prolific/persistent offenders and desistance', in L. Gelsthorpe and R. Morgan (eds) *Handbook of Probation*, Devon: Willan Publishing, pp 352–81.

Farrington, D. P. (1986) 'Age and crime', in M. Tonry and N. Morris (eds) *Crime and Justice: An Annual Review of Research* (Vol 7), Chicago: Chicago University Press, pp 189–250.

Friedan, B. (1963) *The Feminine Mystique*, New York: Norton.

Garrick, J. (2006) 'The humor of trauma survivors: its application in a therapeutic milieu: Leeds Trinity University Library collections', *Journal of Aggression, Maltreatment & Trauma*, 12(1/2): 169–82.

Gbowee, L. and Mithers, C. (2011) *Mighty Be Our Powers: How Sisterhood, Prayer and Sex Changed a Nation at War*, London: Beast Books.

Gelsthorpe, L. and Hedderman, C. (2012) 'Providing for women offenders: the risks of adopting a payment by results approach', *Probation Journal*, 59(4): 374–90.

Gelsthorpe, L., Sharpe, G. and Roberts, J. (2007) *Provision for Women Offenders in the Community*, London: The Fawcett Society.

Gelsthorpe, L. and Wright, S. (2015) 'The context: women as law breakers', in J. Annison, J. Deering and J. Brayford (eds) *Women and the Criminal Justice System: From the Corston Report to Transforming Rehabilitation*, Bristol: Policy Press, pp 39–58.

Giordano, P. C., Cernkovich, S. A. and Rudolph, J. L. (2002) 'Gender, crime, and desistance: toward a theory of cognitive transformation', *American Journal of Sociology*, 107(4): 990–1064.

Greenwood, K. L. (2019) *Statutory and non-statutory service-users experiences of gender-responsive practice in a post-Corston (2007) Women's Centre*, Liverpool John Moore University.

Harding, N. (2018) 'Places on probation: an auto-ethnography of co-produced research with women with criminal biographies', in A. Plows (ed) *Messy Ethnographies in Action*, Malaga: Vernon Press, pp 91–100.

Harding, N. A. (2020a) *Navigating Gendered Criminalisation: Women's Experiences of Punishment in the Community* (PhD), Manchester Metropolitan University.

Harding, N. A. (2020b) 'Co-constructing feminist research: ensuring meaningful participation while researching the experiences of criminalised women', *Methodological Innovations*, 13(2): 34–50.

Healy, D. (2014) 'Becoming a desister exploring the role of agency, coping and imagination in the construction of a new self', *The British Journal of Criminology*, 54(5): 873–91.

Heidensohn, F. (1968) 'The deviance of women: a critique and an enquiry', *British Journal of Sociology*, 19 (republished 2010 in the 60th Anniversary Issue of the *British Journal of Sociology*, 'Shaping Sociology over Sixty Years'), 160–75.

Heidensohn, F. (1985) *Women and Crime*, New York: New York University Press.

Heidensohn, F. (2012) 'The future of feminist criminology', *Crime, Media, Culture: An International Journal*, 8(2): 123–34.

Herman, J. (1992) *Trauma and Recovery: From Domestic Abuse to Political Terror*, New York: Basic Books.

Kreager, D. A., Matsueda, R. L. and Erosheva, E. A. (2010) 'Motherhood and criminal desistance in disadvantaged neighborhoods', *Criminology*, 48(1): 221–58.

Laub, J. H. and Sampson, R. J. (2001) 'Understanding desistance from crime', *Crime and Justice*, 28: 1–69.

MacKeith, J. (2011) 'The development of the Outcomes Star: a participatory approach to assessment and outcome measurement', *Housing, Care & Support*, 14(3): 98–106.

Mallett, S. (2004) 'Understanding home: a critical review of the literature', *The Sociological Review*, 52(1): 62–89.

Masson, I. (2019) *Incarcerating Motherhood : The Enduring Harms of First Short Periods of Imprisonment on Mothers*, London: Routledge.

Masson, I. and Österman, L. (2017) 'Working with female offenders in restorative justice frameworks: effective and ethical practice', *Probation Journal*, 64(4): 354–71.

Ministry of Justice (MoJ) (2018) *Female Offender Strategy*. Available at: https://assets.publishing.service.gov.uk/government/uploads/system/uploads/attachment_data/file/719819/female-offender-strategy.pdf. Accessed: 11 December 2020.

Minson, S. and Condry, R. (2015) 'The visibility of children whose mothers are being sentenced for criminal offences in the courts of England and Wales', *Law in Context: A Socio-Legal Journal*, 32: 28–45.

Minson, S., Nadin, R. and Earle, J. (2015) 'Sentencing of mothers: improving the sentencing process and outcomes for women with dependent children', discussion paper, London: Prison Reform Trust.

Morriss, L. (2018) 'Haunted futures: the stigma of being a mother living apart from her child(ren) as a result of state-ordered court removal', *The Sociological Review Monographs*, 66(4): 816–31.

Österman, L. (2017) *Penal Cultures and Female Desistance*, London: Routledge.

Österman, L. and Masson, I. (2018) 'Restorative justice with female offenders: the neglected role of gender in restorative conferencing', *Feminist Criminology*, 13(1): 3–27.

Shields, R. (1991) *Places on the Margin: Alternative Geographies of Modernity*, London: Routledge.

Smart, C. (1977) *Women, Crime and Criminology – A Feminist Critique*, London: Routledge.

Sommers, I., Baskin, D. R. and Fagan, J. (1994) 'Getting out of the life: crime desistance by female street offenders', *Deviant Behaviour*, 15(2): 125–49.

Stone, R. (2016) 'Desistance and identity repair: redemption narratives as resistance to stigma', *British Journal of Criminology*, 56: 956–75.

Worrall, A. (1990) *Offending Women: Female Lawbreakers and the Criminal Justice System*, London: Routledge.

Worrall, A. (2008) 'The "seemingness" of the "seamless management" of offenders', in P. Carlen (ed) *Imaginary Penalties*, Devon: Willan Publishing, pp 113–34.

Worrall, A. and Gelsthorpe, L. (2009) '"What works" with women offenders: the past 30 years', *Probation Journal*, 56(4): 329–45.

3

Harmful social and cultural practices that exist within South Asian communities in the UK and their impact on women

Zinthiya Ganeshpanchan and Isla Masson

Introduction

Since 1947 there has been an influx of South Asian migrants to the UK for different reasons. Some of this has been motivated by a need to escape civil war, to seek better economic opportunities, for marriage or to join family members. According to the 2011 census, South Asians represent the largest minority group in Britain. Many of these migrants have settled in the UK and are contributing to economic, social and political life (Girishkumar, 2014). Despite the apparent assimilation of South Asian migrants into the UK and their relatively large number, South Asian women migrants in particular continue to face multiple disadvantages. These disadvantages include language barriers, lack of education, lack of skills, poor quality housing, unemployment (Girishkumar, 2014) and specific forms of violence associated with the various cultural and religious practices that define their identity (Raj and Silverman, 2002; Anitha, 2008). These increase the gender-based power imbalance, thereby reinforcing the patriarchal structures of both the host and migrant cultures, which leads to the further marginalisation and victimisation of women (Anitha, 2008; Girishkumar, 2014).

Patriarchy is a system of society in which men hold power and women are largely excluded from it. It is an ideology that is considered to be a major deciding factor when mapping the gender power relations that exist within a society (Anitha, 2008; Girishkumar, 2014). It is suggested that patriarchal structures, combined with other intersecting components such as class, race, culture, religion and family patterns, contribute to the context within which abuse occurs (Gilligan and Akhtar, 2006; Ganeshpanchan, 2017) and oppress women.

Even though patriarchy is considered to be a universal phenomenon, it can intensify depending on the region and culture in which it is practised (Hapke, 2013). In South Asian communities, its manifestation can be widespread, playing a central role in the way women's lives are defined and subjugated (Prasad, 1999; Johnson and Johnson, 2001; Niaz, 2003; Girishkumar, 2014). This chapter, informed by a participatory action research approach (O'Neill, 2006), discusses some of the cultural practices that exist among the South Asian communities living in the UK that negatively impact women and girls.

Methodology

The methodology adopted was qualitative and included a range of face-to-face and telephone interviews, as well as focus groups over a period of 36 months with 107 female survivors of violence from South Asian backgrounds living in Leicester and Leicestershire. The methodology was chosen in order to encourage individuals to fully narrate their lived experiences and for their voices to be heard. Due to the sensitivity of the issues discussed, semi-structured interviews and focus groups were carried out sensitively and ethically, in accordance with the safeguarding policy of the Zinthiya Trust,[1] by the lead author, who is also a researcher trained in documenting the lived experience of women, and in the safeguarding of children and vulnerable adults. Prior to taking part in the research, all participants signed consent forms (which contained information on how to withdraw their responses), and all names have been anonymised to protect their identities. The data was audio recorded, transcribed and then coded into several overarching themes, primarily stemming from the need to be 'good wives' using Braun and Clarke's (2007) thematic analysis. The participants were all involved in 'The Women and Girls' outreach project, with some already engaging with the Zinthiya Trust. The participants ranged from 16 to 70 years of age; most of the girls were single, however the majority of women were married or living in a partnership. All the women identified as South Asian, though they reported practising a range of different religions.

Becoming 'good wives'

One example of patriarchal social and cultural systems in South Asian families is the way in which women are expected to marry early, bear children, manage households and look after the extended family (Goel, 2005). After marriage, women are expected to leave the parental homes and move into living with the husband's family (Kandiyoti, 1988). At times, young girls are moved into the prospective groom's family long before the marriage takes place to be trained as 'good wives'. One woman spoke of how she sent her daughter away to be ready to be a wife:

> 'My daughter is 14 years of age and is no longer in school these days. Her dad sent her to Pakistan to live with her grandma and aunties to learn how to be a good wife. She will learn to work in the fields, cook and clean and manage the household. We have had a marriage proposal for her already. The plan is to invite the groom who is also my husband's nephew to visit her once she returns from Pakistan.' (Damini)

These movements can be either leaving the country of origin or moving between cities in the UK. The research revealed that whichever form the movement is, it weakens women's social position, by taking away any support networks these women have prior to their marriage that they could turn to in times of need, as in the case of Sara, who had to leave her home town suddenly:

> 'I will be getting married in three weeks' time and moving to Bolton to live with his family. My husband-to-be is the eldest of three boys and none of them are married so it will be my responsibility as the daughter in law to take care of his sick mother and therefore, I am not sure when I will get the opportunity to come visit my family and friends in Leicester. I am worried as I don't have any friends in Bolton but maybe I will have to get to know my new family first.' (Sara)

This lack of support intensifies the pressure that women face, such as having to take on new responsibilities associated with being a good wife or facing the anxieties of pregnancies on their own. It may also isolate women if they face problems arising from the practice of dowry, which will be discussed later.

One aspect of being a 'good wife' involves a virginity test, which is a custom prevalent among many South Asian communities across all social classes. This test entails the showing of blood by a bride upon the first act of intercourse as proof of her virginity (Ganeshpanchan, 2017). The elderly women in the family play a role in placing a white cloth on the bed used by the newlyweds on their wedding night. If there is blood on the cloth, then the girl has passed the 'virginity test' or being a 'good wife'. If she failed to prove her virginity, she will be publicly humiliated and sometimes the marriage called off. The failure of the test can also lead to her facing honour-related violence, due to bringing shame on the family, which will be discussed later.

> 'I was raped in the mosque when I went to the toilet. Now I am scared that the boy I am going to marry will find out that I am not a virgin on our wedding day. If this happens I don't know what my parents will do to me, I am scared and can't speak to anyone.' (Lekha)

Virginity testing for many women can lead to lifelong trauma, even if they do 'pass' the test and get married.

> 'On the night of our wedding my husband forced me to have sex with him. I was crying in pain and scared and ran into the hotel bath room but he got more and more angry and forced himself on me and did not stop until he saw the blood to believe that I was a virgin. We have been married for 24 years now but yet I think of that day and cry because now I know what he did that day is rape. There are days I want to leave the marriage but I have to think of my children. Can you imagine having to live with a man who raped you?' (Jyothi)

Many would consider this to be domestic violence. Yet, this cultural practice of virginity tests and the taboo relating to this, along with its links to shame, makes this form of assault very difficult to report and prosecute. Viewing these types of practices through the Western lens of domestic violence may alienate the very women whom practitioners are attempting to support.

Domestic violence/family violence

According to the National Family Health Survey (2007), 40 per cent of a representative sample of Indian women of reproductive age reported having experienced physical violence (35 per cent), sexual violence (10 per cent) or emotional violence (16 per cent) at the hands of their husbands or husband's relatives. One woman, Rupa, who was interviewed for the research, spoke of such physical and emotional violence:

'My family is from Kenya. I was given in marriage to a man in the UK. Once I came to the country we lived with his mother and sister. From the beginning, I had to cook and clean for the family. While his mother and sister just sat and spent their time doing nothing. On top of this he used to beat me for every little thing and at times simply because the women keep saying things about me which are not true. He used to beat me even when I was pregnant and kick me in my stomach. This is the reason that my daughter is ill, she was born with a damaged kidney. When I could take no more I decided to leave. Later I got to know he had done the same thing to another woman before this [and] he had used cigarettes to burn her.' (Rupa)

In addition to such types of physical violence, women who participated in the study spoke about their experience of sexual violence and rape within marriage, such as Vahini:

'My parents arranged a marriage for me to a man in the UK. I only saw him on the day of our wedding. After our wedding, he returned to the UK and I continued to live with my parents. However, he called me via Skype every day. During these conversations, he asked me to perform certain sexual acts which I did not want as I was worried my parents would hear or see. If I refused, then he would pressure me over the phone even calling at midnight so I had to do what he asked. Sometimes he asked me to insert objects into my private area for him to watch. After about six month I got the visa and came to live with him. He picked me from the airport and we went to his flat. That night he repeatedly raped me. Thereafter, he used to force me to drink alcohol with him prior to having sex. He continued to insert objects such as small glass bottles into me. Even when I got pregnant he did not stop. One day I was bleeding heavily and he was forcing me to have sex, when I refused he tried strangling me and I lost consciousness. When I woke up I was in the hospital. Later I was told I had lost my baby. The police interviewed me and I told them what had happened to me and they moved me into a refuge in London. After a short while I was again moved to Leicester in fear that he would find me. Now my visa has expired and I don't know what to do or where to go as I have no one. I can't go back to Jaffna [Sri Lanka] as you know how the situation will be for me there. [She was referring to the interviewer's knowledge of the country, as they were from Sri Lanka.]' (Vahini)

In fact, domestic violence emerged as the single most problematic issue faced by all the women who participated in the interviews and focus groups in this research. Their experience of domestic violence manifested in different ways, including physical, financial and emotional abuse, which deprived the women of their independence and self-esteem. Although domestic violence is not unique to the lives of South Asian women, it is estimated that 37.5 per cent of South Asian women in the UK face abuse at the hands of their husbands/partners in comparison to 24.8 per cent of white British women (Tjaden and Thoeness, 2000).

However, gaining an accurate assessment of the scale of the issue of sexual violence and marital rape in South Asian women is exceptionally challenging. Unfortunately, the research also revealed that there is evidence to suggest that the rate of non-reporting is significantly higher among women from South Asian backgrounds (Leicester, Leicestershire and Rutland DVSV Working Group data, 2018). Such reluctance to report is for a variety of reasons. For example, reporting domestic abuse and domestic violence may be associated with perceived stigma and a sense of shame; and there may be a reluctance to report crimes committed against them by their husbands, but also a failure among the women themselves to recognise themselves as victims of a crime (Niaz, 2003). Bhatia (2012) suggests that this, at least, is in part due to a reluctance to question cultural gender-based norms, as well as a fear of public revelation of their sexual experiences and grievances. Other reasons can include being dependent on the perpetrator or being afraid of the perpetrator, as identified by the interview with Kala:

'He has friends in high places including the police. On several occasions, he told me if I reported him, he will make sure that me and my family in India will pay for it. I have no one in this country so what can I do?' (Kala)

According to the women interviewed for this research, other barriers to reporting or to accessing services include: lack of confidence; fear or mistrust of the authorities; lack of language skills; no alternative accommodation; no access to legal aid; fear of children being taken away by social services; or fear of having to leave the country if they are on a spousal visa.

For example, Kala arrived in the UK in 2018 on a spousal visa; however, within a few weeks of coming to live with her husband and his family, she was subjected to physical, emotional and financial abuse. Not being able to tolerate the violence, she left her home and sought support. Unfortunately, due to her status as no recourse to public funds, she was unable to get a place in a refuge, so a charity made other arrangements to accommodate her. She was encouraged to report the violence to the police, however the police were unable to take a statement due to her inability to speak the language. Kala was unable to answer the phone whenever the interpreter called, and when she returned the call, the operator could not understand her. This went on for nearly two weeks. During that time, Kala was dependent on food banks to support herself in the accommodation. When this was no longer viable and she could no longer cope, against all advice, she returned to her perpetrator. This escalated the violence, as he now had full control of her:

> 'They told me I had no one and no one will care for me … they also told me if I tried to leave they would report me to the Home Office, I was scared and did not know what to do.' (Kala)

On one occasion, her mother-in-law badly beat her and threatened to kill her. Fearing for her life, Kala ran to the women's centre, but was told to return the next day as the caseworker had a meeting to attend. Not knowing what to do, she returned home again and was beaten and raped by her husband for leaving home. The next day, she returned to the women's centre, which had now successfully supported her with her application to the Home Office and made an application for divorce. Kala's story highlights the urgent need to look again at some of the existing immigration policies around spousal visas that are detrimental to women from ethnic minority communities.

In fact, Asian women are also significantly more likely to experience family violence than white women, with the rates of 32 per cent and 19 per cent respectively (Cooper et al, 2006). This is due to a number of reasons, including: their subordinate position within the family unit; living with extended family; moving in to live with in-laws after marriage; lack of suitable housing; lack of financial autonomy resulting from unemployment; as well as having caring responsibilities for multiple family members. The family also plays a key role in reinforcing cultural practices. A traditional South Asian family is a joint patriarchal group with an elderly male figure as the head (Ballard, 1982; Thandi and Lloyd, 2011). There are instances where, in the absence of an elderly man, a stronger elderly female figure takes over the leadership of the family and continues to run the family using the same patriarchal principles and shared beliefs and perpetuating the abuse, thus raising the question of women's capacity to commit violence (Ganeshpanchan, 2017):

> 'My father died a few years ago but since then it is my mother and grandma who is giving me trouble. They don't want me to marry again and are forcing to break up my relationship with X. I was given in marriage when I was 16 years of age in India. For over 15 years in our marriage I suffered and faced abuse and finally three years ago I got a divorce. Now that I have fallen in love again my mother or grandma don't want me to get married. They want me to look after my two sons and wait single forever.' (Rani)

Women's subordinate position within society and the family can leave them vulnerable not only to intimate partner violence but also to other forms of abuse within the family unit involving multiple perpetrators, as in the case of Ram:

> 'I left my home in Luton and went to stay with my friends as I could no longer take the abuse from my husband and in-laws. My husband beat me when he is angry and I can take that as he is my husband but the mental torture I go through at the hands of my mother in law and sister in laws every day is the worse.' (Ram)

Therefore, any progress that is made to encourage women to disclose this form of abuse must consider the additional complexities of South Asian women reporting, as well as considering how ongoing or historical abuse may be present in the lives of those who may come forward.

Despite domestic and wider family-based violence being the biggest issues faced by women, there are other forms of violence that South

Asian migrant women undergo as a result of culture and religion, which are clearly interlinked with being 'good wives'. Women who fail to comply with marriage may be subjected to a forced marriage.

Forced marriage

Forced marriage, is a marriage without free consent of one or both parties often under duress, and is a factor that exists in South Asian communities (Gangoli et al, 2006). It is not the same as an arranged marriage, where the ultimate decision will be made by the bride and groom. However, there can be some overlaps between the two types of marriage, and often a forced marriage will stem from an arranged marriage (Rehman et al, 2013):

> 'My parents have arranged a marriage for me in Dubai where I am from but I don't want to marry him. I want to stay in Leicester and study further. My father has threatened to stop sending money if I don't return home. He has also instructed my cousins who are living in Birmingham to remove me by force and put me on a plane by the end of next month when my course ends.' (Krisha)

> 'I am 28 years of age and am holding a full-time job. My parents want me to marry a man from India who wants to settle in the UK but I don't want to. I was born here and brought up here so how can I live with a man who doesn't even understand the British way of living. Since I said no my father beat me up asked me to leave the house and now I am in rented accommodation. I am scared that he will get to know where I am living, so please don't let anyone know I called you. He is also not allowing me to speak to my mother unless I agree to the marriage.' (Sonal)

In many south Asian families, marriage is viewed as a way of reducing the influence of Western culture over their daughters (and at times their sons), or to end any relationships with 'unsuitable partners' (Gangoli et al, 2006). An unsuitable partner can be someone who does not belong to the same caste, class or religious background:

> 'Her parents did not approve our marriage even though we are from the same town in Sri Lanka because we were form different castes. Her uncles threatened to beat me so

we fled to Germany where we lived as refugees and came to Leicester. I don't have a job but she is working so I am staying at home and looking after the child. Our parents don't want to know where we are.' (Rajiv and Sarda)

Women and girls may be subject to violence in the name of honour, which will be discussed later, as a result of entering into an unsuitable relationship or having a child out of wedlock or, at times, when she wants to flee a violent relationship (Rehman et al, 2013). There are other instances when the marriages are seen as a form of strengthening ties between two families. Girls are often pushed into a marriage through intense duress that may also include physical violence:

'He was the son of a friend of my father. Our parents decided to strengthen the family bonds through our marriage. I did not like him at all but my parents forced me saying if I did not get married they will disown me and I will never be able to see my sisters. My mother also locked me up in a room thinking I will run away. Finally, I had to give in. We were married for four years and have two children. Since lately he has been behaving differently like being very secretive when he talks on the phone and at times come home very late. I was worried that he was having an affair but few days ago I happened to check his phone and found photos of a man. I don't know what to do. I am so ashamed of myself. How can I tell my parents of this?' (Bindu)

Current law in the UK prohibits any form of forced marriage, and victims can get protection through Forced Marriage Protection Orders. However, evidence from this research and from other agencies that operate nationally (such as Karma Nirvana, an agency supporting victims of forced marriage) suggests that there are many marriages still taking place without consent. The evidence from this research identified that women are scared to report the abuse to the police or apply for protection orders due not only to the fear of their families or extended families, but also due to the more complex reasons of breaking family ties, being disowned by the family, bringing shame on the family, feeling that they are hindering the marriage prospects of other female siblings in the family, lack of confidence, and a lack of adequate support if they decide to flee the violent situation:

'My marriage was love marriage. I entered the UK as student and sponsored him. After I got pregnant he left me for another woman. Now I am unable to return home as my parents have asked me not to bring shame on the family. My brother sent me a letter asking me not to return and if I return he will make sure that I will not step [into] my parents' house. He says that if I go home as a divorced woman with a child it will bring shame on our family and no one will marry my younger sisters. I don't have any friends or family here and not sure what I can do to bring up my daughter.' (Sima)

Dowry-related violence and preference for sons

Dowry is practised in many different parts of the world, and is an effective and deeply rooted cultural practice that is used to subordinate and undermine women (Thiruchandran, 1997; Sornarajah, 2004; Ganeshpanchan, 2017). It is also an issue that causes anxiety for many women across caste and class for years to come – even after the marriage. A dowry requires the bride's family to gift excessive amounts of money, jewellery, property and other goods to the groom when the marriage is being agreed. If the dowry is not fulfilled, it may result in post-marital violence towards the woman (Barua and Kurz, 2001; Krishnan, 2005; Rocca et al, 2009):

> 'Tragic that this evil and backward practice continues even in the UK as demands from the boy's side are never ending. Shame on all those who ask for dowry.' (Nirmala)

While dowry can be viewed in the context of a gift to a new couple, it is a more complex patriarchal practice, which not only undermines women, but also acts as a system that can exacerbate violence against women (Thiruchandran, 1997). Through the dowry, the families transfer the ownership of the woman to the family she is marrying into, which symbolises that the family is transferring the 'burden' and paying off the groom's family for taking on their burden (Ganeshpanchan, 2017).

Dowry-related violence is most prevalent in South Asia, in countries such as India, Pakistan, Sri Lanka and Bangladesh, and women of South Asian origin continue to face the negative impacts of this practice in the UK (Thiruchandran, 1997). Women who are unable to pay the demanded dowry can be subjected to abuse for the rest of their married life. The most common forms of dowry-related violence include physical violence, rape, acid throwing, wife burning, abandonment or enslaving of women. Methods of starvation, deprivation of clothing, evictions, and false imprisonment as methods of extortion may also be used:

> 'Can you please help me? I have nowhere to go. The house we are living now is what my father bought me. However, once the marriage was arranged and all invitations were sent out his parents asked my father to transfer the deeds in my husband's name. They told if it was not done then they would cancel the wedding. My father feared that the wedding will be called off and it would bring shame to me so he transferred the house to my husband. Now they want me to leave the house and go but it is my house.' (Seema)

There were also a number of other cases in the research where children were taken away from women for not paying large sums of money as dowry:

> 'My husband is a pharmacist we got married in 2009 and have two children. When our marriage was arranged my father promised to money and property. Unfortunately, he fell ill and passed away before he could write the property to me. Now my brothers are not allowing me to have the property that my father promised. Because of this my in-laws are angry. They have been forcing me to ask my brothers for the property and when I refused, they chased me out of the house. Now I am unable to see my children. My husband said until I get the deeds for the property not to return home.' (Renu)

For many, there are deep-seated levels of shame relating to asking for support. Likewise, unfortunately, the lack of understanding on issues such as the practice of dowry among professionals within the criminal justice system as well as frontline support workers have meant that women often do not get the help they need, even when they come forward to seek assistance:

> 'I suffered abuse at the hands of my husband and mother in law for over two years. Two weeks ago, when I could

not take it any more [I] left the house and [am now] living with a friend. I only took a few clothes and my jewellery that my mother gave me when I got married. Today the police came in search of me and said that my husband and in-laws has lodged an entry in the police station stating that I robbed the jewellery. They [police] asked me to return everything I took or I will be charged with theft. I am scared and don't know what to do, I never robbed anything they are the jewellery that mother gave me.' (Saro)

As discussed previously, in many traditional South Asian families, a girl child is considered to be a burden on the family. Poor families who cannot afford to pay dowries often get into debt that they have to continue paying for the rest of their lives (Thiruchandran, 1997; Ganeshpanchan, 2017). As such, patriarchal practices that are common among south Asian cultures are so detrimental to women that bearing a son is preferable. Women who give birth to girls are considered unlucky and as not fulfilling their duties towards their husband. They can be subjected to physical and emotional violence, including forced abortion:

'I have two daughters and when I was pregnant with my third child my husband and mother-in-law forced me to abort the baby. They said my mother had three daughters so my third child will also be a daughter. Thereafter twice I got pregnant and they made me go through the test to identify the sex of the baby and made me abort. The last abortion was so painful as I did not know that I was pregnant for a while. I could not take any more and I decided to escape. I left my two children in that house and just walked out of the home and I don't want to go back again. Can you please help me get my daughters back?' (Giva)

Girls born to families with such cultural preferences are often sadly abandoned, given up for adoption, subjected to child marriage or forced into prostitution as a way of getting rid of the burden (interview with Child Lanka Staff[2]). Shame is a significant factor for women from these communities, and a much better understanding of the role of shame is needed, to better support these women. Shame is heavily linked to the following two areas of practice: honour within families; and menstruation.

Honour-based violence

Honour or '*Izzat*' is an effective patriarchal tool that is in place to control the lives of South Asian women. Dishonouring your family or community can have a devastating impact on the victims (Rehman et al, 2013). There have been many high-profile cases involving South Asian women being subject to honour-based violence for behaving in a manner that has perceived to be bringing shame on the community. For example:

> Shafilea Ahmed was born in Bradford West Yorkshire, to Pakistani parents and was an A-Level student who hoped to become a solicitor. During a trip to Pakistan in 2003, Shafilea swallowed bleach in what was later reported to be a suicide attempt. Her father claimed however, that it was a mistake: she had drunk it during a power cut, thinking it was a bottle of fruit juice. Shafilea suffered extensive damage to her throat for which she was having regular ongoing care at the time of her disappearance. Later in 2010 it was revealed that her father put a plastic bag into her mouth and suffocated her to death and hid her body. Her parents were jailed for years. (*BBC News*, 2012)

Often there is a relationship between forced marriages and honour-based violence. Many women who were interviewed for this research had been subject to violence due to reasons such as refusing to accept an arranged or forced marriage and bringing shame on the family, or for simply reporting abuse to the police or attempting to access support services.

Another form of violence performed in the name of honour is female genital mutilation (FGM). FGM, which is widely known as 'cutting' or circumcision, is not the same as male circumcision. It has devastating lifelong impacts on women and girls (Forward, 2020). Traditionally, FGM has been viewed as a practice rooted within African cultures and, therefore, less attention has been paid to its impact on South Asian women. Unfortunately, this research has identified that the practice is very much alive within many cultures, including South Asian cultures:

> 'My mother and husband were attempting to take me and my two daughters to Pakistan to perform FGM on my two daughters, I begged my husband not to but since mother came to live with us, she has been forcing him to arrange

for the procedure. If I did not agree he would have divorced me but how can I when I know the consequences of this as I myself was a victim once. The day we were to fly to Pakistan we all left for Heathrow, at the airport I had some money and the passports with me – so once we passed security, in the pretext of taking the girls to the toilet I took them out of sight of my mother and husband and went and alerted the airport staff, they removed us immediately to a safe house and after two weeks transferred me to the refuge. I am due to give birth in a few weeks' time for the third time and I am very scared of what will happen.' (Rosan)

Rosan had some financial capital and was brave enough to protect her daughters, but unfortunately many girls have not been able to escape the violence:

'They took me to Birmingham one day after school and we had a ceremony. I was 11 years of age then. There were four other girls in that house who all went through the procedure. I can't believe that my mum did this to me. I loved her so much, but I cannot trust her now.' (Nandini)

In England and Wales, it is an offence to perform, assist, or fail to protect a girl from FGM (under Sections 1, 2 and 3 of the Criminal Justice Act 2003). Recent campaigns and local authority initiatives to respond to FGM in Britain (Gov.uk, 2020), ensuring that practitioners and frontline workers (for instance in schools) recognise that this continues to be performed on girls and women in South Asian families, might help to reduce this form of honour-based violence.

Stigmatising menstruation

The final cultural practice that ostracises women and girls relates to periods. In many Asian cultures, menstruating women are considered dirty and are stigmatised. The practices around menstruation vary from culture to culture, with a stark contrast between urban and rural societies. For example, based on the author's own experiences of growing up in Sri Lanka, young girls in Sri Lanka who are menstruating for the first time are locked in a room for several days. During this time, they are not allowed to be seen by outsiders other than female relatives. They are allowed out of the room after four to five days at an auspicious time and then bathed in milk and water scented with flowers. Once this is done, they receive new clothes and gifts. It is only after this that they can see their male relatives, including their brothers or fathers.

In countries such as Nepal, under the practice named '*Chhaupadi*', menstruating women are forced to sleep outside the house in huts, where they are often attacked by wild animals and also sexual predators (Nirol, 2017). This ostracisation, which is common in mountainous western Nepal, is due to the belief that menstruating women cause bad luck to the family, crops and cattle, if the god is displeased. Despite the fact that it was outlawed by the Nepalese Supreme Court in 2005, the practice continues and, in 2017, it was taken up in the Nepalese parliament again, because it caused a huge number of deaths in rural areas (interview with Shuma Sharma, Director of Women Can Nepal). In the UK, menstruating women in South Asian communities are often also prevented from entering places of worship, cooking or even sleeping in the same bed as their husband:

> 'When I have my period, I am locked in a room and not allowed to go to the temple or see anyone in the house. My mother in law forces me to sleep on the floor as I am dirty.' (Geeta)

In another interview:

> 'My mother in law has asked me not to wash my clothes with hers. She says because I get periods, I am dirty. So now I have to wash her clothes separate.' (Situl)

Practices such as these around menstruation not only deprive women of their dignity, but also cause ill-health. According to a survey carried out in 2019 in Leicester by the Women's Research Centre (Leicester Women's Research Centre, 2019): 79 per cent women reported that they had never had any information on menstruation health before their first period; 33 per cent revealed that they still use traditional methods of protection, such as rags, during their menstruation; and one in five women reported that they had to use toilet paper instead of sanitary protection during their periods. The reason for this has been primarily the cost of accessing period products as well as stigma around menstruation.

As mentioned previously, there are significant issues with financial independence for South Asian women. For example, according to Bagguley and Hussain (2007, p 1): 'South Asian women, especially Bangladeshi and Pakistani women, remain among the most excluded and lowest paid sections of the labour force'. They are, therefore, forced to rely on others to provide sanitary products. However, stigma often prevents women from these communities from discussing this with their mothers or daughters, and they must overcome the shame of asking a male relative to buy sanitary products for them, if they are unable to do so themselves.

There are, therefore, a number of issues here that need to be addressed. However, it is suggested that greater conversations around sexual health and women's health for *all* children (which would therefore include South Asian girls) would provide a safe, shame-free and taboo-free environment early on. There are many relationship and sex education resources available, and these should be more firmly integrated into personal, social, health and economic (PSHE) classes in schools.

Conclusion and recommendations

Although violence against women and girls is perpetrated in ethnic communities across the world, this research has drawn attention to the specific forms that South Asian women experience – particularly the way in which they are marginalised and victimised, due to a number of social and cultural practices that exist within these communities. Unfortunately, these factors often influence women's ability to report violence or to access support services, leaving them vulnerable to long-term abuse and trauma. While existing UK law around domestic violence, forced marriage and FGM can contribute to the prevention of violence, women are often reluctant to report abuse when this is committed by intimate partners or close family members. Furthermore, some of the cultural practices – such as virginity tests and the stigma around menstruation – are issues that are not discussed in public, due to being considered as taboo. In addition, the current support systems in place for survivors of abuse are designed to address immediate needs rather any historical abuse. Therefore, women who have been subject to historical abuse continue to suffer in silence, as they are not able get legal redress or access to support services such as counselling or therapy. Indeed, the lack of understanding among service providers, including those within the criminal justice system in particular, regarding some of the deep-rooted cultural practices, such as dowry and honour-based violence, has meant that these complex practices are viewed through the lens of domestic abuse, rendering it impossible for the victims to get justice.

It is vital that practitioners gain a better understanding of these cultural practices, so that when attempting to provide support, they do not undermine or dismiss them, as issues that should be dealt with within families. The 'them and us' divide needs to be bridged, to ensure that Western feminism is not imposed upon South Asian feminism, but used to better support these communities.

As discussed in this chapter, there are a number of significant barriers to South Asian women and girls coming forward for support, owing to a culture of shame. This shame pertains to feelings experienced as a direct consequence of the abuse, as well as associated issues that reporting abuse imparts, and especially how it undermines their culture. Knowledge of this shame is therefore incredibly important for improving how support services can be provided. The research presented in this chapter has found that the answer may lie in increased education and awareness on the issues shared by service providers as well as professionals involved in the criminal justice system.

However, it is also essential to raise awareness in the communities themselves, and to work in partnership with communities to address these issues. This joined-up and inclusionary approach could help to break downs myths associated with some of these practices, such as stigma around menstruation and virginity tests.

Reflection points

- What can be done to increase the cultural awareness of practitioners attempting to support women from South Asian communities?
- How can practitioners gain the confidence of South Asian women and girls?
- Who should be responsible for ensuring that research is carried out to raise awareness of the variety of forms of violence that occur within these communities?

Notes
[1] A registered charity in Leicester and Leicestershire that offers support to women from disadvantaged backgrounds: https://www.zinthiyatrust.org/
[2] Child Lanka is an agency working with street children in Sri Lanka, providing alternative education and shelter.

References

Ahamed, F., Riaz, S., Barat, P. and Stewart, D. (2004) 'Patriarchal beliefs and perceptions of abuse among South Asian immigrant women', *Violence Against Women*, 10(3): 262–82.

Amos, V. and Parmar, P. (1984) 'Challenging imperial feminism', *Feminist Review*, 17: 3–19.

Anitha, S. (2008) 'Neither safety nor justice: the UK government response to domestic violence against immigrant women', *Journal of Social Welfare and Family Law*, 30(3): 189–202.

Anthias, F. (2002) 'Beyond feminism and multiculturalism: locating difference and the politics of location', *Women's Studies International Forum*, 25(3): 275–394.

Bagguley, P. and Hussain, Y. (2007) *The Role of Higher Education in Providing Opportunities for South Asian Women*, Bristol: Joseph Rowntree Foundation.

Ballard, R. (1982) 'South Asian families: structure and process in families in Britain', in R. Rapoport and M. Fogarty (eds) *Families in Britain*, London: Routledge, pp 179–204.

Barua, A. and Kurz, K. (2001) 'Reproductive health-seeking by married adolescent girls in Maharashtra, India', *Reproductive Health Matters*, 9(17): 53–62.

Batsleer, J., Burman, E., Chantler, K. and McIntosh, H. S. (2002) *Domestic Violence and Minoritisation: Supporting Women in Independence*, Manchester: Manchester Metropolitan University Women's Studies.

BBC News (2012) 'Shafilea Ahmed murder trial: parents guilty of killing'. Available at: https://www.bbc.co.uk/news/uk-england-19068490. Accessed: 7 December 2020.

Bhatia, M. (2012) 'Domestic violence in India: cases under the protection of women from the Domestic Violence Act, 2005', *South Asia Research*, 32(2): 103–22.

Braun, V. and Clarke, V. (2007) 'Using thematic analysis in psychology', *Qualitative Research in Psychology*, 3(2): 77–101.

Cooper, J., Husain, N., Webb, R., Waheed, W., Kapur, N., Guthrie, E. and Appleby, L. (2006) 'Self-harm in the UK: differences between South Asians and Whites in rates, characteristics, provision of service and repetition', *Social Psychiatry and Psychiatric Epidemiology*, 41(10): 782–8.

Crenshaw, K. (1991) 'Mapping the margins: intersectionality, identity politics and violence against women of colour', *Stanford Law Review*, 43(6): 1241–99.

Forward (2020) 'Female genital mutilation'. Available at: https://www.forwarduk.org.uk/violence-against-women-and-girls/female-genital-mutilation/. Accessed: 7 July 2020.

Ganeshpanchan, Z. (2017) *Bodies as Sites of War – Women and Conflict: A Case Study of Sri Lanka*. UK: Zinthiya Ganeshpanchan.

Gangoli, G., Razak, A. and McCarry, M. (2006) *Forced Marriage and Domestic Violence Among South Asian Communities in North East England*, School for Policy Studies, University of Bristol and Northern Rock Foundation.

Gilligan, P. and Akhtar, S. (2006) 'Cultural barriers to the disclosure of child sexual abuse in Asian communities: listening to what women say', *British Journal of Social Work*, 36(8): 1361–77.

Girishkumar, D. (2014) *Diaspora and Multiculturalism: South Asian Women's Writings* (PhD), Cardiff University.

Goel, R. (2005) 'Sita's trousseau: restorative justice, domestic violence and South Asian culture', *Violence Against Women*, 11(5): 639–65.

Gov.uk (2020) *Female Genital Mutilation: Resource Pack*. Available at: https://www.gov.uk/government/publications/female-genital-mutilation-resource-pack/female-genital-mutilation-resource-pack#prevalence-of-fgm-in-england-and-wales. Accessed: 12 July 2020.

Hapke, H. M. (2013) 'Theorizing patriarchy development paradoxes and the geography of gender in South Asia', *Gender, Technology and Development*, 7(1): 1–29

Johnson, P. S. and Johnson, J. A. (2001) 'The oppression of women in India', *Violence Against Women*, 7(9): 1051–68.

Kandiyoti, D. (1988) 'Bargaining with patriarchy', *Gender and Society*, 2(3), Special Issue to Honor Jessie Bernard: 274–90 .

Krishnan, S. (2005) 'Gender, caste, and economic inequalities and marital violence in rural south India', *Health Care for Women International*, 26: 87–99.

Leicester Women's Research Centre (2019). Available at: https://womensresearchcentre.wordpress.com/contact/. Accessed: 9 February 2021.

National Family Health Survey (2007) *National Family Health Survey (NFHS-3), 2005–06: India*, Mumbai, Maharashtra, India: International Institute for Population Sciences and Macro International.

Niaz, U. (2003) 'Violence against women in South Asia', *Archives of Women's Mental Health*, 6(3): 173–84.

Nirol, I. (2017) 'Chaupadi a tradition in Nepal turns menstruating women into untouchables'. Available at: https://www.statnews.com/2017/02/17/nepal-tradition-chaupadi-menstruation/. Accessed: 7 July 2020.

O'Neill, M. (2007) 'Feminist knowledge and socio-cultural research: ethno-mimesis, feminist praxis and the visual turn', in T. Edwards (ed) *Cultural Theory: Classical and Contemporary Positions*, London: Sage, pp 211–30.

Prasad, S. (1999) 'Medicolegal responses to violence against women in India', *Violence Against Women*, 5(5): 478–506.

Raj, A. and Silverman, J. (2002) 'Violence against immigrant women: the roles of culture, context, and legal immigrant status on partner violence', *Violence Against Women*, 8(3): 367–98.

Rehman, Y., Kelly, L. and Sidiqui, H. (2013) *Moving in the Shadows: Violence on the Lives of Minority Women and Children*, London: Routledge.

Rocca, C. H., Rathod, S., Falle, T., Pande, R. P. and Krishnan, S. (2009) 'Challenging assumptions about women's empowerment: social and economic resources and domestic violence among young married women in urban South India', *International Journal of Epidemiology*, 38: 577–85.

Sornarajah, N. (2004) 'The experiences of Tamil women: nationalism, construction of gender, and women's political agency', *Lines*, 4: 3..

Thandi, G. and Lloyd, B. (2011) ' "This is a man's problem": Strategies for working with South Asian male perpetrators of intimate partner violence'. Available at: https://www.jibc.ca/sites/default/files/research/pdf/This-is-a-man%27s-problem_REPORT.pdf. Accessed: 7 July 2020.

Thiruchandran. S. (1997) 'The construction of gender in the social formation of Jaffna; some thematic observations', *Nevidini Journal of Gender Studies*, 5(2): 50–83.

Tjaden, P. and Thoeness, N. (2000) *Full Report of the Prevalence, Incidence, and Consequences of Violence Against Women*. Available at: https://www.ncjrs.gov/pdffiles1/nij/183781.pdf. Accessed: 7 July 2020.

4

Exploring shame, love and healing within women's recovery: an analysis of a trauma-specific intervention

Alexandria Bradley, Kirsty Day and Rose Mahon

Introduction

Within the field of criminology and women's recovery and rehabilitation there has been increasing interest among academics, practitioners and policy makers, to move towards a trauma-informed approach across the criminal justice system (Bloom and Covington, 2008; Bradley, 2017; Ministry of Justice, 2018; Jewkes et al, 2019; One Small Thing, 2019[1]). This approach aims to recognise the ways in which trauma can manifest within the behaviour and lives of individuals. The trajectory of the 'becoming trauma-informed' movement, has steadily infiltrated women's services and policy strategies within the UK since the early 2000s.

The focus on women's vulnerabilities and experiences of previous trauma intensified following the release of the Corston Report (2007), which encouraged the greater use of safe women-only spaces, women's centres and tailored services. In order to improve engagement within such facilities, it was argued that centres should provide onsite childcare and access to multiple services within a 'one-stop-shop' environment, to better support women with a variety of needs (Gelsthorpe et al, 2007).

Women with histories and experiences of sex work are a hidden demographic and the statistics currently available are outdated. It is suggested that 21 per cent of women within one prison had experienced sex working (National Offender Management Service, 2012). Out of those women, 74 per cent specified that they did so, in order to fund a drug habit, while 26 per cent stated that they had been abused. Between 2011 and 2012 it was estimated that 723 women referred to women's centres were identified as needing sex-work-specific support due to their lived experiences (Prison Reform Trust, 2014).

However, there continues to be a paucity of research in academia, policy and practice to examine effective responses to the distinct and often trauma-infused experiences of women with sex-working histories.

Methodology

The data presented in this chapter was collected as part of a qualitative evaluation of the Griffin Programme[2]. It was designed following a research project that examined support services for women with histories of sex work (Tate, 2015). The voices of women who had completed the programme, and staff who had facilitated the programme, were collected, in order to explore the impact, value and nuances from a dual perspective. The reflections of the women and staff were gathered using qualitative methods and were explored using thematic analysis (Braun and Clarke, 2007).

To better enhance all of our understandings of the programme the experience of the specialised Griffin Programme, seven women took part in two separate focus groups. One focus group was conducted with four women who had completed numerous cycles of the programme and referred to themselves as the 'veterans'; the other focus group interview included three women who were in the middle of their first Griffin Programme cycle. In addition, semi-structured interviews were conducted with five staff who had either facilitated the Griffin Programme or who had had strategic involvement in the development stages. The qualitative methodology was chosen, in order to hear and explore the experiences of both staff and women accessing support from the Nelson Trust[3]. It was important to nurture shared experiences and feelings of safety within the focus group, to explore the impact of the programme (Hollander, 2004.

Alternatively, to capture staff reflections in a safe environment, anonymity was required, in order to ensure that vicarious identification was reduced. Therefore, one-to-one semi-structured interviews were conducted with staff, in order to respect their privacy and to increase trust and the depth of discussion between the staff and the researcher (Brown and Danaher, 2017).

All of the participants created their own pseudonyms. However, during focus group transcription, it was not possible to definitively identify each of the women. In addition, due to the nature of the research, it is imperative that the anonymity of the women is prioritised. The data from the two focus groups with women have been combined and fully anonymised. Therefore, only the staff have pseudonyms within this chapter.

The aims and objectives of the evaluation were to provide an analysis of the merit of the trauma-specific intervention and to examine challenges from the perspectives of experienced women and staff. This chapter begins with a consideration of the trajectory of trauma-informed working, to provide a guided landscape of good practice. Following this, the authors explore the 'becoming trauma-informed' evolution, to outline the progression towards becoming trauma-responsive and then trauma-specific. This provides a practical foundation to investigate the evidenced-based, trauma-specific Griffin Programme. The chapter considers the importance of providing trauma-specific programmes to support women healing from sexual trauma and substance misuse (Covington, 2008). Following on from contextual discussions, the chapter considers the positionality of this research within the broader field of women, families, and crime and justice studies. Furthermore, there is a consideration of three key themes that emerged from the evaluation:

- relational association: healing, shame and intimacy;
- implicit knowing;
- nurturing, love and healing.

Each of these themes is explored using a combination of data from the women and staff who took part in the evaluation.

Innovation within rehabilitation: becoming trauma-informed

More recently, there has been a more rapid and haphazard application of trauma-informed practices. This, ultimately, has led to a disregard of the methodical implementation plans and conditions first outlined by Harris and Fallot (2001) (discussed later), as well as a dilution of the core values identified by Covington (2008). The core values required and prioritised within a trauma-informed approach are safety, trust, choice, collaboration and empowerment (Covington, 2008). However, for these to flourish within an organisation, the conditions for the implementation of trauma-informed approaches must be considered.

Harris and Fallot (2001) were the first to introduce five key conditions to facilitate change within organisational culture and structure:

- administrative commitment to change;
- universal screening;
- training and education;

- hiring principles;
- review of policies and procedures.

These conditions form a top-down strategy, to ensure that the appropriate foundation is in place to embed the trauma-informed approach. The conditions relate to organisations providing resources in order to increase trauma awareness effectively across their service and programme delivery. In addition, they reiterate the importance of screening all individuals accessing services, to understand lived experiences and histories of trauma. The skills and understanding required for this are to be embedded within staff training, education and hiring principles. This ensures that organisations demonstrate consistency across the organisation to revisit and prioritise the staff team's trauma awareness. Therefore, it is important to note that the implementation follows a top-down approach, to ensure consistency in policies, organisational culture and leadership buy-in before it can be embedded in staff practices and approaches. It is suggested that a significant issue within the implementation of trauma-informed practice is due to the lack of attempt to evaluate progress, provide quality assurance or evidence to suggest that a service or organisation is actually delivering a 'trauma-informed' service (Bradley, 2017; Bradley, 2020a).

The lack of quality assurance and accreditation development has led to the trauma-informed approach becoming 'an elastic term for rehabilitation services to demonstrate innovation, during a challenging climate of perpetual competitive funding' (Bradley, 2020a, p 4). Research exploring the funding landscape of women's only services presents particular vulnerabilities such as limited sources of income and ration of assets to income (Hirst and Rinne, 2012). The same research compared the assets, income concentration and administrative ratio of other service providers to equivalent women-only organisations. However, women-only organisations were nearly 16% less likely to survive than comparative local service providers. As such, it is even more important for women-only services to demonstrate innovation (such as becoming trauma-informed) within a challenging climate. In the context of the prison service, it is acknowledged that some academics within the field of prison research and senior prison staff have described trauma-informed care and practice (TICP) as 'fashionable' and 'faddish' (Jewkes et al 2019, p 2). However, the current authors argue that if properly implemented, trauma-informed care and practice has the potential to succeed in providing holistic practices that align with the environment in which they are delivered.

Therefore, any criminal justice organisation or institution can embed trauma-informed working, if dedication to the implementation plan is demonstrated and the appropriate resources are available to do so. This must also be accompanied by the prioritisation of quality assurance and regular evaluation of the organisation's or institution's progression towards trauma-informed working. Often, the ongoing and reflective nature associated with implementation of trauma-informed care and practice is often underestimated and underresourced. This can result in implementation fatigue, leading to poor quality trauma-informed working and limited cultural and/or practical change.

In addition, it is argued that women's services need to ensure successful implementation of trauma-informed and trauma-responsive practices, prior to considering progression towards providing a trauma-specific intervention. It is important to recognise the distinction between the phases when working with trauma. For an organisation to become trauma-informed, it must be able to demonstrate cultural, relational and environmental recognition of the many ways that trauma can impact upon an individual's life and behaviour. To move towards becoming trauma-responsive, requires the application of the above trauma-infused knowledge, in order to focus on 'moving from knowing to doing and being' (Triesman, 2018, p 10). It is not possible to be one without the other. Furthermore, this process should be recognised as a progression and continuum, while placing the emphasis on the commitment to consistently reflect on service delivery.

However, to support women towards healing from trauma, the Substance Abuse and Mental Health Services Administration[4] (2014) in the US outlines that there are many approaches and treatment modalities within trauma-specific services, in order to treat traumatic stress and facilitate recovery. These can include cognitive behavioural therapy, relaxation and breathing strategies to support individuals to cope with anxiety, and the use of stories to explore events in the lives of individuals, to increase their understanding of their behaviour.

To facilitate shared experiences within a safe space, the foundation of the Griffin Programme was relational and strength based. It was designed from emerging research (Tate, 2015) that argued for the development of trauma-specific and safety-based groups for women with sex-working histories.

Recognising violence and trauma in sex work

It has been well documented that sex workers have continued to experience a range of violence, sexual trauma, human rights violations, abuse and stigma globally (Deering et al, 2014). The marginalisation experienced by sex workers can often intersect with gender-based violence, addiction, as well as mental and physical health issues (SWARM,[5] 2017). These can lead to longer-lasting and pervasive impacts, relating to sex-working experiences.

It is important to highlight that all women have diverse experiences and, as such, it is important not to conflate all sex-working experiences within the context of violence against women. However, this chapter acknowledges the voices of women who seek recovery and healing from sex-work-associated trauma and those who identify as survivors of the industry. In order to respond to the violence and abuse experienced by sex workers, there is a critical need for community-led interventions (Deering et al, 2014).

Introducing the Griffin Programme

The Griffin Programme adopts a triad of theory, experience and practice. It is a combination of past-focused and present-focused approaches. The combination of approaches enables women to explore their trauma histories, behaviours and triggers, as well as their current coping mechanisms, to provide a meaningful holistic intervention. The programme consists of nine weekly sessions.

It has a theoretical underpinning, which recognises addiction theory, trauma theory and relational theory (Bloom and Covington, 2008). The combination of theories supports the recognition of gender-specific adversities and sexual trauma that may have been experienced by women with histories of sex work. The intervention has three key aims:

- to bring women with a sex-working history into an emotionally safe setting and create an optimum space for sharing experiences to support the building of emotional connection;
- to consider and discuss, through group sessions, the pervasive shame and trauma symptoms as a result of sex working;
- to process emotional realities, to rewrite internal narratives and instil hope.

The programme design embeds the common experiences that sex-working women face within group sessions, to facilitate the combating of shame without the pressure of disclosure. The women who take part in the Griffin Programme have had a variety of sex-working histories;

however, most of the women have experienced street sex working or survival sex working.

The first cycle of the programme occurs while women are seeking support in residential recovery and rehabilitation. However, women can revisit the same Griffin Programme content again, once they are living outside of residential services, to take part in another two cycles in order to put their learning into practice.

The groups are kept small, to promote trust between a maximum of seven women. Women are initially referred to the residential recovery services from all over the UK. Once women are stable within their recovery from drugs and alcohol, and are ready to engage in group work, they can refer themselves onto the Griffin Programme. The programme is facilitated by two staff members and all sessions are held in a therapeutic group room at their hub academy in Stroud, Gloucestershire.

Designing and delivering a programme that is trauma-specific for women healing from sexual trauma, substance abuse and sex-working histories is not straightforward. For example, due to the pervasive nature of shame, being exposed to judgement or discrimination could further compound shame and reinforce the experience. To revisit a buried experience within a group produces an additional level of vulnerability to consider. Within the Griffin Programme, the facilitators and group members strive to develop a safe environment, and to encourage honest narratives and enhanced trust, to provide a reparative experience.

The following section examines the first theme emerging from data collected with women who took part in at least one cycle of the Griffin Programme.

Relational association: healing, shame and intimacy

The term 'relational association' was coined from the findings of this research. The term relates to the depth of trust and meaningful relationships formed within the group, which encourage women to share very difficult experiences – including histories of sexual trauma and violence. The sharing of experiences and the powerful nature of 'relational association' is significant for the group, as many of the women within this research stated that this was the first time that many of them had realised that they were not alone.

Facilitating the discussion of painful experiences within a group is a challenging task. Consequently, the environment and safety developed within the group play a key role. Some of the challenges identified in

Tate's (2015) research acknowledged that shame is a significant barrier for women who are exiting sex work. In support of this, Sauer (2019, p 329) argues that shame is fundamentally attached to sex worker emotional experiences and stigmatisation within the double standards of the 'patriarchal bourgeois interpretation'. Therefore, women continue to engage in a double battle of societal stigma and the internal feelings of shame (Månnson and Hedin, 1999), compounding the experience of trauma. In turn, these experiences intertwine to make both exiting sex work and disclosing sex working to support services particularly difficult for women.

If women do disclose their histories of sex work and they receive negative or stigmatic responses from individuals, this can result in disclosure becoming a further trauma (Ullman and Peter-Hagene, 2014; Tate, 2015). In support, Mott (2014, n.p.) states, 'I can speak to multiple rapes, I can speak to knowing physical, mental, sexual torture'. Abolitionist movements have included the voices of individuals with lived experience to highlight the 'violence against women and a traumatic bodily experience' and the 'daily genocide of the prostituted class' (Mott, 2014, n.p.). This highlights the need to discuss some of the long-lasting stigma and trauma experiences of some women with sex-working histories.

Although much has been done to end the stigmatisation of sex work and to transform shame into pride (Laing et al, 2015), there are still significant challenges in disclosure for women. This results in services not recognising or responding to the needs of women with sex-working histories. Gidron et al (1996) argue that it is important for women to feel comfortable to disclose their experiences of trauma and sex work, as it is helpful for their recovery journey. Valandra (2007) posits that the safe spaces created by survivor-led groups are more likely to promote healthy recovery experiences for women with histories of sexual trauma. This approach has been adopted in both design and evaluation of the programme. In the following quotes, women and staff consider the importance of sharing experiences in the group:

'My relapse lasted many years and, whereas when I first got clean my experience of sex working had all been escorting and getting paid lots of money and in a fairly safe environment, when I relapsed it just went down to street level working and so the shame that I felt when I came back was on so many levels that I just didn't think that I'd ever be free of that. I just felt that I was a failure on every level. I remember my very first Griffin group, I cried my eyes out, cried my eyes out 'cos I felt hope. I thought, "Oh my God, this might be just something that is gonna set me free from all that labels and all that stuff that's inside me". And I did. I really got that from doing the course.'

As illustrated previously, the emotional impact of 'selling sex' can be far reaching and long lasting (Sanders, 2004). Attendance at the Griffin Programme enabled women to liberate themselves from the legacy of psychological and emotional harm, and to counteract feelings of stigma and shame. In addition, this quote highlights that shame is also associated with relapsing and alterations to the nature of the sex working. Therefore this could be an additional hurdle for academics and practitioners to consider for women accessing support. This is supported by Månsson and Hedin (1999), who suggest that breaking away from sex work is characterised by relapses and regressions. This reiterates the importance of services recognising that setbacks are a normal aspect of recovery, rather than failure.

The power of shame has been described as one of the biggest barriers for women accessing support services (Clawson et al, 2008). Yet, within the Griffin Programme, women are supported to share their experiences of shame and trauma in a safe environment, sometimes for the very first time. The following quotes highlight the need for honest discussions of shame within the group, to build trust and crucial 'relational association':

'I mean, I've blurted things out, and I've felt full of shame and I've thought, "Oh my God. Can't believe I've just said that!" and then they'll go, "You ain't alone! We've done that too!" and all of a sudden that shame is lifted and you think "Ahhh. Okay. I'm glad I'm not the only one".'

The group was able to provide a safe environment for women to share experiences that had previously made them feel isolated. This provided an opportunity for 'relational association' to develop:

'It's like you get vulnerable and then everyone else meets you there, and we all hold that vulnerability together.'

The impact of carrying shame can be pervasive and long-lasting (Balfour and Allen, 2014). This shared experience of vulnerability within the group encouraged all of the women to share things that they have kept to themselves for a long time:

> 'Because you never talked about anyone you think that you're the only one and that carries a lot of shame. Especially the topics that we talk about. For me it was massive, really massive hearing not just one, not just two but three other women identifying with this stuff that I've never been able to tell anyone. Stuff that literally makes me curl up in shame because I feel disgusting. I feel dirty but actually speaking to women who'd had the same experiences as me, it's sort of like, okay. It's not just me and I think that's invaluable. Absolutely invaluable.'

> 'I felt so disgusting and so bad about myself I just literally wanted to unzip my skin and throw it on the floor and it was like, almost like shame and it was horrible, and I went in there and literally I'd kept all that feeling all day and not knowing what to do with it anywhere else, not wanted to share it with anyone and I just kind of broke down and the other women in there were just so amazingly supportive and I was allowed to get those feelings out, say what it was without feeling all that shame and it was like just shedding off a load of bricks that I'd been carrying around with me all day.'

The experiences of shared shame provided resilience building within the small-group setting. The group was able to honour each experience with respect and dignity, in order to facilitate empowerment and healing. The voices of the women highlight the importance of sharing trauma and lived experience, in order to experience 'relational association'. This can facilitate relationships described by the women as 'intimate':

> 'It just feels like it's intimate on another level and I think that connection between a group of women is so powerful … there's something so powerful about having, maybe, been hurt by men and looked for healing in men, misguidedly, to then find it in a group of women, there's something really powerful about that.'

The 'intimacy' described by women highlights the depth of connection within the group. This enabled women to build a space of love and healing. This is particularly important for the development of healthy relationships after leaving sex work. Some of the key emotional issues identified following leaving sex work are 'vulnerability, helplessness, fear and disempowerment' (Gorry et al, 2010, p 497). Therefore, the women accessing the Griffin Programme may bring experiences into the group which are painful, retraumatising or triggering for one another, yet they described the environment as intimate, powerful and a space of love. This is testimony to the evidenced-based and trauma-specific design and delivery of the Griffin Programme.

Furthermore, the data collected with facilitators of the Griffin Programme and women indicated that the depth of connection within the group was inimitable and certain qualities associated with a Griffin facilitator were 'untrainable' and intrinsic. However, in order to promote transparency within Griffin Programme facilitator recruitment and selection criteria, in a recent evaluation The Nelson Trust were encouraged to identify specific qualities associated with the desirable skill set to enhance staff development, and to consider how they could make the recruitment process more transparent for staff (Bradley, 2020b).

The following section considers the second theme emerging from this research: implicit knowing.

Implicit knowing

The term 'implicit knowing' has been coined by the authors to explain the depth of connection, compassion and nurturing between a Griffin Programme facilitator and women within the group. In this section, the perspectives of staff and women explore the unique and specialised skill set required in order to be a successful Griffin Programme facilitator.

According to Starhawk (2011, pp 203–4): 'We can make ourselves available to listen, actively, empathetically, hearing emotion as well as content. We don't have to fix the situations or relieve the pain. Indeed, we cannot. A good listener is a witness, not a problem solver or an advice giver'. To bear witness to a woman's trauma is a privilege; therefore, it is crucial that practitioners honour the experience shared, without interruption, discomfort or pity:

> 'We don't dance around the edges with it; we're right in there. We talk very deeply about sexual experiences, the kind of humour behind certain situations, all that kind of stuff ... it's in there and the person I've got co-facilitating

is not afraid to come there. I think that's what it is. You need to be able to go to those places with those women and be alongside them and to be able to hold the space I think is the other thing with it is. There's a saying somewhere around, to be able to be a good facilitator you need to be able to go into the darkness with them and I think that's what makes the people that I know so far that have facilitated Griffin have all had, for whatever reason ... doesn't necessarily mean the history stuff ... but the ability to go with them and be side-by-side with them ... The thing about Griffin is that very few people can facilitate it because of the nature of the subject that we're talking about. You can't really train people to do it – that sounds like a strange thing to say – you've either got it or you haven't, kind of thing with it, because it's different from any of the other groups that we run here, some of the generic addiction groups or even the other trauma groups, it's very different. To have an all-female space that is safe enough for the women to be able to talk about the stuff that they need to talk about is a very unique environment for them and we've had some previous people who've come and facilitated and it hasn't really worked out ... So someone who knows when to laugh at the right time, cry at the right time, hold space at the right time and just somebody – I don't want to get emotional – someone who isn't afraid to stand at the edge of somebody's darkness and just be there. Just be there. No judgement, no movement, no noise, no sound, no nothing. Just someone who has the ability to stand at the edge and understands what a true gift the women give you when they allow you to witness and doesn't do anything. It's like standing on the edge of a perfectly still pond and not doing anything to cause a ripple. Do you know what I mean? Someone who's not afraid of that.' (Naomi)

Notably, Covington et al (2008) indicate that some staff members may feel uncomfortable when talking about trauma with women, due to potential unresolved personal experiences of trauma. This is an important consideration for organisations running trauma-specific programmes. Prioritising staff safety is as crucial as selecting the right facilitator. In addition, due to the nature of the Griffin Programme, the staff all receive external therapeutic supervision, debriefing opportunities and an extensive training programme (Bradley, 2020b).

Staff tried to explore a word or phrase that encompassed the work of a Griffin facilitator, and none could articulate it. They all felt that the skills were not trainable; rather, it was an intrinsic quality:

> 'They haven't allocated a word to it but all the basic stuff like trauma-informed stuff, the passion, the love, the care, but the love of boundaries [laughs]. Yeah, the care. You're equal to them in that place so it's faith. Do you know what I mean? You don't have to have gone through it but you have this thing that you can't teach that, it lives within you.' (Willomena)

When staff were asked to consider the perfect 'ingredients' to create a Griffin facilitator, they shared examples of characteristics, but found it very difficult to pinpoint the specific skills required. The facilitators came from a range of backgrounds – some had lived experiences, while others did not. However, all of the facilitators had worked with women within the criminal justice system for many years, building up experience and knowledge associated with trauma-informed working. When asked about the skills required to be a Griffin facilitator, the staff stated that it was something more than having lived experience, more than love and compassion, and more than being trauma-informed, but all were unable to articulate the precise expertise associated.

The authors refer to this as 'implicit knowing', which we argue is an essential ability of a Griffin facilitator. This ability enables facilitators to bear witness to a woman's trauma and to honour that experience, in order to encourage healing. In addition, 'implicit knowing' is the non-verbal communication – or vibe – between a woman and facilitator, whereby non-verbal interaction and environmental cues are utilised in order to gather information and understand emotional responses. This provides a depth of interaction, which elicits feelings of safety, understanding and the inherent recognition of 'I see you, I hear you and I am with you'.

The power of 'implicit knowing' can also be explored in the voices of women who have completed the programme:

> 'On every level of this organisation, there are women not with just lived experience but that seem to really understand the importance of the process.'

Women shared examples of support provided by the staff. They stated that the depth of relationship that they had with staff made them feel more connected in comparison to other services:

> 'I find that the relationships are much more personal here and it's not just like, "right, it's five o'clock and I've finished work, so I don't care about your problems anymore", it was really like, yeah, personal relationships and if you were feeling a certain way it's not so strictly regimed [sic] and I think that really helps 'cos it's real people it's not just somebody in a role in a job. It's somebody who's got experience and then doing it because they have so much passion for this stuff. And I think that really makes a difference it's not just a job and a role. We're not like client and whatever; it's equal.'

This emphasises the relational approach within the organisation. However, all of the women agreed that the selection of specialised and nurturing staff is essential:

> 'If it wasn't for the staff that manage it and I think they're very careful as to what staff they get to facilitate it. Not every member of staff would be able to facilitate this group.'

The experiences between the group highlighted the different dynamic and relational approach, due to the careful selection of Griffin Programme facilitators by the creator of the intervention. The selection process is therefore critical to ensuring that the group runs in a meaningful and safe way for the staff and women.

The final section explores the third theme within this research, whereby staff and women both acknowledged the group sessions as providing a place for love and healing.

Nurturing, love and healing

It is recognised that therapeutic relationships are mutually respectful, empathetic and compassionate (Covington, 2008). In the US, the Substance Abuse and Mental Health Services Administration (2011) acknowledged that women who have histories of addiction find supportive therapies more beneficial. Further analysis indicates that the term 'love' exists within the context of self-nurturing to promote empowered connectiveness within self-work. These are enhanced feelings of 'love and generosity that transcended self, reaching towards spiritual understandings and a sense of belonging in the world' (Kearney, 1998, p 508).

In this study, the women acknowledged experiencing love throughout the Nelson Trust women's residential treatment programme:[6]

> 'You can tell that they've got love and compassion and understanding. You can just feel it throughout the whole of the [Nelson] Trust, for me. Especially the women's service, I can't really speak for the mixed service, but the women at the women's service are just amazing. The support that they give you, and understanding, is invaluable. And you also know, I think, you get a feeling that they understand, they've been there for the most extent of it. You know it's not just textbook learning that they actually have been through this and they care deeply about what happens to the women in the service.'

The previous quote indicates that staff have demonstrated love and compassion towards women accessing their programme. This is a testament to the organisation and staff approach to working in a trauma-responsive way. This is an advanced level of practice which organisations can demonstrate following the long-term implementation of trauma-informed practice. This is where the approach transitions from recognising and responding to trauma in order to demonstrate good practice in supporting long-term healing and recovery from trauma.

> 'It really is a full package, down to the programme content and the staff who deliver it, it's the room and the space, the welcome, the silence, the holding with love and the bean bags.'

Some of the women highlighted the importance of the environment that the organisation has created:

> 'I've never been in a group before where you have an emotional bond. I quite like the word "transcend"; I feel like this group transcends in every way. It's just deeper and further, and it is holding a space of love.'

Many of the women agreed that the group consisted of love. They discussed this as 'the holding of love' and the 'space of love', which is felt within the entire group and between Griffin facilitators and the women:

> 'It's taught me how to have a lot more compassion and love for other people, therefore you can't help but to start giving that to yourself. And the stuff that I've learned here continues to help me.'

The activities and discussions transformed their thinking to compassionately understand others in the group, as well as learning to love themselves. This long-term behaviour change stemming from the programme is significant for trauma working, as self-confidence can be impacted due to the experiences of shame. However, this group demonstrates healing and recovery in perceptions. The trust built within the group also supports the staff to facilitate honest exchanges:

> 'And by that time the trust within the group itself the fact that it's a closed group so you've been with those same women from day dot, you've got that trust, literally. And the love and compassion in the room, you know.' (Charlie)

As demonstrated previously, the importance of love within women's healing from trauma lies in the experience of relationships and reconnection (Duncan and Mason, 2011). When a woman 'disconnects', this is usually caused by relationships that are disempowering and when a woman feels 'unheard' or when women have experienced violence, abuse or sexual trauma (Substance Abuse and Mental Health Services Administration, 2014). It is acknowledged that trauma can impact upon the relational experiences of women, and the way that women engage with staff and peers (Rosenbaum and Varvin, 2008). Therefore, it is particularly powerful that women are able to associate 'love' with their healing experience on the Griffin Programme:

> 'I say all of the time, much of the work we do here is just loving them back to life, you know. You can't do this work without love.' (Naomi)

This final quote symbolises the approach taken by the organisation and staff who support women to heal from trauma and sexual violence.

Concluding thoughts

This chapter has explored the value of a trauma-specific intervention for women who are recovering from trauma and shame, related to their sex-working histories. The three key themes will now be explored in more depth, highlighting future directions for organisations hoping to design trauma-specific programmes. This final discussion focuses on the importance for nurturing and love within the context of women's recovery and rehabilitation.

The voices of the women explored the power of 'relational association', particularly when they shared personal experiences of shame. It was argued that the term should be considered when trying to explain the depth of connection between the women on the Griffin Programme. The shame and stigma of sex working was discussed by all of the women in this research. Women within the programme felt able to disclose painful memories and experiences that they had kept to themselves for many years. This is an area of interest for practitioners and academics, as shame and a fear of rejection can be a significant barrier for women with sex-working histories, when attempting to access associated support.

Tate's (2015) research indicated that women with sex-working experiences may not be disclosing their needs and lived experiences to services. Therefore, many organisations are unaware of potential rehabilitation or recovery needs within the women accessing their support. It is therefore important to prioritise the reduction of shame and to promote the safe discussion of sex-working histories within organisations. Practically, this could be improved with additional trauma-informed training, which specifically considers the pervasive aspect of shame intertwined with experiences of sexual trauma and sex work. In addition, the inclusion of survivor-led groups (Valandra, 2007) may be a potential way to facilitate transformative recovery experiences through 'relational association'.

The experiences of the women outlined the feeling of shame as a trauma. For example, women considered shame at every level of their experiences, including the application of labels and stigma both after their relapses and during their sex work. This led to one woman stating that she wanted to "unzip my skin and throw it on the floor", which demonstrates the pervasive impact of shame and trauma – and how these can influence identities and perceptions of the self. However, many of these disclosures of shame within the group facilitated 'relational association', which enabled women to share their vulnerability and shame in order to feel relief. This relief was described by two women as being "lifted" and being "set free". This emphasises the power of 'relational association' through the shared experiences within the Griffin Programme. The relationships and trust constructed in the group were fundamental in achieving such a safe environment. This emphasised the importance of the environment in delivering a trauma-specific programme.

One of the most significant findings of this research indicated the power of the programme in producing intimacy between women through shared vulnerability and 'relational association'. As the term 'intimacy' is not traditionally used in this field, this is an important consideration within relational approaches. The women described it as transformative for their relationship building. They stated that they typically focused on finding healing from men, yet this programme supported them to develop healthy relationships with women instead.

Furthermore, this chapter has demonstrated that the Griffin Programme provides two distinct approaches to combating shame. First, an environment is created whereby the unspeakable becomes the relational group norm, as the content supports discussions of experiences that women often struggle to verbalise. Second is the power of 'relational association', whereby women are profoundly impacted when they see and hear another woman sharing the same or similar shame experiences. This encourages a flood of emotional connection, solidarity, sisterhood, hope, optimism, love and a desire to stand up and say "me too".[7] For women to know that they are not the only ones who have experienced what they have experienced, or did what they did, this has the power to reduce shame.

Another theme presented in this chapter relates to the term 'implicit knowing'. This finding from the research relates to the inherent untrainable skills and characteristics required in order to be a Griffin Programme facilitator. Therefore, careful and considered selection of staff is vital in this context. The instances of staff support provided in this chapter are powerful, demonstrating the passion and advanced trauma awareness of the team delivering the programme. 'Implicit knowing' has been considered here as a non-verbal connection and communication, which generates an understanding between staff and women. This interaction provides a depth of trauma-responsiveness, without providing verbal communication, in order to articulate challenging emotions. In addition, the depth of the interaction produces more meaningful and safe relationships between women and staff.

Crucially, the findings indicate that while lived experience is valued, this does not always equate to 'implicit knowing'. Importantly, staff are encouraged to feel real emotion within the delivery – to cry, to laugh and to be present with women as they revisit to some of their trauma(s) and just to be present. This reiterates the work of Starhawk (2011) – to bear witness, rather than attempting to relieve pain, interrupt or solve problems.

Indeed, this emphasises the need to consider more ways that women can share openly within further trauma-specific recovery contexts. Although it is a challenging political climate within women's community services, the women highlighted that the personal relationships with the staff enhanced their experience on the programme. Subsequently, future directions should focus on encouraging more meaningful experiences within rehabilitation and recovery as an important relational tool to support women's engagement and transformation within services.

The final theme in this chapter considered the role of 'nurturing, love and healing' within the programme. This is the crescendo which unites the previous themes, as there is no place for 'relational association' and 'implicit knowing' without there being an environment that is nurturing, loving and healing. The data indicated that women felt love and compassion from the facilitators. The women described the space of love and an emotional bond within the group that 'transcends' in every way. This is particularly powerful from the women's perspective, as it recognises the relationship development, support and staff engagement as love; they felt that the staff cared both genuinely and deeply about them. Moreover, the love demonstrated in the group enabled one woman to begin to love herself, which is particularly transformative, considering the pervasive impact of shame discussed earlier in this chapter.

A future direction for practitioners and academics is to question why the term 'love' is seldom used within criminology, rehabilitation and recovery from addictions. As such, the authors argue that the current system requires a cultural and philosophical shift, in order to accept that relationships and loving approaches are key to the successful recovery of women healing from trauma and sex-working histories.

In line with the future directions presented, it is crucial to acknowledge the wellbeing of staff who deliver trauma-specific programmes. Therefore, care needs to be taken to ensure that staff do not experience vicarious trauma during or following the delivery of the programme. An example of good practice from the Nelson Trust centres around their prioritisation of post-programme debriefs for staff as well as external trauma-informed supervision. While, it is important to provide love within trauma healing, staff will be unable to deliver the best service to women, if nurturing and safety are not also prioritised for them.

This research has also demonstrated the importance of academics and practitioners working collaboratively on publications in this area. This offers a good practice approach to strengthening the perspectives and capitalising on the modernisation within women's rehabilitation services. Overall, the success of trauma-specific programmes will be unsustainable, if changes are not made both culturally and financially within the precarious and insecure funding landscape of women's rehabilitation and recovery.

Reflection points

- When working with trauma-specific programmes, is it relevant to consider trauma histories of staff?
- Is 'implicit knowing' a trainable skill and, if so, how would you facilitate this?
- When working with women who have experienced multiple traumas, how important a tool is love for recovery and healing?
- Could 'relational association' be used in another rehabilitation or recovery context?

Notes

[1] One Small Thing is a registered charity (https://charitylist.ab3.uk/posts/charity-11/80/1180782.html https://onesmallthing.org.uk/people/tag/One+Small+Thing) devoted to creating efficacy and cultural change within the criminal justice system. The charity provides training for frontline staff, to enable a greater understanding of the pervasive impact of trauma.

[2] The Griffin Programme is a trauma-specific intervention, which has an evidence base originating from Tate's (2015) Griffin research at the University of Cambridge. It was designed by a staff member working at The Nelson Trust. Specialist Nelson Trust staff are recruited to deliver the programme.

[3] A charity that brings belief, hope and long-term recovery to people whose lives have been torn apart by addiction and the multiple and complex needs that come with it. They provide residential addiction treatment to men and women. They also support women in the community who are in contact with the criminal justice system.

[4] The Substance Abuse and Mental Health Services Administration – a US agency within the Department of Health and Human Services.

[5] Sex Worker Advocacy and Resistance Movement (SWARM) – a UK-based, sex-worker-led grassroots collective.

[6] The women-only residential treatment programme is a safe and therapeutic environment, where women can work together to address underlying issues of

safety. The care plans are designed for a period of 12 to 24 weeks to meet the personal needs of each woman, to provide abstinence-based residential treatment and recovery from drug and alcohol addiction.

[7] See: Me Too (2018) *History and Vision*. Available at: https://metoomvmt.org/about/. Accessed: 20 February 2020.

References

Balfour, R. and Allen, J. (2014) *A Review of the Literature on Sex Workers and Social Exclusion*. Available at: https://www.nswp.org/sites/nswp.org/files/nosilencetoviolence-swarmdec17.pdf. Accessed 12 September 2020.

Bloom, B. E. and Covington, S. S. (2008) 'Addressing the mental health needs of women offenders', in R. Gido and L. Dalley (eds) *Women's Mental Health Issues Across the Criminal Justice System*. Columbus, OH: Prentice-Hall, pp 160–176.

Bradley, A. (2017) 'Trauma-informed practice: exploring the role of adverse life experiences on the behaviour of offenders and the effectiveness of associated criminal justice strategies' (doctoral thesis), Northumbria University.

Bradley, A. (2020a) *A Qualitative Evaluation of the Nelson Trust Bridgwater Women's Centre*, Gloucester: The Nelson Trust.

Bradley, A. (2020b) *A Qualitative Evaluation of the Nelson Trust Griffin Programme*, Gloucester: The Nelson Trust.

Braun, V. and Clarke, V. (2007) 'Using thematic analysis in psychology', *Qualitative Research in Psychology*, 3(2): 77–101.

Brown, A. and Danaher, P. A. (2017) 'CHE principles: facilitation authentic and dialogical semi-structured interviews in educational research', *International Journal of Research and Method in Education*, 42(1): 76–90.

Clawson, H. J., Salomon, A. and Goldblatt Grace, L. (2008) *Treating the Hidden Wounds: Trauma Treatment and Mental Health Recovery for Victims of Human Trafficking*. Available at: https://aspe.hhs.gov/report/treating-hidden-wounds-trauma-treatment-and-mental-health-recovery-victims-human-trafficking. Accessed: 2 January 2020.

Corston, J. (2007) *The Corston Report—A Report by Baroness Jean Corston of a Review of Women with Particular Vulnerabilities in the Criminal Justice System: The Need for a Distinct, Radically Different, Visibly-led, Strategic, Proportionate, Holistic, Woman-Centred, Integrated Approach*, London: Home Office.

Covington, S. S. (2008) 'Women and addiction: a trauma-informed approach', *Journal of Psychoactive Drugs*, 40(5): 377–85.

Covington, S. S. and Bloom, B. E. (2007) 'Gender-responsive treatment and services in correctional settings', *Women and Therapy*, 29(3): 9–33.

Covington, S. S., Burke, C., Keaton, S. and Norcott, C. (2008) 'Evaluation of a trauma-informed and gender-responsive intervention for women in drug treatment', *Journal of Psychoactive Drugs*, 40(5): 387–98.

Crews, D. A. (2016) 'The use of yoga to build self-compassion as a healing method for survivors of sexual violence', *Journal of Religion and Spirituality in Social Work*, 35(3): 139–56.

Deering, K. N., Amin, A., Shoveller, J., Nesbitt, A., Garcia-Morena, C., Duff, P., Argento, E. and Shannon, K. (2014) 'A systematic review of the correlates of violence against sex workers', *American Journal of Public Health*, 104(5): 42–54.

Duncan, J. and Mason, R. (2011) 'Older women reconnecting after sexual violence through group work', *Women Against Violence: An Australian Feminist Journal*, 23: 18–28.

Elliott, D. E., Bjelajac, P., Fallot, R. D., Markoff, L. S. and Reed, B. G. (2005) 'Trauma-informed or trauma-denied: principles and implementation of trauma-informed services for women', *Journal of Community Psychology*, 33(4): 461–77.

Gelsthorpe, L., Sharpe, G. and Roberts, J. (2007) *Provision for Women Offenders in the Community*, London: Fawcett Society.

Gidron, Y., Peri, T., Connolly, J. F. and Shalev, A. Y. (1996) 'Written disclosure in posttraumatic stress disorder: is it beneficial for the patient?', *Journal of Nervous Mental Disease*, 184(8): 505–7.

Gorry, J., Roen, K. and Reilly, J. (2010) 'Selling your self? The psychological impact of street sex work and factors affecting support seeking', *Health and Social Care in the Community*, 18(5): 492–9.

Harris, M. and Fallot, R. D. (2001) *Using Trauma Theory to Design Service Systems*, San Francisco: Jossey-Bass.

Hirst, A. and Rinne, S. (2012) *The Impact of Changes in Commissioning and Funding on Women-only Services*. Available at: https://www.equalityhumanrights.com/sites/default/files/research-report-86-the-impact-of-changes-in-commissioning-and-funding-on-women-only-services.pdf. Accessed 16 February 2020.

Hollander, J. A. (2004) 'The social contexts of focus groups', *Journal of Contemporary Ethnography*, 33(5): 602–37. Available at: https://journals.sagepub.com/doi/10.1177/0891241604266988. Accessed: 12 December 2020.

Jennings, A. (2004) *Models for Developing Trauma-Informed Behavioural Health Systems and Trauma Specific Services*. Available at: http://theannainstitute.org/MDT.pdf. Accessed: 23 December 2019.

Jewkes, Y., Jordan, M., Wright, S. and Bendelow, G. (2019) 'Designing "healthy" prisons for women: incorporating trauma-informed care and practice (TICP) into prison planning and design', *International Journal of Environmental Research and Public Health*, 16(20): 1–15.

Kearney, M. H. (1998) 'Truthful self-nurturing: a grounded formal theory of women's addiction recovery', *Qualitative Health Research*, 8(4): 495–512.

Laing, M., Pilcher, K. and Smith, N. (eds) (2015) *Queer Sex Work*, London: Routledge.

Månsson, S. A. and Hedin, U. C. (1999) 'Breaking the Matthew effect on women leaving prostitution', *International Journal of Social Welfare*, 8: 67–77.

Ministry of Justice (2018) *Female Offender Strategy*, London: HMSO.

Mott, R. (2014) *Speech at Launch of End Demand*. Available at: https://zeromacho.wordpress.com/2014/10/27/end-demand-in-uk-rebecca-mott-speech/. Accessed: 3 January 2020.

Najavits, L. M. (2007) 'Psychosocial treatments for posttraumatic stress disorder', in P. E. Nathan and E. M. Gorman (eds) *A Guide to Treatments that Work*, New York: Oxford University Press, pp 513–30.

National Offender Management Service (2012) *A Distinct Approach: A Guide to Working with Female Offenders*, London: NOMS.

One Small Thing (2019) *Learn*. Available at: https://onesmallthing.org.uk/. Accessed: 4 December 2019.

Petrillo, M., Thomas, M. and Hanspal, S. (2019) *Healing Trauma Evaluation Report,* London: One Small Thing.

Prison Reform Trust (2014) *Brighter Futures, Working Together to Reduce Women's Offending*, London: Prison Reform Trust.

Rosenbaum, B. and Varvin, S. (2008) 'The influence of extreme traumatization on body, mind and social relations', *The International Journal of Psychoanalysis*, 88(6): 1527–42.

Sanders T. (2004) 'A continuum of risk? The management of health, physical and emotional risks by female sex workers', *Sociology of Health & Illness*, 26(5): 557–74.

Sauer, B. (2019) 'Mobilizing shame and disgust: abolitionist affective frames in Austrian and German anti-sex-work movements', *Journal of Political Power,* 12(3): 318–38.

Sex Worker Advocacy and Resistance Movement (SWARM) (2017) *No Silence to Violence*. Available at: https://www.nswp.org/sites/nswp.org/files/nosilencetoviolence-swarmdec17.pdf. Accessed: 4 February 2020.

Starhawk (2011) *The Empowerment Manual: A Guide for Collaborative Groups*. Gabriola Island: New Society Publishers.. Available at: https://sustainabilitypopulareducation.files.wordpress.com/2014/05/the-empowerment-manual_nodrm.pdf. Accessed: 12 December 2020.

Substance Abuse and Mental Health Services Administration (2011) *Essential Components of Trauma-informed Judicial Practice*. Available at: https://www.nasmhpd.org/sites/default/files/JudgesEssential_5%201%202013finaldraft.pdf. Accessed: 12 September 2019.

Substance Abuse and Mental Health Services Administration (2014) *Trauma-informed Care in Behavioral Health Services*. Available at: https://www.ncbi.nlm.nih.gov/books/NBK207201/. Accessed: 4 December 2019.

Sweeney, A., Clement, S., Filson, B. and Kennedy, A. (2016) 'Trauma-informed mental healthcare in the UK: what is it and how can we further its development?', *Mental Health Review Journal*, 21(3): 174–92.

Tate, K. (2015) *Losing my Voice: A Study of the Barriers and Facilitators to Disclosure for Sex-working Women in Residential Drug Treatment*. Available at: https://www.thegriffinssociety.org/system/files/papers/fullreport/griffins_research_paper_2015-02_final.pdf. Accessed: 1 December 2019.

Treisman, K. (2018) *Becoming a More Culturally, Adversity, and Trauma-informed, Infused, and Responsive Organisation*. Available at: https://www.wcmt.org.uk/sites/default/files/report-documents/Treisman%20K%202018%20Final.pdf. Accessed: 12 January 2020.

Ullman, S. E. and Peter-Hagene, L. (2014) 'Social reactions to sexual assault disclosure, coping, perceived control and PTSD symptoms in sexual assault victims', *Journal of Community Psychology*, 42(4): 495–508.

Valandra (2007) 'Reclaiming their lives and breaking free: an Afrocentric approach to recovery from prostitution', *Affilia*, 22(2): 195–208.

5

Reducing the enduring harm of short terms of imprisonment

Isla Masson

Introduction

Despite a growing body of literature on prisons, and how these are experienced by those held within their walls, this literature remains predominantly focused on the male estate due to their overwhelming majority status (Ministry of Justice (MoJ), 2020a). Women continue to 'remain marginal to the study and practice of imprisonment' (Moore and Scraton, 2014, p 1), despite knowledge that they have very specific and particularly painful experiences in prison. Short periods within prison are particularly common for women. For example, 43 per cent of all first receptions into female prison establishments between 2016 and 2019 were remand prisoners (either unconvicted or unsentenced), and over 81 per cent of first sentenced female prison receptions were serving under 12 months (the majority of which were under six months) (MoJ, 2017, 2018c, 2019c, 2020a).

While these experiences are frequently short, the need for prison is questionable, given that the women are rarely violent offenders and thus typically represent a low risk to public safety (MoJ, 2017, 2018c, 2019c, 2020a). Furthermore, use of short terms of incarceration is problematic for both the government, as a financially costly procedure, and for the women, as it represents a disproportionate punishment due to the enduring harms caused. Neither remand nor short prison sentences provide support to women, often instead causing tangible issues with finances, education, employment and housing, or consequences to health and wellbeing, which include physical health, addictions and psychological harm.

Prison is rarely a fitting punishment for women with non-violent offences and thus low-risk status. It is argued that the harms caused are typically disproportionate to the original offences, and while these punishments have attracted recent attention from academics, practitioners, penal reformists and policy makers (for example Baldwin and Epstein, 2017; MoJ, 2018b), there has been little change in their use.

Towards rebalancing this injustice and learning from the voices of those who have already suffered, the current research explores the enduring harms of first short terms of imprisonment with the aim of providing practical recommendations to mitigate future harm. The results of a number of post-custody interviews with 16 mothers aged between 25 and 51 are presented here. Each of the women identified as a mother and had experienced a short period in prison for the first time (on remand or sentenced to less than 12 months) for a non-violent offence. Each of the mothers and their families had endured prison, and yet continued to be deeply and complexly impacted by their experience post-custody.

Sykes (1958) outlined five specific pains of imprisonment: deprivation of liberty; deprivation of goods and services; deprivation of heterosexual relations; deprivation of personal autonomy; and deprivation of security. Most prisoners will experience elements of these pains while in custody. However, there are a number of structural and systemic gendered issues which mean that women experience them differently to men, and are likely to suffer from them more acutely (Crewe et al, 2017; Soffer and Ajzenstadt, 2010).

Furthermore, for those interviewed in this research, the harms of short periods in prison were much more varied and persistent, and included the insecurities associated with living in limbo, feelings of injustice, fear of the unknown, and feelings of guilt. Women often hold a complex range of roles and responsibilities, and when they enter prison, they often bring in a number of complex needs (see, for example, Corston, 2007). A short period in prison does little to facilitate positive developments in many important aspects of life, including attendance at education, securing and maintaining employment and accommodation, and supporting good mental health. With limited time to secure any meaningful support in any of these areas, these 'short' punishments are often experienced as ongoing trauma.

Certainly, the intense and perpetuating consequences of such an experience brings into question the proportionality of the punishment they received in comparison to the original offence. As will be discussed, the mothers' narratives highlight how short terms of imprisonment have meaningful long-term consequences for themselves and their families, with harms enduring long after they left the prison gates. For a more detailed analysis of the women and their children's experiences – and the specific enduring harms – see Masson, 2019.

One central recommendation following the identification and recognition of such enduring harms from short terms of imprisonment is to minimise their use in exchange for appropriate alternatives, for example community sentences or women's centres. However, despite official recognition of this (MoJ, 2018b), their use remains ongoing. As such, it seems most useful, in the interim or while other recommendations are overlooked or ignored, to instigate an adoption of better practices, to minimise the unintended and often arbitrary harms caused. Driven by the experiences of the mothers interviewed, recommendations for the provision of information and practical changes required prior to, during, and post, custody are discussed. We begin with what provision should be available to support women and their families prior to incarceration.

Preparation for prison

For many women, a particularly painful aspect of their incarceration is the fact that it involves being separated from their children. Many women in prison prior to being incarcerated have dependent children (for example, HMIP, 2012; HMCIP, 2018, 2019a, 2019b, 2019c, 2019d). Often, the women are the primary caregivers (Beresford, 2018). Women with infants may be eligible to have their babies with them in a mother and baby unit, however the spaces are infrequently used (Women in Prison, 2013; Abbott, 2015; Sikand, 2015). This is either through personal choice (the mother or caregiver not supporting an application), or issues with the process (for example, Sikand (2015) reported issues with high rates of lost or unaccounted for applications and the applications to a space in the MBU is rejected).

As such, many women leave their children in the community while they are incarcerated for short terms. The number of children left is not insignificant. For example, Kincaid et al (2019) estimated that 17,000 children each year are separated from their mother due to imprisonment, and given the number of women incarcerated for short terms, a significant number of these children would be affected by short terms of incarceration. However, there is no single body responsible for attaining an accurate figure, nor providing guidance to children of incarcerated parents, despite repeated calls for appropriate data collection (for example, Joint Committee on Human Rights (JCHR), 2019).

Therefore, it is suggested that the system is failing to prepare mothers, and their children, for prison. Preparation for custody was a significant support deficit identified with many of the women interviewed; some received false hope from professionals regarding the reality of a custodial sentence, and most were originally unaccepting of the reality of the situation. For some, the shame associated with the process was such that it prevented them from warning and preparing their children for the possibility of separation (see Chapter 4 and Chapter 9 for further discussions regarding shame), as well as then hiding the truth about their incarceration, to protect their children. The consequences is that children can become confused as to whether they are loved, and whether their actions resulted in the separation (Hairston, 2008; Sazie et al, 2011), as well as dealing with feelings of deception if the truth is found out through other means (Poehlmann, 2005; Light and Campbell, 2007).

For the women interviewed, no advice or guidance was offered to support them to engage their children in dialogue, or how to explain their absence. No clear recommendations are readily available from the extant literature to suggest how best to raise this with children, or how to overcome denial and shame. However, there has been initial work to identify several problematic practices (for example, Glover, 2009; Sutherland and Wright, 2017; Minson, 2020). In order for this to be properly addressed, this work needs to be considered and, where appropriate, adopted by all agencies. Those working in the community should have a duty of care to advise women and alternative caregivers, in order to minimise harms to the children. However, appropriate funding needs to be ringfenced, in order to allow this to happen. Prior to sentencing, legal advisors should also be a key stakeholder in providing realistic – but potentially worse-case scenario – guidance.[1]

A central step forward in supporting preparation for prison is sentencing reform, including a statutory responsibility to acknowledge the rights of the child as laid out in, for example, the Convention on the Rights of the Child (United Nations General Assembly, 1989) and the Bangkok Rules (United Nations General Assembly, 2010). It is suggested in this chapter that the impact that a mother's incarceration could have on the wellbeing of her child should be addressed in a pre-sentence report. However, these are used 'inconsistently and ineffectively in many cases' (Booth, 2019, p 2) and are 'not usually female-specific' and often do 'not differentiate the needs of women from those of men' (HM Inspectorate of Probation, 2016, p 8).

The prison system is often failing to support mothers upon their arrival, with lack of early intervention – as previously highlighted by HM Inspectorate of Prisons (2010). During the reception process, or in the first night centre, it seems beneficial for women to be given guidance about what to say to their children about their absence, and to receive help in making prompt contact with home. Both of these suggestions are in line with the commitment to minimise the harms associated with women's imprisonment post-Corston. However, a preferred solution to assisting women prior to, or upon arrival in, prison with what they should tell their children is for a delayed imprisonment for non-violent, first-time prisoners. This would preferably be 24 hours, but potentially even longer, to allow a clearer transition (a delay which has been echoed by others, for example Baldwin and Epstein, 2017; JCHR, 2019). This would allow for the implementation of proper caregiving arrangements (discussed later) as well as the opportunity for face-to-face interactions with the child before separation. Such practice would likely reduce women's anxieties, as they are involved with, and in control of, what children are told. This would also bring benefits to the children, as they may be better supported to manage the negative emotions related to separation, which can cause enduring harm to a child of any age.

Given the short length of time in prison, further preparation should also be encouraged, to support accommodation post-prison (Prison Reform Trust, 2016). Regaining custody of children is frequently dependent on secure housing, yet for the women interviewed, the loss of housing was common and caused ongoing harm. As such, greater support to prevent this happening needs to be implemented prior to the period of incarceration. Female prisoners often lose their home due to the lack of consistent rent payments, due to the lack of funding secured by employment, or by losing housing benefits by being absent from the property for more than 13 weeks. As receipt of benefits is somewhat more common in women than men (Fawcett Society, 2005), the latter issue is particularly pertinent in the female estate. As such, loss of housing, while not intended as part of the punishment, is a common experience for imprisoned women.

While providing support prior to or during custody might seem obvious, it is not commonplace. The women interviewed reported no guidance being offered, whether that be to retain or replace their accommodation. This support deficit is reflected in the poor accommodation outcomes reported in the literature for women exiting prison (MoJ, 2018b). A number of changes in post-custody provision have been implemented (as discussed shortly), however issues surrounding inappropriate support for accommodation persist (Wilson, 2017). This is to such an extent that the House of Commons Committee of Public Accounts (2016, p 10) stated that 'the offender housing problem is deteriorating', with many 'feeling that help with housing has got worse since the probation reforms'.

Although suggestions to improve the Bail Accommodation and Support Service for women exiting prison in the Female Offender Strategy (2018) are welcomed (Booth et al, 2018), more needs to be done to protect and allocate longer-term housing for this vulnerable group (this is further discussed by McMahon, 2019). Budget cuts need to be minimised, the shortage of social housing needs to be rectified, and one body should be made responsible for overseeing the maintenance and securing of suitable accommodation for this vulnerable group.

A culture change is important, whereby the importance of accommodation is recognised, prioritising greater support for women on their first short-term prison stay. Grants or loans to help to protect tenancies, and amendments to the 13-week rule would represent vital steps forward in addressing these issues. Any of these recommendations could help to mitigate the long-term harms caused by the lack of preparation. For example, it would likely reduce the number of women and mothers released with debt, or inappropriate accommodation, which may negatively impact the women's psychological wellbeing as well as their opportunities to regain custody of children.

Effective and tailored healthcare and education

Given 'their previous life experiences, gynaecological needs and the cultural demands made on women outside prison, certain aspects of imprisonment formally imposed on men and women equally are likely to occasion more pain for women than males' (Carlen, 2002, p 9). Any length of incarceration can compound or create additional psychological or physical issues (Gelsthorpe et al, 2007), contributing to women's pains of incarceration (Carlen, 2002; Centre for Mental Health, 2011). The complexity of harms experienced means that prison represents a particularly damaging place for women, highlighting a need for far more accountability for the exacerbation of existing problems, and creation of new ones, as well as much greater action towards reducing these often enduring harms (Masson, 2019).

Linking back to the impact on children left behind, it is suggested that incarcerated mothers may also 'carry the burden of a criminal conviction and the violation of societal norms about what good women and mothers are supposed to be' (Snyder, 2009, p 38). Homes, and children, are vital to women's identities, and thus 'to take this away from them when it may be all that they have causes huge damage to women' (Corston, 2007, p 16).

Highlighting the emotional toil of prison, women continue to account for a disproportionate level of all prison self-harm incidents (Corston, 2007; MoJ, 2020b). Incidents of self-harm are disproportionately attempted by prisoners on remand and occur within the first month of arrival (MoJ, 2021). Such statistics indicate that this initial period of incarceration is difficult to manage and can cause the greatest trauma (Prison Service Order 4800, 2008; Public Health England, 2018). There is potential for those incarcerated for short terms to be released before these negative feelings can be resolved, with the potential for significant enduring consequences to, for example, substance misuse or mental ill-health.

For a number of women, self-harm can often escalate towards suicidal thoughts, again with high risk levels occurring during the early stages of incarceration (Shaw et al, 2004; Prisons and Probation Ombudsman, 2014; Walker and Towl, 2016). Indeed, many of the women interviewed experienced this spiral in mental health and reported that mental ill-health continued to be problematic for significant periods of time post-custody. Despite positive changes within the female estate to reduce this (Covington, 2015; Bradley, 2017), further work is required. First, mental health needs should be continuously assessed and actioned, treating this as an immediate and ongoing priority for this prison population. Second, greater support needs to be provided during early periods, in order to reduce the amount of self-harm carried out.

Appropriate support also needs to be put in place to monitor both self-harm and suicidal thoughts and escalation of behaviour. Given how self-harm and suicidal thoughts are often interconnected, accurate risk assessments are challenging without specialist input (Walker and Towl, 2016). The women interviewed were typically prescribed anti-depressants by prison authorities to meet mental health needs. However, based on best practices established, this should also be supported with psychological support (for example talking therapy), to have the greatest chance of both managing and resolving the short- and long-term consequences of the depression caused (NHS, 2018).

If incarceration is deemed necessary, prison should be seen as an opportunity to reflect and grow. However, this can only be done in a supportive environment. Additional resources are desperately needed within the female estate, to better support mental ill-health, for example more appropriate levels of psychological therapy. More also needs to be put in place to provide an environment in which women can work on improving poor mental health.

The physical health needs of women entering prison also require much greater attention and action. All prisoners should 'have access to the same range and quality of services appropriate to their needs as are available to the general population through the NHS' (Department of Health and HM Prison Service, 2001, p 5). However, prison healthcare is under-prioritised and 'under-resourced and the concept and practice poorly understood' (Watson et al, 2004, p 125). Declines in physical health as a result of the prison environment were a common experience of the women interviewed, including lack of access to fresh air, exercise and food, as well as issues sourcing appropriate medication, communication problems between community and prison arrangements, and poor accessibility of medical staff (which echoes other work, for example Carlen, 2002; Lord Farmer, 2019).

Sadly, physical problems did not cease once they were released, with prison placing an ongoing detrimental pressure on this aspect of their life. Prison should be seen as an opportunity to improve a person's health, given the removal of some stresses present at home and the fact that continuity of care can be provided. Rather than managing deteriorating health, a culture change is necessary, whereby those working in prisons could be expected and supported to improve a person's health. Greater provision for exercise as well as autonomy over meals should be encouraged.

It is also vital for the systems and processes across the estate to fully and quickly adapt to meet the women's requirements, respond more quickly to issues, and provide appropriate medication and support. The results of such actions would be lessened anxiety with respect to healthcare in custody, and women exiting prison with better physical health. It is also hoped that the implementation of the Health and Justice Information Services (HJIS) (NHS, 2019) will allow for continuity of care due to greater communication between prison and community healthcare. Under this system, patient records can be transferred between the community and prison when a person is incarcerated, and transferred back again when they are released. These practices are likely to be of benefit in, for example, reducing the amount of time before receiving medication for pre-existing conditions. Time will tell how successful the HJIS is, and it is important to note that 'data sharing alone will not ensure continuity of care, as this population includes many vulnerable people who may need additional support to engage and remain engaged with health service' (Clinks, 2018, p 3). Therefore, wider levels of support are required in the community for recently released prisoners, particularly those with known mental health issues, in order to reduce deaths immediately following custody (MoJ, 2019a).

Responding more quickly to issues is a recurring requirement within the female estate, and thus all prison support should be re-evaluated for efficiency. Delays disproportionally impact those who are there for relatively short periods, with greater time in limbo and less time to benefit from the experience. A good opportunity to develop oneself in prison is through education. However, there are ongoing issues with this. For example, prison education 'remains by far the lowest performer in the Further Education sector. Ofsted rated 44 per cent of prisons as "requires improvement" or "inadequate" in 2016/17' (MoJ, 2018a p 12). In addition, being incarcerated for short terms creates further barriers to these opportunities because of the length of courses or waiting lists. As such, programme development focusing on basic skills – rather than modular courses or qualifications – should reflect an immediate priority, created specifically for those on remand or serving short sentences. Opportunities are being missed, as those incarcerated for short periods could benefit from one-day or half-day courses. In addition to building confidence, skills in DIY, finance or home economics seem likely to be of benefit. To minimise the investment in resources necessary, it is entirely possible that prisoners with previous experience in these areas could teach such groups, allowing more informal peer-learning opportunities, as well as opportunities for paid employment for prisoners.

However, it was particularly frustrating to see that in the MoJ Education and Employment Strategy (2018a), there were no specific directions as to how to best support those incarcerated for short periods. Likewise, sadly, short-term prisoners remain ineligible for Prisoners' Education Trust (2019) grants, which can be used for distance learning courses or art/creative hobby materials. It is felt that these opportunities to support this vulnerable group will continue to be lost within the prison estate, if this is not addressed shortly. Nonetheless, use of digital in-cell learning represents a promising opportunity, which 'can help engage and educate hard-to-reach and vulnerable prisoners' (MoJ, 2018a, p 11). While this is yet to be rolled out in the female estate, it is hoped that this will be achieved soon.

Any of these attempts to increase the educational opportunities for women in prison for short terms of incarceration may reduce the enduring harm of custody, through helping them to gain confidence, as well as secure post-custody employment, which significantly helps with housing, debt, mental ill-health and recidivism levels.

Children and communication

As mentioned previously, many women in prison are separated from dependent children in the community when they are incarcerated. Despite the significant number of families affected by this, there is currently no single body responsible for providing support to the mothers or the alternative caregivers during the period of absence. We continue to have no way of finding out about the caregiving arrangements put in place for their children (Kincaid et al, 2019).

Across the mothers interviewed in this research, there were a number of concerns surrounding the standard of care for children, despite often being looked after by family and friends. Many mothers worried about the financial and emotional support given to their children's alternative carers. In order to properly protect all parties (children, mothers and alternative caregivers) during these periods of change, better information needs to be gathered about these more informal arrangements, and greater financial and emotional support needs to be provided for families affected by imprisonment (Booth, 2020). Greater support and resources should also be available to caregivers supporting children with mothers incarcerated for the first time. Vital support to children and families of prisoners are currently offered by voluntary organisations like the Prison Advice and Care Trust (Pact) (2020) and Children Heard and Seen (2020). Linking to arguments that are made in chapter 6 regarding funding, unfortunately, these initiatives currently have limited and inconsistent funding. Likewise, this type of support should not be solely provided by the third sector, as there is a duty of care by the state to assist those left behind when a woman is incarcerated, even if only for a short time. In line with the JCHR (2019), providing better support during the period of separation will not only make the time in prison less painful, but will also assist with reintegration post-custody and speed up the healing process.

Maintaining mother–child contact while the mother is incarcerated can also contribute towards reducing the enduring harm of short terms of imprisonment. It is suggested that this benefits both parties (Houck and Loper, 2002; Poehlmann, 2005; Hanlon et al, 2007; Hoffmann et al, 2010; Farmer, 2019) and is well reflected within prison system paperwork. In fact, Lord Farmer (2019, p 26) recently argued that 'the importance of family and other relationships needs to be a golden thread running through the criminal justice system' (see Chapter 8 for further discussion of this golden thread) – something that is particularly important for women in our prison system. However, there appears to be a gap as to which department is responsible for providing support for these families (see, for example, Burrows, 2020).

Likewise, according to recent HM Chief Inspector of Prisons inspections, a significant percentage of women say that staff do not encourage them to keep in touch with their family and/or friends (74 per cent at HMP Styal (HMCIP, 2018); 69 per cent at HMP New Hall (HMCIP, 2019d); 64 per cent at HMP Bronzefield (HMCIP, 2019a); 62 per cent at HMP Eastwood Park (HMCIP, 2019b) and 59 per cent at HMP Foston Hall (HMCIP, 2019c)). Regardless of the level of involvement in the child's care, recognising a woman's mother status is important (Baldwin, 2015). Thus this feeling of staff ambivalence represents a significant missed opportunity for minimising harm to both mothers and their children, particularly as there are many means by which possible contact can be made. An immediate consideration for visits, telephone calls and letters is cost (Baldwin, 2017; Booth, 2018a), causing an unnecessary barrier and a missed opportunity for benefits to the women and their families. Levels of visitation within the female estate are particularly low (Prison Service Order 4800; Social Exclusion Unit, 2002).

As such, greater support should be provided to encourage visits, be that financial or practical, for example through the implementation of regular prison buses in rural locations. It was encouraging to see that in recent inspections at both HMP New Hall (HMCIP, 2019d) and Bronzefield (HMCIP, 2019a), women identified as not receiving visits would be given telephone credit in order to help maintain these family ties, as well as the installation of in-cell telephones to reduce issues accessing phones. Both should be standard practice across the whole estate.

While contact is vital for both parties, these contact experiences need to be properly cultivated to realise their benefits. For example, visits are not inherently positive (Bloom and Steinhart, 1993; Young and Smith, 2000; Parke and Clarke-Stewart, 2001; JCHR, 2019) and can cause greater distress, leading to further deficits in contact (O'Malley and Devaney, 2015; Booth, 2018b). As such, greater support is needed for alternative caregivers, in addition to women, to support quality contact, regardless of the medium (see Rees et al, 2017). It is also suggested that family days, where children are given longer periods of time with their parents, often in more relaxed settings (see Booth, 2018b), should be more consistently offered throughout the prison estate, as these tend to be rated very positively. Every prison should actively encourage frequent family days; however, there should be greater inclusivity, by welcoming children regardless of age, and with financial assistance for first-time prisoners, to maximise engagement.

Developments in technology also present more opportunities for accessible and cost-effective contact that encourage mother–child communication. For example, Booth (2018a, p 164) suggests that in-cell telephones 'would benefit mother–child contact, and most likely, all relational ties for prisoners and their families'. Likewise, StorybookMums offers mums the opportunity to record a story for their child via CD. This practice is seen as particularly beneficial for minimising harm to children, as it can be played and repeated whenever necessary in comfortable home environments (StorybookDads, 2018).

Likewise, while not adopted by any of the mothers interviewed, emailaprisoner (2020) is another service popularly advertised in most prisons. While it represents a simple and low-cost communication channel, to work most effectively it does rely on there being a 'reply' service which, according to the website, was until recently not currently available in many female prisons. The women interviewed were aware of the service, but felt they knew relatively little about it and thus had not adopted it. Better advertising is therefore needed, along with the reply service in order for two-way communication to be had.

Voicemail services are also inexpensive and have been adopted in some prisons, for example HMP Bronzefield. However, most internet-mediated communication services that could fill the contact deficit, were previously not supported due to restrictions on internet access. Indeed, 'most prisoners are placed at the far end of the digital divide' (Champion and Edgar, 2013, p iii). Farmer (2017) initially encouraged greater adoption of 'virtual visits', and in his later report (Farmer, 2019, p 16) said: 'the Women's estate in its entirety to be prioritised for roll-out of virtual visits with all women routinely able to use facilities, where there are no security concerns, because of the disproportionately positive impact on children'. One consequence of the COVID-19 pandemic (see Chapter 1 for a further discussion of the impact of this virus) has been the roll-out of virtual (purple) visits in many prisons in England and Wales. While these virtual visits have not been without criticism, there is an opportunity for them to be of great benefit to women in prison to complement the positives of regular physical visits.

Greater support for communication initiatives that add to existing channels (rather than replacing them), that are clearly communicated to prisoners and which have few barriers to engagement, are of priority. However, it is vitally important that any digital technology implemented does not replace existing methods of communication, but only replaces these when existing methods have to be reduced or stopped (Booth and Masson, 2021), for example in the recent COVID-19 pandemic.

Support during and post custody

Lack of support both during and after custody was a theme present throughout the interviews conducted. Broadly, the extent of, and the consistency in, the negative experiences highlight the importance of receiving appropriate support from those working in prison. While it may be easier to compartmentalise the different needs, tending to the most immediate needs (for example detox for prisoners on short-term sentences), a more holistic consideration of needs would likely highlight opportunities to support and rehabilitate the women (as found by Lord Farmer, 2019).

The much-anticipated Offender Management Model in Custody (OMiC) could provide this additional support through the proposed introduction of 'key workers'. Under this model, every prisoner (sentenced and remanded) in the male closed estate will receive a 45-minute session every week with a dedicated key worker: 'whose responsibility is to engage, motivate and support them throughout the custodial period ... within this allocated time, key workers can vary individual sessions in order to provide a responsive service, reflecting individual need and stage in the sentence' (MoJ and HM Prison & Probation Service, 2018, pp 6 and 9). It was the intention that the model would be fully embedded within the male estate, prior to the launch of a model 'tailored for the needs of women, which considers complexity alongside risk, and introduces key worker time to provide more focused support to individual offenders' (MoJ, 2018c, p 33). There is much merit to a 'bespoke' model that 'recognises the different needs of women and the challenges and opportunities in the women's estate' (Crozier, 2019). However, it is vital that key workers taking on such an important role fully understand the complexities faced by those incarcerated in female prisons, and do not see their allocated time as a tick-box exercise, but fully commit to providing appropriate support.

Likewise, there have been some rather inevitable delays with the rollout across both the male and female estate. This is primarily due to the fact that 'the implementation of OMiC is dependent on the recruitment of sufficient staff, the numbers of whom had been falling prior to the model's conception' (House of Commons Justice Committee, 2019), as well as issues with funding, multiple elections, different ministers of state for prisons, Brexit and, more recently, COVID-19. Despite attempts to recruit new officers, staffing levels remain problematic, with particularly high turnover rates in some prisons and high resignation levels across the estate. Therefore, given the issues with properly embedding this model, particularly within the female estate, there is not yet any evidence available to determine whether these plans have achieved the desired benefits (NAPO, 2018).

For women in prison for short periods, it will be of particular interest to explore whether such key worker time is sufficient to implement, and thus improve, their experiences. Rather than relying on OMiC alone, it is vital that support services are coordinated and that probation services, social workers, family engagement workers, and the plethora of professionals engaged in supporting both women and families, contribute towards a collaborative and caring approach to reducing the enduring harm of short terms of imprisonment. This could potentially be through Farmer's (2019) suggestion of employing prison-based social workers, who will act as a liaison between the prison and the community. However, in order for any of this to happen, significantly greater levels of funding need to be allocated to this support.

Post-custody support is also greatly needed by this vulnerable group. Prior to the implementation of the Offender Rehabilitation Act 2014, only those serving longer sentences received statutory supervision post-custody from the National Offender Management Service. Post-custody support to those serving short sentences was provided by other public bodies (National Audit Office, 2010). Although post-custody support is welcomed, as releasing such vulnerable prisoners into the community with no support is both morally problematic and dangerous, the compulsory 12 months of post-custody supervision for any short term of incarceration under two years is excessive. It is overly punitive, and does little but result in more women returning to prison, because they breach their licence conditions. This is demonstrated by the fact that, according to the MoJ (2017, 2018c), 280 more women serving a sentence of less than 12 months were recalled to prison in 2017 compared to 2016.

This form of net widening is a startling reminder of the consequences of ill-conceived plans that do not consider the reality of such changes. As with the suggested help provided in the female estate, post-custody support needs to be holistically, rather than financially, driven, exploring the different challenges facing vulnerable women in a supportive rather than punitive environment. Sadly, until recently, financial savings appeared to be driving decisions about the implementation and delivery of this post-custody support, with organisations bidding for 'payment by results' contracts (MoJ, 2013). Thankfully these payment by results contracts have been terminated, and the probation service has been re-nationalised (Grierson, 2019) – but only after an additional £22 million a year was allocated 'to improve through-the-gate support' (Gov.uk, 2018) and many women's centres closed due to lack of funding.

We again wait to see how this change in post-custody support will play out in reality and whether women who have been incarcerated for short terms benefit from these modifications. Given their unique vulnerabilities and experiences prior to and during custody, this support now provided by probation needs to be tailored towards women's needs, rather than being adapted from best practice with men. As with support provided in prison, post-custody support needs to be holistic and to address the plethora of issues experienced by each woman, rather than dealing with each issue individually.

Summary and recommendations

The punitive nature of prison, particularly female prisons, is well established within the literature. The interviews carried out for this research demonstrate that this harm continues long after women are released from their short periods of incarceration; these pains are significant and enduring. Despite agreement that these short terms of incarceration should not be used, we still have a large number of women (often mothers) in prison for a 'short, sharp, shock'. It is the author's continued argument that:

> in their current form short terms of imprisonment are unconscionable because of the uncontrolled nature of the punishment that the women suffer. This punishment is not an intended component of their sentence or period on remand, and should be addressed because these women's Human Rights ... are violated ... It is therefore argued that drastic steps should be taken to reduce the use of short terms of imprisonment, as the proportionality of a period of incarceration should take account of the impact of the punishment on the individual and others directly affected. (Masson, 2019, p 228)

However, until these punishments desist, there is a moral obligation of those in power to change the way these negative punishments are experienced by some of our most vulnerable members of society. This chapter has outlined a number of practical ways in which the enduring harms associated with these forms of punishment can be alleviated.

The recommendations start with work prior to the incarceration of a woman, including consideration of advice received by third-sector organisations as well as those providing legal guidance to best prepare her for difficult conversations with dependent children. Lack of appropriate support prior to a potential custodial sentence does not benefit children, and uncomfortable conversations need to be had prior to custody, or once a custodial sentence is temporarily delayed.

Housing is also a fundamental concern for many women in prison, yet accommodation continues not to be properly protected prior to and during custody. Again, greater levels of support and advice need to be implemented, in order to protect or obtain appropriate future housing, which reduces vulnerability post-custody and assists with reinstigation of caregiving duties.

Given the previous experiences of many women entering prison, greater levels of tailored support need to be provided within a short timeframe. More can be achieved to address some of the vulnerabilities within the female estate: physical and mental health can be improved through better provision of healthcare as well as more continuity between community and custody provision; and more money needs to be injected into providing psychological support, rather than simply giving anti-depressants. Education also provides a golden opportunity to give women greater ownership over their lives. This education should again be made available to all within a short timeframe, and post-release opportunities should be explored and encouraged. Every prisoner, no matter how long they are incarcerated for, should be given the opportunity for rehabilitation and to maximise their potential in a supportive environment.

In order to best support children left behind through the incarceration of women, it is imperative that we gain a better understanding of, first, the number of children affected, as well as the identity of who continues to provide care during their mother's absence. These alternative caregivers are predominantly ignored by the criminal justice system, and a lack of understanding about their needs and how these fit with the women's experiences demonstrate the willingness of those in power to turn a blind eye to the harm caused through the incarceration of women for short terms. Likewise, more needs to be done to support meaningful contact between mother and child, when it is in the best interest of both parties. Greater funding needs to be available to support more embedded methods of communication and also those made possible through advances in technology.

Tailored support should extend to other areas of the women's lives while they are incarcerated, and time and money need to be spent in providing support to address pre-existing issues in the mothers' lives. All relevant bodies and individuals need to acknowledge their responsibility for this support during custody, and funding must be prioritised in order for this to be implemented properly across the female estate. Support should not cease once women exit prison. Individualised support, rather than additional punitive monitoring, is required, to help women move away from previous vulnerabilities and to reduce the enduring harm of short terms of incarceration. This support needs to be delivered by individuals who understand the importance of gendered support and are driven to help the women make positive changes.

Those entering female prisons do so with a number of differing vulnerabilities, and much research (including the author's own) has demonstrated that pre-existing problems are worsened by incarceration. It is argued that 'these morally significant harms are not proportionate to the offences committed by these women, and they appear to be distributed in an arbitrary fashion: there is no logic in how they are distributed, they are seemingly unregulated. These unintended punishments are not unavoidable' (Masson, 2019, p 228). It is important to note that many others have made suggestions to reform the female prison estate in the past. There is an 'an embarrassment of riches' (Booth et al, 2018, p 430),[2] yet these have been slow to come to fruition – 'the triumph of inertia' (Player, 2013, p 276).

However, that does not mean we should give up. We must continue to demand change. It is hoped that, if implemented, with the ongoing backing of those in power and holding the purse strings, then some of the recommendations suggested in this chapter will minimise the collateral damage to this already vulnerable group – and therefore significantly reduce disproportionate and unnecessary pains of short terms of incarceration.

Reflection points

- Who should be held accountable for the implementation of any of these practical recommendations?
- Does the Female Offender Strategy (Booth et al, 2018) provide the much-anticipated guidance that is required to improve the female estate?
- What further failures within the female estate will it take for the government to support the reduction of the use of short terms of incarceration?
- How long is it deemed acceptable for short periods of incarceration to negatively impact so many aspects of a person's life?
- How can we – as academics, students, practitioners, activists or law makers – change our own practice in order to minimise harm?

Notes

[1] For example, the JCHR (2019, p 22) suggests that 'where possible, the court should give advance notice that it is considering a custodial sentence, so that care arrangements can be made'. Likewise, in the Government Response to the JCHR (2019b, p 9), the MoJ states that it has 'developed easy-to-read guides for people attending court, which include a section on information for people who have children and may be facing custody'.

[2] For more information regarding the reasons why limited progress has been made in penal reform in the female estate, see Booth et al (2018) and Player (2013).

References

Abbott, L. (2015) 'A pregnant pause: expecting in the prison estate', in L. Baldwin (ed) *Mothering Justice: Working with Mothers in Social and Criminal Justice Settings*, East Sussex: Waterside Press, pp 185–210.

Baldwin, L. (2015) *Mothering Justice: Working with Mothers in Social and Criminal Justice Settings*, East Sussex: Waterside Press.

Baldwin, L. (2017) 'Tainted love: the impact of prison on maternal identity, explored by post prison reflections', *Prison Service Journal*, 233: 28–34.

Baldwin, L. and Epstein, R. (2017) *Short But Not Sweet: A Study of the Impact of Short Sentences on Mothers and their Children*. Available at: https://www.dora.dmu.ac.uk/bitstream/handle/2086/14301. Accessed: 11 December 2020.

Beresford, S. (2018) *What About Me? The Impact on Children When Mothers are Involved in the Criminal Justice System*. Available at: http://www.prisonreformtrust.org.uk/portals/0/documents/what%20about%20me.pdf. Accessed: 14 May 2019.

Bloom, B. and Steinhart, D. (1993) *Why Punish the Children? A Reappraisal of the Children of Incarcerated Mothers in America*, San Francisco: National Council on Crime and Delinquency.

Booth, N. (2018a) 'Disconnected: exploring provisions for mother–child telephone contact in female prisons serving England and Wales', *Criminology & Criminal Justice*, 20(2): 150–68.

Booth, N. (2018b) 'Family matters: a critical examination of family visits for imprisoned mothers and their families', *Prison Service Journal*, 238: 10–15.

Booth, N. (2019) *Written evidence from Dr Natalie Booth (CMP0016) to Joint Committee on Human Rights. The right to family life: children whose mothers are in prison*. Available at: http://data.parliament.uk/writtenevidence/committeeevidence.svc/evidencedocument/human-rights-committee/the-right-to-family-life-children-whose-mothers-are-in-prison/written/92187.html. Accessed: 17 March 2020.

Booth, N. (2020) *Maternal Imprisonment and Family Life: From the Caregiver's Perspective*, Bristol: Policy Press.

Booth, N. and Masson, I. (2021) 'Loved ones of remand prisoners: the hidden victims of COVID-19', *Prison Service Journal* 253: 23–31.

Booth, N., Masson, I. and Baldwin, L. (2018) 'Promises, promises: can the Female Offender Strategy deliver?', *Probation Journal*, 65(4): 429–38.

Bradley, A. (2017) *Trauma-informed practice: exploring the role of adverse life experiences on the behaviour of offenders and the effectiveness of associated criminal justice strategies*, (doctoral thesis) Northumbria University.

Burrows, S. (2020) @SarahBurrows100, 18 June 2020. Available at: https://twitter.com/SarahBurrows100/status/1273558237401530369. Accessed: 12 May 2020.

Carlen, P. (2002) *Women and Punishment: The Struggle for Justice*, Devon: Willan Publishing.

Centre for Mental Health (2011) *Mental Health Care and the Criminal Justice System*, London: Centre for Mental Health.

Champion, N. and Edgar, K. (2013) *Through the Gateway: How Computers Can Transform Rehabilitation*, London: Prison Reform Trust.

Children Heard and Seen (2020) *Children Heard and Seen*. Available at: https://childrenheardandseen.co.uk/. Accessed: 19 June 2020.

Clinks (2018) *Clinks Response to the NHS Long Term Plan for Health and Justice*. Available at: https://www.clinks.org/sites/default/files/2018-10/Clinks%20response%20to%20the%20NHS%20long%20term%20plan%20for%20health%20and%20justice.pdf. Accessed: 17 June 2020.

Corston, Baroness J. (2007) *The Corston Report: A Review of Women with Particular Vulnerabilities in the Criminal Justice System*, London: Home Office.

Covington, S. S. (2015) *Becoming trauma-informed: a core value in effective services*. Available at: https://www.stephaniecovington.com/assets/files/FINAL-BTI%2C-A-Core-Element-in-Womens-Treatment%2C-Counselor-Magazine-Aug-2015.pdf. Accessed: 14 December 2020.

Crewe, B., Hulley, S. and Wright, S. (2017) 'The gendered pains of life imprisonment', *The British Journal of Criminology*, 57(6): 1359–78.

Crozier, S. (2019) *Letter to NAPO from Sonia Crozier, Chief Probation Officer and Director of Women, HM Prison and Probation Service, regarding OMiC, dated 5 September 2019*. Available at: https://www.napo.org.uk/sites/default/files/Napo%20re%20OMiC%202019%2009%2005.pdf. Accessed: 21 March 2020.

Department of Health and HM Prison Service (2001) *Changing the Outlook: A Strategy for Developing and Modernising Mental Health Services in Prisons*, London: Department of Health.

Emailaprisoner (2020) *Emailaprisoner.* Available at: emailaprisoner.com/content/howitworks. Accessed: 20 June 2020.

Farmer, Lord M. (2017) *The Importance of Strengthening Prisoners' Family Ties to Prevent Reoffending and Reduce Intergenerational Crime.* Available at: https://assets.publishing.service.gov.uk/government/uploads/system/uploads/attachment_data/file/642244/farmer-review-report.pdf. Accessed: 20 June 2020.

Farmer, Lord M. (2019) *The Importance of Strengthening Female Offenders' Family and other Relationships to Prevent Reoffending and Reduce Intergenerational Crime.* Available at: https://assets.publishing.service.gov.uk/government/uploads/system/uploads/attachment_data/file/809467/farmer-review-women.PDF. Accessed: 20 June 2020.

Fawcett Society (2005) *Who Benefits? A Gender Analysis of the UK Benefits and Tax Credits System,* London: Fawcett Society.

Gelsthorpe, L., Sharpe, G. and Roberts, J. (2007) *Provision for Women Offenders in the Community,* London: Fawcett Society.

Glover, J. (2009) *Every Night You Cry: The Realities of Having a Parent in Prison.* Available at: https://www.bl.uk/collection-items/every-night-you-cry-the-realities-of-having-a-parent-in-prison. Accessed: 19 June 2020.

Gov.uk (2018) *Justice Secretary Outlines future Vision for Probation.* Available at: https://www.gov.uk/government/news/justice-secretary-outlines-future-vision-for-probation. Accessed: 1 August 2018.

Grierson, J. (2019) *Probation Will be Renationalised after Disastrous Grayling Reforms.* Available at: https://www.theguardian.com/society/2019/may/16/part-privatisation-probation-sevices-to-be-reversed-offender-management-nationalised-chris-grayling. Accessed: 16 May 2019.

Hairston, C. (2008) 'Children with Parents in Prison: Child Welfare Matters', in T. LaLiberte and E. Snyder (eds) *Children of Incarcerated Parents,* Saint Paul, MN: University of Minnesota, Centre for Advanced Studies in Child Welfare, p 4.

Hanlon, T., Carswell, S. and Rose, M. (2007) 'Research on the caretaking of children of incarcerated parents: Findings and their service delivery implications', *Children and Youth Services Review,* 29(3): 348–62.

HM Chief Inspector of Prisons (HMCIP) (2018) *Report on an Unannounced Inspection of HMP & YOI Styal,* London: HMIP.

HMCIP (2019a) *Report on an Unannounced Inspection of HMP & YOI Bronzefield,* London: HM Inspectorate of Prisons (HMIP).

HMCIP (2019b) *Report on an Unannounced Inspection of HMP Eastwood Park*, London: HMIP.

HMCIP (2019c) *Report on an Unannounced Inspection of HMP & YOI Foston Hall*, London: HMIP.

HMCIP (2019d) *Report on an Unannounced Inspection of HMP & YOI New Hall*, London: HMIP.

HMIP (2010) *Women in Prison: A Short Thematic Review*, London: HMIP.

HMIP (2012) *Remand Prisoners: A Thematic Review*, London: HMIP.

HM Inspectorate of Probation (2016) *A Thematic Inspection of the Provision and Quality of Services in the Community for Women who Offend*. Available at: https://www.justiceinspectorates.gov.uk/hmiprobation/wp-content/uploads/sites/5/2016/09/A-thematic-inspection-of-the-provision-and-quality-of-services-in-the-community-for-women-who-offend.pdf. Accessed: 20 June 2020.

Hoffmann, H., Byrd, A. and Kightlinger, A. (2010) 'Prison programs and services for incarcerated parents and their underage children: results from a national survey of correctional facilities', *The Prison Journal*, 90(4): 397–416.

Houck, K. and Loper, A. (2002) 'The relationship of parenting stress to adjustment among mothers in prison', *American Journal of Orthopsychiatry*, 72: 548–58.

House of Commons Committee of Public Accounts (2016) *Transforming Rehabilitation: Seventeenth Report of Session 2016–17*, London: Committee of Public Accounts, House of Commons.

House of Commons Justice Committee (2019) *Prison population 2022: Planning for the Future*. Available at: https://publications.parliament.uk/pa/cm201719/cmselect/cmjust/483/report-files/48308.htm#footnote-359. Accessed: 19 May 2020.

Joint Committee on Human Rights (JCHR) (2019) *The Right to Family Life: Children whose Mothers are in Prison*. Available at: https://publications.parliament.uk/pa/jt201719/jtselect/jtrights/1610/report-files/161007.htm#footnote-059. Accessed: 21 May 2020.

Kincaid, S., Roberts, M. and Kane, E. (2019) *Children of Prisoners: Fixing a Broken System*. Available at: https://static.wixstatic.com/ugd/89643c_a905d6cf4f644ee5afb346e368bb9e0e.pdf. Accessed: 21 May 2020.

Light, R. and Campbell, B. (2007) 'Prisoners' families: still forgotten victims?', *Journal of Social Welfare and Family Law*, 28(3–4): 297–308.

Masson, I. (2019) *Incarcerating Motherhood: The Enduring Harms of First Short Periods of Imprisonment on Mothers*, Abingdon: Routledge.

McMahon, T. (2019) *A Sense of Place: A Study of Accessing Housing for Women Exiting Custody – Housing First Not Housing Last*. Available at: https://www.thegriffinssociety.org/system/files/papers/fullreport/griffins_research_paper_2016-02_-_full_paper.pdf. Accessed: 19 May 2020.

Ministry of Justice (MoJ) (2013) *Press release: 12 months supervision for all prisoners on release*. Available at: https://www.gov.uk/government/news/12-months-supervision-for-all-prisoners-on-release. Accessed: 1 April 2014.

MoJ (2017) *Offender Management Statistics Quarterly: October to December 2016*, London: Ministry of Justice.

MoJ (2018a) *Education and Employment Strategy*, London: Ministry of Justice.

MoJ (2018b) *Female Offender Strategy*, London: Ministry of Justice.

MoJ (2018c) *Offender Management Statistics Quarterly: October to December 2017*, London: Ministry of Justice.

MoJ (2019a) *Deaths of Offenders in the Community, England and Wales, 2018/19*. Available at: https://assets.publishing.service.gov.uk/government/uploads/system/uploads/attachment_data/file/843140/deaths-offenders-community-2018-19-bulletin.pdf. Accessed: 19 June 2020.

MoJ (2019b) Government Response to the Joint Committee on Human Rights Twenty-Second Report of Session 2017–19: the right to family life: children whose mothers are in prison. Available at: https://assets.publishing.service.gov.uk/government/uploads/system/uploads/attachment_data/file/844737/government-response-jchr-22-report-session-2017–19.pdf. Accessed: 20 June 2020.

MoJ (2019c) *Offender Management Statistics Quarterly: October to December 2018*, London: Ministry of Justice.

MoJ (2020a) *Offender Management Statistics Quarterly: October to December 2019*, London: Ministry of Justice.

MoJ (2020b) *Safety in Custody Statistics: Self-harm Annual Tables, 2004–2019*, London: Ministry of Justice.

MoJ (2021) *Safety in Custody Quarterly: Update to September 2020*, London: Ministry of Justice.

MoJ and HM Prison & Probation Service (2018) *Manage the Custodial Sentence Policy Framework*. Available at: https://assets.publishing.service.gov.uk/government/uploads/system/uploads/attachment_data/file/789926/manage-custodial-sentence-pf.pdf. Accessed: 20 March 2020.

Minson, S. (2020) *Maternal Sentencing and the Rights of the Child*, London: Palgrave Macmillan.

Moore, L. and Scraton, P. (2014) *The Incarceration of Women: Punishing Bodies, Breaking Spirits*, Basingstoke: Palgrave Macmillan.

National Association of Probation Officers (NAPO) (2018) *Offender Management in Custody – Napo View*. Available at: https://www.napomagazine.org.uk/wp-content/uploads/2018/04/OFFENDER-MANAGEMENT-IN-CUSTODY-NAPOS-VIEW.pdf. Accessed: 5 October 2018.

National Audit Office (2010) *Managing Offenders on Short Custodial Sentences*, London: National Audit Office.

National Health Service (NHS) (2018) *Antidepressants*. Available at: http://www.nhs.uk/conditions/Antidepressant-drugs/Pages/Introduction.aspx. Accessed: 25 September 2018.

NHS (2019) *Health and Justice Information Services*. Available at: https://digital.nhs.uk/services/health-and-justice-information-services. Accessed: 21 June 2020.

O'Malley, S. and Devaney, C. (2015) 'Maintaining the mother–child relationship within the Irish prison system: the practitioner perspective', *Child Care in Practice*, 22(1): 1–15.

Pact (2020) *Prison Advice and Care Trust*. Available at: https://www.pact.co.uk/. Accessed: 20 June 2020.

Parke, R. and Clarke-Stewart, A. (2001) 'Effects of parental incarceration on young children', in *From Prison to Home: The Effect of Incarceration and Reentry on Children, Families, and Communities* (conference), US Department of Health and Human Services.

Player, E. (2013) 'Women in the criminal justice system: the triumph of inertia', *Criminology & Criminal Justice*, 14(3): 276–97.

Poehlmann, J. (2005) 'Representations of attachment relationships in children of incarcerated mothers', *Child Development*, 76(3): 679–96.

Prisoners' Education Trust (2019) *Distance Learning Curriculum*. Available at: https://www.prisonerseducation.org.uk/wp-content/uploads/2019/04/Distance-Learning-Curriculum-2018.pdf. Accessed: 19 June 2020.

Prisons and Probation Ombudsman (2014) *Learning from PPO Investigations: Risk Factors in Self-inflicted Deaths in Prisons*, London: Prisons and Probation Ombudsman.

Prison Reform Trust (2016) *Home Truths: Housing for Women in the Criminal Justice System*. Available at: http://www.prisonreformtrust.org.uk/Portals/0/Documents/Women/Home%20Truths%20Updated.pdf. Accessed: 19 June 2020.

Public Health England (2018) *Gender Specific Standards to Improve Health and Wellbeing for Women in Prison in England*. Available at: https://assets.publishing.service.gov.uk/government/uploads/system/uploads/attachment_data/file/687146/Gender_specific_standards_for_women_in_prison_to_improve_health_and_wellbeing.pdf. Accessed: 10 March 2020.

Rees, A., Staples, E. and Maxwell, N. (2017) *Evaluation of Visiting Mum Scheme*. Available at: http://orca.cf.ac.uk/112243/1/Final-PACT-report-Final-version.-12.7.17.pdf. Accessed: 4 September 2018.

Sazie, E., Ponder, D. and Johnson, J. (2011) *How to Explain Jails and Prisons to Children: A Caregivers Guide*, Oregon: Inside Oregon Enterprises.

Shaw, J., Baker, D., Hunt, I., Moloney, A. and Appleby, L. (2004) 'Suicide by prisoners: national clinic survey', *The British Journal of Psychiatry*, 184: 263–7.

Sikand, M. (2015) *Lost Spaces: Is the Current Procedure for Women Prisoners to Gain a Place in a Prison Mother and Baby Unit Fair and Accessible? The Griffins Society Research Paper*, London: The Griffins Society.

Snyder, Z. (2009) 'Keeping families together: the importance of maintaining mother-child contact for incarcerated women', *Women & Criminal Justice*, 19(1): 37–59.

Social Exclusion Unit (2002) *Reducing Re-Offending by Ex-Prisoners*, London: Office of the Deputy Prime Minister.

Soffer, M. and Ajzenstadt, M. (2010) 'The multidimensionality of "pains of imprisonment" among incarcerated women in Israel', *Women and Health*, 50(6): 491–505.

Storybook Dads (2018) *Storybook Dads*. Available at: http://www.storybookdads.org.uk/. Accessed: 20 June 2020.

Sutherland, L. and Wright, P. (2017) *Supporting Children and Families Affected by a Family Member's Offending – A Practitioner's Guide*. Available at: https://www.nottinghamshire.gov.uk/media/120226/supportch ildrenfamiliesfamilymemberoffending.pdf. Accessed: 19 May 2018.

Sykes, G. (1958) *Society of Captives: A Study of Maximum-Security Prison*, Princeton, NJ: Princeton University Press.

United Nations General Assembly (1989) *Convention on the Rights of the Child*. United Nations: Treaty Series, vol. 1577.

United Nations General Assembly (2010) *United Nations Rules for the Treatment of Women Prisoners and Non-custodial Measures for Women Offenders (the Bangkok Rules)*, United Nations General Assembly.

Walker, T. and Towl, G. (2016) *Preventing Self-Injury and Suicide in Women's Prisons*, Hook: Waterside Press.

Watson, R., Stimpson, A. and Hostick, T. (2004) 'Prison health care: a review of the literature', *International Journal of Nursing Studies*, 41(2): 119–28.

Wilson, W. (2017) *Housing Support for Ex-Offenders (England and Wales) Briefing Paper Number 2989*, London: House of Commons Library.

Women in Prison (2013) *State of the Estate Report: Women in Prison's Report on the Women's Custodial Estate 2011–12*, London: Women in Prison.

Young, D. and Smith, C. (2000) 'When moms are incarcerated: the need of children, mothers, and caregivers', *Families in Society: The Journal of Contemporary Human Services*, 81(2): 130–41.

6

'Without it you're lost': examining the role and challenges of family engagement services in prisons

Erin Power

'Without it [family support] you're lost. I was lost before I spoke to [the family engagement worker]. I couldn't deal with the emotions I was dealing with, with the children, not knowing what was going on.' (Elle, quoted in Dominey at al, 2016, p 62)

Introduction

Drawing from current literature, policy and recent reviews of family engagement services (FES) in prison, this chapter explores the role and challenges of implementing FES in the public prison sector.[1] Situating current services in a neoliberal context, the chapter examines barriers and potential for delivering high-quality and caring FES in the women's prison estate.

FES in prisons are defined as 'a specialised casework service based in prison which aim to build and maintain contact between prisoners and their family members' (Dominey et al, 2016, p 7). They offer emotional and practical support to prisoners and their families, intending to improve wellbeing and minimise the trauma of family separation as far as possible, as well as aiming to increase life chances for prisoners' children (Dominey et al, 2016). FES were identified by prisoners as lifting moods, offering hope, reducing self-harm and providing consistent care and support (Dominey et al, 2016). In recent years, the perception of FES by prisons has shifted from an optional, albeit useful, service (Hucklesby and Corcoran, 2016) to one that is essential and contributes to prisoner safety and wellbeing (Dominey et al, 2016) in a prison landscape severely affected by overcrowding and understaffing (Prison Reform Trust, 2019). While this recognition of the benefit of FES is evidence-based and valued by family service organisations, the necessary integration of family service organisations into prisons can pose practical and ideological challenges, as this chapter examines.

This chapter explores the role of FES predominantly from the view of the Prison Advice and Care Trust (Pact). Pact was founded in 1898 (as the Catholic Prisoners Aid Society) and was integral to the development and implementation of FES in prisons. This chapter utilises my own experience as a Pact employee in groupwork and family roles across the prison estate. Literature examining family services in prisons is limited, therefore the chapter draws heavily from recent research commissioned by Pact, *Bridging the Gap: A Review of the Pact Family Engagement Services* (Dominey et al, 2016). The review interviewed prisoners, prisoners' families, prison staff and family service staff in both male and female prisons, to offer a broad, gendered perspective of Pact's family service work in prisons. However, it is important to note that Pact is not the sole provider of family engagement work in prisons in England and Wales. Extensive programmes are delivered in prison by Partners of Prisoners (POPS), North East Prison After Care Society (Nepacs), Barnado's and Spurgeons, alongside smaller local voluntary sector organisations (VSOs), and many of the concepts in this chapter will be applicable to wider FES organisations.

FES, alongside most prison-based services, originated in the male estate and the service follows the same structure across all prisons. However, the family service work carried out in women's prisons differs both in terms of the practical and the more emotional relational elements of the work. Women's experience of prison varies greatly to men's (for example, Carlen, 2002; Corston, 2007). Women tend to commit less serious offences than men, with 80 per cent of women in prison having committed a non-violent offence (Ministry of Justice [MoJ], 2019a) and 62 per cent serving sentences of 6 months or less (MoJ, 2019b). Self-reported data indicates that 65 per cent of women in prison describe having a mental health issue and, despite making up 5 per cent of the prison population, women account for approximately 19 per cent of incidents of self-harm across the prison estate (MoJ, 2019c). An MoJ report (2012) on prisoners' family backgrounds found that 53 per cent of women in prison experienced abuse as a child, with research showing that many women's reasons for imprisonment include a relational element (Chesney-Lind, 1997; Owen, 1998; Moe, 2004). This context means that delivering FES with women in prison holds additional importance alongside practical, emotional and relational challenges.

An estimated 66 per cent of women in prison are mothers of dependent children (Caddle and Crisp, 1997), although, given the date of this source, the current figure is likely to be higher (Baldwin and Epstein, 2017). Therefore, FES in the women's estate have a more significant focus on children and on joint work with carers and children's services, due to women in prison being far more likely than men to be sole or primary carers for their children (Beresford, 2018), and the child protection issues arising from the imprisonment of a child's primary carer. Emotionally, family engagement work with mothers differs from work with fathers, as a sense of parental responsibility and feelings of guilt are more evident in the women's estate (Farmer, 2019). Dominey et al (2016) identified that motherhood, and feelings of failure around mothering from prison, can impact on mental health issues including depression, self-harm and suicide. Mothering from prison is a unique emotional trauma (Baldwin, 2017; Masson, 2019) compounded by pre-existing pressures on women to conform to ideals of motherhood (Mauthner, 1998), the societal stigma of women who deviate from feminine norms (Rowe, 2011), and the trauma of physical separation from children (Masson, 2019). This chapter acknowledges these differences and needs, particularly when exploring the challenges of delivering a care-based service in a neoliberal prison environment.

What are family engagement services (FES)?

Prior to the development of family engagement workers (FEWs) in the late 2000s, few formal family services were being delivered inside prisons. Most face-to-face family engagement work took place in visitors' centres outside of the prison gates, and focused on supporting prisoners' families. Pact's first move inside the prison gates was as a first night service, with members of non-uniformed Pact staff and volunteers working alongside uniformed prison staff on the prison reception. The intention was that when people first arrived, non-uniformed staff could offer 'a more human face' (Woodall et al, 2009, p 17), as they had done for prisoners' families in the visitors' centres. The first night service allowed staff to offer support to new prisoners separated from their families, especially if they had children. This tackled a barrier specifically relevant to women, as many primary or sole carers would be reticent to inform prison staff of their children, in order to avoid social service involvement. This wariness of statutory agencies is a recurring theme throughout the prison estate (Edgar et al, 2012), especially for prisoners who were primary carers for their children (Baldwin, 2015; Masson, 2019).

The first night service enabled FES staff to identify that the children of women in prison were often cared for by family members or family friends who had few legal rights or formal support. Pact responded to this finding with the development of 'kinship carer support', which aimed to support carers with the practical, emotional and legal implications of caring for the child of an imprisoned parent. While this scheme no longer runs, this support persists as a significant component of family work in its current form, especially in the women's estate, and is one of the few avenues of support available to families of prisoners (Booth, 2017; Masson, 2019).

In 2008, the National Offender Management Service (NOMS, now Her Majesty's Prison and Probation Service) first began to respond to a gap in policy and practice around prisoners' families and introduced a 'children and families' pathway into its seven pathways for reducing reoffending (MoJ, 2008). In the development of the practical considerations for this pathway, Pact played a role in identifying the need for a family worker, comparing the post to that of drug workers, who were prevalent in prisons at the time (MoJ, 2010). Pact CEO Andy Keen Downs (2016, p 2) states that he was struck that:

'whilst everyone was talking about how we needed to strengthen family, and support people in having healthy relationships, there were next to no casework practitioners in prisons working on these agendas.'

The identification of this need led to funding for pilot family support workers in three male prisons (Dominey et al, 2016). These support workers later became known as 'integrated family support workers' (Keen Downs, 2016, p 2). After a successful pilot, Pact was invited to tender to supply integrated family support workers in further prisons. They joined with Nepacs, a FES VSO in the North East, and were successful in their bid to run family support at HMP Low Newton. This was the catalyst for partnership working and the development of family engagement work in prisons on a national scale.

Due to ongoing governmental concerns about the term 'support' and whether it was the state's responsibility to support families of prisoners, integrated family support workers were renamed Family Engagement Workers (Keen Downs, 2016, p 2). This was intended to shift the focus towards engaging families to support the offender in desistance[2] and therefore reduce reoffending. This sees FEWs in their current iteration across the prison estate.

Current family engagement services

The current role of family engagement work in prisons has developed beyond one-to-one support. Family engagement charities also run visits halls, support families and children in the community, provide a helpline for families of prisoners and deliver groupwork programmes in prisons, although FEWs still provide the most recognised and common service (Dominey et al, 2016). The 2016 review demonstrated much evidence of family engagement work reducing distress for prisoners separated from their families. The FEW role was recognised as primarily consisting of supporting prisoners with family-related issues by: liaising with community agencies; offering information and advice; liaising with family members; and offering emotional support to prisoners (Dominey et al, 2016).

The review also identified some of the challenges of delivering family engagement work in prisons. These include high caseloads, emotional strain and, in some cases, lack of training. While some FEWs come from social work or counselling backgrounds, the FEW role is not a protected job title. This risks gaps in training for the role and a subsequent inconsistency in the service across the prison estate, alongside low wages relative to other, protected or statutory social care jobs in similar fields. High caseloads were identified as a potential catalyst for stress and burnout.

My own experiences of delivering family engagement work across two women's prisons, alongside the experiences of current FEWs, demonstrate that FEWs held caseloads far higher than the recommended 25–30 for prisons that hold around 300 women. Indeed, many FEWs identified that they avoided advertising their services due to their inability to meet the needs of all the prisoners in an establishment. In the 2016 review, FEWs explained the gap between the need and the service as "I think there's a lot of prisoners and not a lot of us" (Dominey et al, 2016, p 32), highlighting how the underresourcing of family work in prison directly limits prisoners' opportunities to access high-quality, careful and targeted family interventions.

While family engagement is a relatively new service to prisons, it has already gone through multiple iterations under successive governments. In order to adequately analyse the changes made to FES in such a short space of time, it is necessary to situate it in the relevant sociopolitical context. This chapter explores FES through a neoliberal lens.

Family engagement services in a neoliberal context

Neoliberalism originated as a set of economic doctrines employed on the political stage (Whitehead and Crawshaw, 2012). First outlined by economist Friedrich Hayek, it is broadly characterised by five steering principles: 'privatisation of state assets, liberalisation of trade, monetarism and the control of inflation, the deregulation of labour and the marketisation of society through public–private partnerships and commodification' (Whitehead and Crawshaw, 2012, p 12). Since the 1980s the UK has taken a distinctly neoliberal turn both ideologically and in terms of policy, and neoliberalism has permeated and shaped the social and public sphere. A neoliberal rhetoric of individualism and responsibilisation has affected prisons through a shift in power relations (Crewe, 2007) and a move towards individual prisoner self-regulation (Crewe, 2011).

Neoliberalism has also impacted prisons through increased privatisation (Prison Reform Trust, 2018), budget cuts which have seen a 25 per cent decrease of frontline staff between 2011 and 2017 (MoJ, 2019d), despite more recent attempts to recruit and retain prison officers, and with the introduction of benchmarking mechanisms. Benchmarking is a set of modifications to the running of prisons through increased competition between prisons and by measuring establishments' performances against one another with the intention to increase efficiency and minimise spending. This has contributed to a reduction in staffing numbers, particularly of experienced staff members, more restrictive regimes in many institutions and a negative shift in physical safety across the prison estate (Crowhurst and Harwich, 2016, p 16).

Hucklesby and Corcoran (2016) examine ways in which contemporary neoliberal policies have impacted VSOs in prisons. They recognise that a reduction in public spending has resulted in VSOs relying largely on short-term and insecure sources of funding 'which have resulted in ad-hoc, patchy and short-term service provision with little strategic direction' (Hucklesby and Corcoran, 2016, p 1). The rhetoric of efficiency and cost effectiveness has resulted in a trend towards competitive commissioning. This can be seen in the retendering process that is required of FES in prisons every five years. The most recent retendering process was in 2016, and led to significant reshaping of FES across England and Wales.

FES retendering

In order to ensure more consistent distribution of FES funding, the MoJ established the total amount spent on commissioning FES across the prison estate, though identifying the actual funds allocated has been a frustrating and unfruitful task. This unknown figure was used to identify the amount spent per prisoner and this budget was then divided between each prison, based on the number of prisoners, with a slight weighting towards the women's estate due to recognition of a higher need, particularly for mothers. Governors and senior leadership teams were then able to specify which services their prisons required, and voluntary sector service providers were invited to bid to provide these services, attempting to offer the most quality services for smaller budgets, in order to negotiate a competitive neoliberal market and secure contracts.

At the time of the initial surveys to identify FES spending across the prison estate, only 60 per cent of prisons were commissioning FES. When this budget was split over 100 per cent of prisons in England and Wales, prisons already commissioning FES were significantly affected. While all women's prisons requested FEWs, at the time of writing, not all public sector women's prisons had a full-time worker devoted solely to family engagement work despite the fact that, as identified by Dominey et al (2016), the need for family engagement work far exceeds the capacity of one FEW. While some women's prisons have a full-time FEW, other FEWs have duties that are split between FEW work and managing visitors' centres, or managing other staff. Some FEW contracts were part time due to the need to employ other FES staff such as visit managers or play workers.

The 2016 retendering process impacted Pact and other voluntary sector FES providers in a number of ways. This included an increased reliance on fundraising to supplement services, and a restructuring of services which has meant some job losses, particularly within play services where frontline roles have become part time, and frontline staff have assumed managerial responsibilities with no decrease in caseload. The changes risk staff burnout, increased staff turnover and reduced staff morale – and therefore significantly impact the quality of services delivered.

Family engagement as an outsourced service

The fact that FES in public prisons are outsourced to VSOs, rather than delivered by Her Majesty's Prison and Probation Service (HMPPS), reflects a neoliberal principle of welfare state retraction and marketisation of society through public–private partnerships (Whitehead and Crawshaw, 2012). Ilcan (2009) examines shifts in the undertaking of welfare responsibilities under a neoliberal government.

She identifies what she terms a privatising of responsibility as movement in social responsibilities from the state to private companies and VSOs. Ilcan (2009) notes that governments are not only increasingly privatising and outsourcing public services, but that private companies and other agencies are also now undertaking work that used to be the responsibility of the state.

In a prison context, Garland terms this 'responsibilization strategy' (1996). While Crewe's (2011) thoughts on responsibilisation link predominantly to prisoners in terms of self-regulation and individualism, Garland conceptualises the term on a structural level. He explains the 'responsibilization strategy' as an example of governments acting upon crime in an indirect manner that transfers some responsibilities from statutory organisations such as the police, social workers and the prison service to non-statutory organisations, for example Pact and other VSOs. Ilcan (2009) notes that this intertwining of the state and voluntary sector contributes to a necessary development of VSOs engaging in neoliberal partnerships, marketisation and competition, purportedly to encourage cost and service efficiency.

In the 2016 review (Dominey et al), a senior prison staff member identified Pact as 'a good quality voluntary sector provider' (Dominey et al, 2016, p 31) due to their evidence-based practice, their willingness to evaluate their services and impact, and the fact that their work 'complemented the priorities of NOMS' (Dominey et al, 2016, p 31). This demonstrates that the success of strategies of responsibilisation in the prison sector can depend on VSOs' abilities to integrate into the establishment and their aims and values. While this can be a necessity for organisations in order to successfully deliver their work with as few barriers as possible, Hucklesby and Corcoran (2016, p 2) warn that: 'The long term ambition rendering VSOs fit for purpose to deliver public services necessarily incorporates them into the pervasive managerial, audit and performance management systems that operate in the statutory sector'.

This reflects what Ritzer termed 'McDonaldization'. Ritzer's (1993) theory is based on the idea that much can be learned about contemporary society by examining how it operates through the lens of global fast food chain McDonalds. Ritzer's theoretical lens encompasses four dimensions through which contemporary society reflects the McDonalds chain: efficiency; calculability, or an emphasis on the quantitative aspects of a service; predictability, or uniformity of service; and control, both over workers and consumers of a service. This can be seen in the voluntary sector through audits, targets and retendering processes employed to ensure efficiency, calculability and predictability.

These processes also exert control, by necessitating that VSOs must compete against one another and adhere to prison values and guidelines in order to succeed. Ritzer also poses a potential fifth dimension, 'the irrationality of rationality' (Ritzer, 1993, p 20). Through this, he suggests that 'rational systems inevitably spawn irrational consequences' (Ritzer, 1993, p 20) and that the implementation of the first four dimensions can result in systems which are so rigid that they deny human reason. This is an interesting tension to consider in the context of FES which are, at their core, based on humanity and relationships.

The McDonaldisation of VSOs in the criminal justice system risks 'social justice' based charities necessarily aligning with the values of a system that represents injustice (Hucklesby and Corcoran, 2016) in order to increase their efficacy, calculability and predictability, and therefore continue to operate in the contemporary prison estate. Reflecting Ilcan's ideas of responsibilisation, Hucklesby and Corcoran note that many charities working within the criminal justice system have transformed from providing supplementary 'nice to have' services to delivering core services which were once the state's responsibility (Hucklesby and Corcoran, 2016, p 4). Maguire (2012) warns that the integration of VSOs into integral parts of the prison system risks co-opting parts of charitable services into the apparatus of the state. This has the potential to jeopardise a charity's social mission (Independence Panel, 2014), by forcing it to reproduce the very systems it was created to advocate against (Ilcan, 2009).

One example of integration into the system potentially impacting on a charity's social mission is the prison Incentives and Earned Privileges (IEP) scheme[3]. During Ben Crewe's ethnographic research with male prisoners, 'one prisoner argued that the IEP scheme "individualized you from each other" but was 'profoundly indifferent to you as an individual' (Crewe, 2007, p 264), reflecting neoliberal values and agendas by pitting individuals against one another without recognising need or difference. The link between the IEP system and prisoner access to visits has a significant impact on the implementation of FES. Although the system no longer determines the amount of visits prisoners can access in the women's estate (Evans, 2015), it can impact women's abilities to access family visit days, which differ from usual visits in the length of the visits, activities available and prisoners' abilities to move from their seat and engage in activities, particularly if they are 'on basic'. In the 2016 review, one FEW is quoted as saying 'I would always say "if you end up going onto basic it's beyond my control, I won't be able to get you onto the family day, so you do need to do the right thing, otherwise ..."' (Dominey et al, 2016, p 48). Although it is rare for family service workers to implement or effect the IEP system themselves, the IEP system does impact their work, as it exacerbates a power imbalance and emphasises the punitive potential of the relationship. While voluntary sector services may be based around care, relationships or social justice, a strategy of responsibilisation has forced them into aligning themselves with neoliberal values of individualisation and personal responsibility.

The impact of integrating FES into the prison estate on the social mission of VSOs is further highlighted by the link between FES and the reducing reoffending agenda. This link is evidenced by the inclusion of 'family ties' in the NOMS pathways to reducing reoffending (Ministry of Justice, 2008). Ilcan (2009, p 30) warns that as responsibilities are shifted and privatised, VSOs can become more focused on 'managing' people, rather than campaigning and advocating on their behalf. The use of FES, whose original mission is rooted in values of care and justice, as a tool to meet the objectives of the reducing reoffending agenda reflects Ritzer's 1993 'irrationality of rationalisation' (Ritzer, 1993). As such, we might argue that where FES were historically established to minimise the relational damages caused by imprisonment, they risk reproducing these harms as their perceived 'value' becomes assimilated by neoliberal discourses of reformation and rehabilitation.

Another challenge of integrating VSOs into the prison regime is that VSOs with precarious funding can be unable to offer consistent services. The quality of FES is dependent on adequate and long-term funding, as opposed to inconsistent funding streams and a high staff turnover. Consistent staffing allows for the development of relationships with staff of all grades across the establishment, which is key to much of the success of family engagement work (Dominey et al, 2016). These relationships allow staff to implement boundaries around partnership working, and deliver a service supported by frontline staff which contributes to staff safety, alongside ensuring that women are unlocked from their cells and are able to access activities, that FEWs can access spaces and that groupwork can be delivered successfully. The 2016 review found that the extent to which FEWs felt valued within the prisons they worked in, and were able to successfully deliver their work, was dependent on the prison staff's engagement with the service. The review highlighted that some officers did not feel that family engagement was relevant to their own work, providing barriers to the successful running of FES. As one governor explained, officers need to know 'why they are unlocking the door for Pact' (Dominey et al, 2016, p 33). Scribano et al (2018) note that outsourcing in the workplace has resulted in a weakening in solidarity among workers. This is particularly critical to FES staff whose working environment is divergent to other frontline staff, in that they are often lone workers, employed by a VSO with differing agendas to HMPPS/HMPS, and are attempting to deliver a caring serving against and within the more punitive backdrop of prison.

Delivering care in a neoliberal prison environment

Within this neoliberal context of individualisation and the erosion of formalised care services (Thompson, 2015), the concept of care is crucial to delivering services based around relationships in punitive environments, particularly for women in prison, given the complexities of their emotional and relational needs (Owen, 1998). Care can be defined as a:

> complex, contested, multilayered concept that refers not just to actions and activities, but to relationships and to values and attitudes about our responsibility for others and for our own being in the world. It is at once an activity or form of work, as a system of social relationships that extends from the intimate and personal to a broader set of ties acknowledging our mutual dependency, and an ethical position that involves an approach to self and a commitment to others. (Fine, 2006, p 4)

This can be seen in FES which require a series of actions, ongoing relationships, commitment to others and an acknowledgment of both the personal and professional. Care ethicist Maurice Hamington notes that 'the caring act also takes place in a social and political milieu that is negotiated. We bump up against norms of behaviour' (Hamington, 2015, p 17).

Care was a recurring theme in the 2016 review, which identified that FEWs were involved in complex and sensitive labour and needed a wide range of skills in order to fulfil their role successfully. The report noted that FEWs built successful and trusting relationships because they were able to communicate what felt like genuine empathy to prisoners; successful FEWs were able to demonstrate their empathy and care by being non-judgemental, showing genuine enthusiasms for their work and remembering personal details of individual prisoners and their family circumstances (Dominey et al, 2016). This reflects Hamington's (2015) assertion that care is not simply one act of kindness, but an ongoing action, or habituation of learning about others in varied and meaningful ways. This ongoing action undertaken by FEWs can be viewed as 'bumping up against the norms' of a neoliberal prison environment which, by its nature, can be anonymous and uncaring (Foucault, 1979).

Hamington (2015, p 2) contends that 'if the human will to care exists, even repressive circumstances cannot stop it'. Having worked as both an arts practitioner and in FES in women's prisons, this will to care has been witnessed many times in the ways in which women care for one another and offer support, advice and a listening ear in prison. A recent example of this could be found during the pilot for the Mothers Inside and Out (MIO) course, an evidence-based programme, co-delivered by myself and Lucy Baldwin, based on Baldwin's research (2015, 2017), which focused on maternal identity and roles in and after prison.[4] The course intended to explore emotions around mothering from prison and develop support networks and coping strategies. During this, the women demonstrated a sense of community and collective responsibility, sharing stories of their children, offering advice and building up relationships which were carried back onto the wings. Many of the incidents of care were seen during the more informal moments of the course, in conversations in breaks, or in throwaway comments of support, advice or even gentle teasing. These were the moments which allowed bonds to be formed, creating a space that was more relaxed than the usual prison environment and subsequently aiding deeper exploration and learning than a traditional classroom.

Within my PhD research, I have come to know these as 'in between moments', instances of human interaction which cannot be planned, prescribed or quantified, but which allow for relationships to develop and emotions to be felt and honoured. In a FES context these 'in between' moments can be seen in the informal conversations between FEWs and women on the wing, women seeking out family workers to update them on their worries or successes, supporting women with materials to make birthday cards or attending award ceremonies to celebrate their achievements. These moments are key to successfully building up relationships yet, as services are 'McDonaldized' for maximum efficiency and cost effectiveness, through auditing and retendering processes, financial cuts and increasing workloads, the space for these 'in between' moments, which cannot be measured or quantified by a neoliberal agenda, becomes increasingly limited.

This is particularly pertinent and problematic, as building trusting relationships in a punitive environment requires empathy, thought and skill. Bourriard (2002) argues that the intimate and interpersonal should be acknowledged and welcomed as an important source of our values and politics, rather than disregarded as irrelevant to the professional sphere. However, insecure funding streams result in reduction in staff members or reshaping of roles as funding contracts come to an end. This leaves many FEWs as lone workers, presenting the potential for high levels of stress and burnout, which, alongside high staff turnover or the conclusion of funding contracts, poses a significant risk of creating a service which relies overwhelmingly on the FEW's individual capacity for empathy, enacting care and building up relationships.

Another potential barrier to caring is the absence of a protected job title within family work, which can result in some FEWs feeling untrained or underprepared (Dominey et al, 2016). However, this also allows staff to be recruited based on their personal skills and perceived ability to empathise, to listen, to work under pressure and to form relationships. As the FEW role is still relatively new, and not widely recognised outside of FES providers, the details of the role vary by establishment. This leaves potential for flexible and targeted work, which adequately cares for, and meets, the needs of the prisoner. Despite this, it can also risk inconsistent quality and expectations of the service and work that is too heavily reliant on the individual (Dominey et al, 2016), especially for the many prisoners who are moved between establishments.

The lack of a formalised role also leaves FEWs vulnerable to undertaking work that is not their responsibility or specialism. For example, the review found that many FEWs felt that they were undertaking the duties and responsibilities of mental health staff in the emotional support they provided to distressed individuals, especially as cuts to mental health services mean that they can be difficult to access in prisons (House of Commons Committee of Public Accounts, 2017). One FEW was quoted in the 2016 review report as saying: 'Cos, ok, you could refer [the prisoner] on to the IAPT [Improving Access to Psychological Therapies] team or mental health – but that could be a while. What is being done for them during that time and that process?' (Dominey et al, 2016, p 59). As will be discussed later, a recent plan for a pilot scheme introducing family-based social workers into prisons adds further complications to the lock of the formalisation of the FEW role.

The future of family engagement services

Lord Farmer Reviews

In 2017, Lord Farmer was commissioned to review the importance of strengthening family ties in the male prison estate. The report offers recommendations for the prison estate including: 'There should be a clear and simple structure for accountability as regards prisoners' contact and relationships with their family'; and 'The importance of "Maintaining and developing family relationships" must be explicitly stated as part of the purpose of prison, to protect the agenda from being de-prioritised or dropped under future governments' (Farmer, 2017, pp 9–10). The report attempts to 'hammer home' the principle that 'relationships are fundamentally important if people are to change' (Farmer, 2017, p 4), emphasising the value of services which support the maintenance and improvement of family relationships. Sadly, these recommendations are positioned much through a neoliberal discourse of individualism and personal responsibility.

The 2017 Farmer review impacted on FES in the prison estate in a number of ways. It ensured that the provision of FES is a focus for prison management teams and has placed a new government emphasis on family work, despite no additional or permanent funding for VSOs delivering family services. As a result of this, a policy document was developed (MoJ, 2019e), which dictates that the government has a role and responsibility in supporting families and prisoners to maintain family ties. The document mandates that every prison must have a family strategy, and that family performance measures and audits will be implemented alongside visits surveys and consultations for prisoners and their families. This is intended to lead to more consistency in the quality of delivery of FES, and highlight any issues in relation to visits that may compromise this quality for families and prisoners. This national and mandatory survey will offer a channel for issues to be reported which does not rely on individual prisons acting on FES workers' concerns. The intention behind this is to create a mechanism that can provide consistent and reliable communication streams, as well as identifying and (hopefully) responding to the challenges that can arise from outsourcing FES.

However, these measuring tools can also be viewed as examples of the 'McDonaldization' of social care in their attempts to create a service which is efficient, calculable, predictable and controlled. They pose a risk of quantifying the unquantifiable; forcing services into a 'one size fits all' model and discounting the flexibility and 'humanness' required to deliver a service based around relationships and care. As such, they may be understood as implementing Ritzer's fifth dimension of denying human reason for rational systems. While the sharing of family service responsibility between the state and VSOs may offer some consistency, accountability and regulation of services, it is important to consider this move critically, in order to ensure that hearing and responding to the emotions and challenges faced by prisoners and their families continue to be at the centre of FES.

In 2019, a second review into FES was undertaken by Lord Farmer, focusing on the women's estate. The review found that FES were just as important in the female estate as in the male, and that it is vital to enable women 'who have to be in custody', to build and maintain relationships (Farmer, 2019, p 79). The women's review placed more of a focus on mental health, primary care for children, and domestic abuse than the one for males, and recommended that additional FEWs should be funded in all women's prisons and on-site social worker roles should be created within each women's prison, and funded by the Ministry of Justice (Farmer, 2019). However, the practical implications following this review remain to be seen due to its fairly recent publication and ongoing political unrest in the UK. Given Brexit negotiations, alongside an election, and the more recent COVID-19 pandemic, little political importance has been placed on prisons (Booth et al, 2018).

Inclusion of social workers in FES

Although a minority of prisons employ social workers, a pilot programme to place family social workers in prisons is presently being implemented in direct response to the Lord Farmer Review, as noted earlier. In contrast to Lord Farmer's suggestion, this will not be run by the MoJ but by family service VSOs. MoJ funding has not currently been secured beyond the pilot programme, which will take place in two prisons.

This pilot may have many benefits for the women's prison estate. As the 2016 review of FES (Dominey et al) indicates, much work in the women's estate has an element of child protection and safeguarding, and therefore liaison with social services is crucial to the current family engagement role. However, the report also acknowledges that FEW relationships with social workers can often be strained and social workers are often unable to respond to FEW queries in a timely manner due to sickness, leave or high caseloads, or not viewing children's maintained contact with their imprisoned mothers as a priority (Dominey et al, 2016). These issues are often reflected in prisoners' attitudes towards social workers, which can include feelings of frustration and mistrust, alongside the stereotype that social workers' motivations centre around separating children from their parents (Leigh, 2017). This is recognised in the 2019 Lord Farmer review, which acknowledges that 'frequently women in prison do not see social services as being there to help them' (Farmer, 2019, p 93). These perspectives demonstrate that the role of a family service social worker could be problematic, and careful thought must be given to role and responsibility division between FEWs and social workers when they share the prison space, especially given the lack of formalisation of the FEW role.

This new potential role is intended to contribute to the professionalising of FES. This risks adding to the 'McDonaldization' of FES, through its attempts to implement efficiency and predictability. It could, however, also be of benefit, as it may integrate staff with statutory agency status, training and knowledge, into a service centred around relationships and care, as well increasing social workers' understanding of, and willingness to engage with, female prisoners and the subsequent spaces they inhabit, such as mother and baby units (Sikand, 2017). Furthermore, it may assist in the reduction and manageability of the workload of FEWs, allowing them more space and freedom to utilise their skills in developing relationships through 'in between moments' and enacted care.

Conclusion

This chapter has examined the history and the benefits of family engagement services, including their services' ability to offer practical and emotional support to prisoners and their families by facilitating contact, supporting visits, mediating conversations and liaising with statutory agencies. By situating FES in a contemporary neoliberal context, the chapter has raised issues around the potential 'McDonaldization' of the service, the shifts between state and voluntary sector in social responsibilities, the risks of integrating a service based around care into a punitive environment, and the challenges of staff turnover and lone working related to insecure funding streams.

The chapter notes a complex and nuanced tension between professionalising FES in order to ensure quality and consistency and the potential to 'McDonaldize' these services through imposing rigid audits and measures. Neoliberalism seemingly necessitates that FES must conform to formalised prison practices in order to integrate FES into the establishment, ensuring fewer barriers to delivery. However, any integration into the system poses a risk of minimising or even losing the 'in between' moments which are integral to a service centred around relationships and care. It is a complex and nuanced position, which reflects Ritzer's (1993) 'irrationality of rationalisation' – in formalising a service, we risk compromising its morals and values, the very reason it was created.

In highlighting these issues, this chapter risks dismissing the careful, thoughtful and valuable FES work that currently takes place in prisons nationally. FES and FEWs can be crucial to the wellbeing of prisoners. In the 2016 review, female prisoners commented: '[The FEW] takes the burden, a bit, for us' (Dominey et al, 2016, p 46); and 'she's such a caring person as well, you know? … she just listens to you. And I think that's what you need when you're in prison you know?' (Dominey et al, 2016, p 52).

FES provide comfort, advice and practical and emotional support, often at times when it feels like little is available. However, in order to continue this work in the same careful, caring and flexible manner, critical thought, alongside a consideration of the prisoner voice, must be given to the role and position of FES in prisons. It is necessary to consider how the service can ensure consistency, while continuing to value individual skillsets and avoid 'McDonaldization', in order to ensure that care, relationships and humanity remain at the core of family service work.

Reflection points

- What can the differences in women's experiences of the prison context teach us about women's relationships with power and responsibility in a wider social context? How do we best address these lessons?
- FES were developed during a period when VSOs had already begun to hold public sector responsibilities. The chapter notes a potential shift in some responsibility towards government, and a partial integration of family services into the prison estate. If this is the case, how can VSOs work to ensure a service that continues to have the care of prisoners and their families at its heart?
- How does the responsibilisation of service providers across the prison estate impact on women in prison? Does the responsibilisation of VSOs reflect a responsibilisation of prisoners as individuals, who are encouraged to take responsibility for, and self-regulate (Crewe, 2011), their own behaviours and rehabilitative journey?

Notes

[1] This chapter focuses on public sector prisons, as some private prisons have integrated family service teams and, as private sector funding is structured differently to public sector funding, not all reflections made are applicable to private prisons.

[2] Hart and van Ginneken (2017, p 1) define desistance as 'the process by which an individual ceases to engage in criminal activity'.

[3] As of 2020 The IEP system consists of three levels: Basic (for those whose behaviour is deemed as poor; they are not entitled to access any more family contact,

association time or entertainment than is required by law); Standard (for prisoners who take part in prison activities, show a commitment to rehabilitation and are deemed to behave well; entitles individuals to more visits and letters and they may also be allowed a TV in their cell, or to spend more of their money in the prison canteen); Enhanced (for prisoners who show commitment to rehabilitation, take part in work and other activities, and follow prison rules for at least three months; may be allowed to wear their own clothes, have more visits, a TV in their cell, or to spend more money). (MoJ & HMPPS, 2020).

⁴ Following the successful pilot, the programme is now being rolled out across the female estate and has become a licensed, accredited programme, which will be run by family engagement workers.

References

Baldwin, L. (ed) (2015) *Mothering Justice; Working with Mothers in Criminal and Social Justice Settings*, Hampshire: Waterside Press.

Baldwin, L. (2017) 'Tainted love: the impact of prison on maternal identity, explored by post prison reflections', *Prison Service Journal*, 233: 28–34.

Baldwin, L. and Epstein, R. (2017) *Short But Not Sweet: A Study of the Impact of Short Sentences on Mothers and their Children*. Available at: https://www.dora.dmu.ac.uk/bitstream/handle/2086/14301. Accessed: 11 December 2020.

Beresford, S. (2018) *What About Me? The Impact on Children when Mothers are Involved in the Criminal Justice System*, London: Prison Reform Trust.

Booth, N. (2017) 'Prisoners' children and families', *Criminal Law and Justice Weekly*, 181(15): 246–48.

Booth, N., Masson, I. and Baldwin, L. (2018) 'Promises, promises: can the Female Offender Strategy deliver?', *Probation Journal*, 65(4): 429–38.

Bourriard, N. (2002) *Relational Aesthetics* (trans. S. Pleasance and F. Woods with M. Copeland), Dijon: Les Presses du Réel.

Caddle, D. and Crisp, D. (1997) *Imprisoned Women and Mothers*, London: Home Office.

Carlen, P. (2002) *Women and Punishment: The Struggle for Justice*, Cullompton: Willan.

Chesney-Lind, M. (1997) *The Female Offender: Girls, Women and Crime*, Thousand Oaks, CA: Sage Publications.

Corston, J. (2007) *The Corston Report: A Report by Baroness Jean Corston of a Review of Women with Particular Vulnerabilities in the Criminal Justice System*, London: Home Office.

Crewe, B. (2007) 'Power, adaptation and resistance in a late-modern men's prison', *The British Journal of Criminology*, 47(2): 256–75.

Crewe, B. (2011) 'Depth, weight, tightness: revisiting the pains of imprisonment', *Punishment & Society*, 13(5): 509–29.

Crowhurst, E. and Harwich, E. (2016) *Unlocking Prison Performance*, London: Reform.

Dominey, J., Dodds, C. and Wright, S. (2016) *Bridging the Gap: A Review of the Pact Family Engagement Services*, Centre for Community, Gender and Social Justice, Institute of Criminology, University of Cambridge.

Edgar, K., Aresti, A. and Cornish, N. (2012) *Out For Good: Taking Responsibility for Resettlement*, London: Prison Reform Trust.

Evans, J. (2015) *Locked Out: Children's Experiences of Visiting a Parent in Prison*, Essex: Barnardo's.

Farmer, M. (2017) *The Importance of Strengthening Prisoners' Family Ties to Prevent Reoffending and Reduce Intergenerational Crime*, London: Ministry of Justice.

Farmer, M. (2019) *The Importance of Strengthening Female Offenders' Family and other Relationships to Prevent Reoffending and Reduce Intergenerational Crime*, London: Ministry of Justice.

Fine, M. D. (2006) *A Caring Society?: Care and the Dilemmas of Human Services in the 21st Century*, Hampshire: Palgrave Macmillan.

Foucault, M. (1979) *Discipline and Punish. The Birth of the Prison* (trans. A. Sheridan), New York: Vintage Books.

Garland, D. (1996) 'The limits of the sovereign state: strategies of crime control in contemporary society', *The British Journal of Criminology*, 36(4): 445–71.

Hamington, M. (2015) 'Politics is not a game: the radical potential of care', in D. Engster and M. Hamington (eds) *Care Ethics and Political Theory*, New York, NY: Oxford Scholarship Online, pp 272–92.

Hart, E. L. and van Ginneken, E. F. J. C. (eds) (2017) *New Perspectives on Desistance: Theoretical and Empirical Developments*, London: Palgrave Macmillan.

House of Commons Committee of Public Accounts (2017) *Mental Health in Prisons: Eighth Report of Session 2017–19*, House of Commons.

Hucklesby, A. and Corcoran, M. (2016) *The Voluntary Sector and Criminal Justice*, Basingstoke: Palgrave Macmillan.

Ilcan, S. (2009) 'Privatizing responsibility: public sector reform under neoliberal government', *Canadian Review of Sociology*, 46(3): 207–34.

Keen-Downs, A. (2016) 'Foreword' in Dominey, J., Dodds, C. and Wright, S. (eds) *Bridging the Gap: A Review of the Pact Family Engagement Services*, Cambridge: Centre for Community, Gender and Social Justice, Institute of Criminology, University of Cambridge.

Leigh, J. (2017) 'Atmospheres of mistrust and suspicion: theorising on conflict and affective practice in a child protection social work agency', *Qualitative Social Work*, 18(2): 212–28.

Maguire, M. (2012) 'Big Society, the voluntary sector and the marketization of criminal justice', *Criminology and Criminal Justice*, 12(5): 483–505.

Masson, I. (2019) *Incarcerating Motherhood: The Enduring Harms of First Short Periods of Imprisonment on Mothers*, Oxford: Routledge.

Mauthner, N. S. (1998) '"It's a woman's cry for help": a relational perspective on postnatal depression', *Feminism & Psychology*, 8(3): 325–55.

Ministry of Justice (MoJ) (2008) *Strategic Plan for Reducing Re-offending 2008–11: Working in Partnership to Reduce Re-offending and Make Communities Safer: A Consultation*, National Offender Management Service.

Moe, A. M. (2004) 'Blurring the boundaries: women's criminality in the context of abuse', *Women's Studies Quarterly*, 32(3/4): 116–38.

MoJ (2010) *Integrated Drug Treatment System PSI 45/2010*, National Offender Management Service.

MoJ (2012) *Prisoners' Childhood and Family Backgrounds*, London: Ministry of Justice.

MoJ (2019a) *Offender Management Statistics Quarterly: April to June 2019*, London: Ministry of Justice.

MoJ (2019b) *Offender Management Statistics Quarterly, Prison Receptions 2018*, London: Ministry of Justice.

MoJ (2019c) *Safety in Custody Statistics, England and Wales: Deaths in Prison Custody to March 2019 Assaults and Self-harm to December 2018*, London: Ministry of Justice.

MoJ (2019d) *HM Prison and Probation Service Workforce Statistics: September 2019*, London: Ministry of Justice.

MoJ (2019e) *Strengthening Prisoners' Family Ties Policy Framework*, London: HM Prison and Probation Service.

MoJ and HMPPS (2020) Incentives Policy Framework. Available at: https://assets.publishing.service.gov.uk/government/uploads/system/uploads/attachment_data/file/898621/incentives-policy-framework.pdf. Accessed: 22 February 2021.

National Offender Management Service (2013) *PSI 30/2013: Incentive and Earned Privileges Scheme*, London: National Offender Management Service.

Owen, B. (1998) *In the Mix: Struggle and Survival in a Women's Prison*, New York: State University of New York Press.

Prison Reform Trust (2018) *Bromley Briefings Factfile Autumn 2018*, London: Prison Reform Trust.

Prison Reform Trust (2019) *Bromley Briefings Prison Factfile Winter 2019*, London: Prison Reform Trust.

Ritzer, G. (1993) *The McDonaldization of Society: An Investigation into the Changing Character of Contemporary Social Life*, Thousand Oaks, CA: Pine Forge Press.

Rowe, A. (2011) 'Narratives of self and identity in women's prisons: stigma and the struggle for self definition in penal regimes', *Punishment and Society*, 13(5): 571–91.

Scribano, A., Timmermann Lopez, F. and Korstanje, M. E. (2019) *Neoliberalism in Multi-Disciplinary Perspective*, London: Palgrave Macmillan.

Sikand, M. (2017) *Lost Spaces: Is the Current Procedure for Women Prisoners to Gain a Place in a Prison MBU Fair and Accessible?*, London: The Griffins Society.

Thompson, J. (2015) 'Towards an aesthetics of care', *Research in Drama Education*, 20(4): 430–41.

Whitehead, P. and Crawshaw, P. (eds) (2012) *Organising Neoliberalism: Markets, Privatisation and Justice*, London: Anthem Press.

Woodall, J., Dixey, R., Green, J. and Newell, C. (2009) 'Healthier prisons: the role of a prison visitors' centre', *International Journal of Health Promotion and Education*, 47(1): 12–18.

7

What are the challenges and opportunities for schools in supporting children of people in prison?

Anna Jones

Introduction

It is estimated that there are 341,900 children in England and Wales who 'are/will be affected by paternal and maternal imprisonment ... in 2020' (Kincaid et al, 2019, p 20). It is most likely that the children who fall into this group will have experienced the imprisonment of their father, since the prison population in the UK is 95 per cent male (Prison Reform Trust, 2018). However, more recently, research by Baldwin and Epstein (2017), Minson (2018), Beresford (2018) and Masson (2019) has specifically looked at the effects of maternal imprisonment on children. Findings repeatedly show that few children remain in the family home when their mother is imprisoned, because the mother is usually the primary carer. While it is acknowledged that outcomes may be adverse for any child experiencing parental imprisonment, having a mother imprisoned may cause more negative outcomes for the child than having a father imprisoned.

However, despite the significant numbers of children estimated to be experiencing familial imprisonment, largely these children continue to remain a hidden group. It is suggested that schools appear to be unaware of children in their communities who may be affected, or, seemingly, choose not to engage with this as an issue (Shaw, 1992, cited in Morgan et al, 2013b). While schools remain largely ill-informed as to the children in their communities affected by familial imprisonment, this is not an issue specific to schools but rather, there is a lack of information regarding these children across all agencies and it is well established that there is 'no systematic identification of children of prisoners' (Kincaid et al, 2019, p 11) or their needs. The Joint Committee on

Human Rights report in relation to children whose mothers are in prison states 'it is not clear from the evidence we have received whether women entering prison are always asked whether they have dependent children' (House of Commons and House of Lords Joint Committee on Human Rights, 2019, p 13). Although this report refers to women, it can be assumed that this same oversight can be applied to the children of men in the criminal justice system and despite the system noting 'the presence of children at different stages [of their parent's journey through the criminal justice system] their wellbeing remains in many cases ignored' (Kincaid et al, 2019, p 23). However, it is not to say that people entering the criminal justice system would disclose this information for fear of their child/ren being taken into care or other repercussions (Scharff Smith, 2014).

Despite being required to do so under the guidance of the European Convention on Human Rights, Article 8 and the Bangkok rules, magistrates do not regularly take into account the presence or needs of children in sentencing (Baldwin and Epstein, 2017). There are no official records of children affected by family imprisonment and, therefore, schools are not informed by the police or other agencies as a matter of course. This means that it is often the responsibility of the remaining carer to inform the school; however, whether they wish to do so, or feel comfortable about doing so, is another matter.

The lack of reliable data on the numbers of children who have a parent in prison is, of course, of great concern to those working in schools and local authorities who must understand the needs of the learners in their care, in order to be able to provide the most appropriate support to achieve the best outcomes for the child. In 2007, a joint review considering how to support children of prisoners and their family, by the Department for Children, Schools and Families (DCFS) and the Ministry of Justice (MoJ) made strong recommendations to 'use parental entry into prison to trigger a process which enables the secure sharing of relevant information between agencies, and systematic assessment and support of the child' (DCFS and MoJ, 2007, p 17). However, over ten years later, this remains a real issue, so much so that the Joint Committee on Human Rights made the same recommendation in 2019 and stated that 'mandatory data collection and publication must be urgently prioritised by the Ministry of Justice' (House of Commons and House of Lords Joint Committee on Human Rights, 2019, p 3).

Research consistently shows that 'the outcomes for children of prisoners are poor' (DCFS and MoJ, 2007, p 9). While having a parent in prison is not proven to be the cause of poorer outcomes, there is a strong correlation between the two affecting the experiences these children have in different areas of their lives, not least in their schooling. It is acknowledged by researchers that 'the effects of parental imprisonment on children may differ according to both the child's and family's characteristics and the wider social context in which the child lives. However, the experience for the child is generally negative' (DCFS and MoJ, 2007, p 6).

While much of the research which focuses on parental imprisonment does not differentiate between the impact of a father or mother's imprisonment on the child, 'the research available shows that the absence of an imprisoned mother often has a greater impact' (Beresford, 2018, p 5). In fact, children and young people in Beresford's (2018, p 7) research said 'the experience of having their mother sent to prison is particularly hard. A mother is supposed to be there for her children, so her absence is more unusual and therefore difficult to explain to others'.

It has been established in some research that children of people in prison are more likely to have mental health issues, to suffer emotional distress caused by trauma and therefore exhibit 'challenging' behaviour. They are also more likely to be placed in care, to experience poverty or homelessness, and to be absent from and/or excluded from school compared to their peers (DCFS and MoJ, 2007; Murray et al, 2008; Roberts, 2012; Morgan et al, 2013b; Prison Advice and Care Trust, 2018). This, coupled with the fact that these children are often an 'invisible group' (Kincaid et al, 2019) within our schools, means that there are a number of challenges and implications for school staff in providing an inclusive education which meets the needs of all learners. However, with every challenge comes opportunities to tackle these and, therefore, schools also have a wide range of opportunities through targeted support to address the needs of all learners in spite of their circumstances.

Given that an estimated 42 per cent of the current prison population were excluded from school (Prison Reform Trust, 2018) and went on to experience social exclusion through being incarcerated, it is vital that all learners are given the opportunity to succeed and be included in school. This is all the more important for the children who it is known are vulnerable and at risk of poor outcomes – children of people in prison, for example. It is argued that it is vital that schools, which play a key role in supporting children of people in prison, enable them to experience good outcomes both educationally and personally. It is already known that children of people in prison are also more likely to be at risk of, or are, excluded from school. Therefore, it is hardly surprising that 'a landmark study showed that 63% of prisoners' sons went on to offend themselves' (Farrington et al, 1996, cited in Farmer, 2017, p 18). Although simply being a child of a person in prison does not in itself lead to offending behaviour, schools can – and should – seek to do all they can to reduce exclusions, so that the cycle of potential intergenerational offending which leads to social exclusion (through being incarcerated in prison) might also start to decline. Schools would be in a better position to do this by understanding and addressing the needs of children of people in prison at an early stage, so that they are included.

The Farmer review (2017) highlighted the importance of maintaining family ties for offenders and their families, as this has been shown to have a significant impact on reducing reoffending and improving rehabilitation for the prisoner. There can also be benefits in maintaining family relationships for the child/ren as well as the prisoner themselves. Children of people in prison and their families may experience their family member's imprisonment in the same way as they might a bereavement, and may suffer insecure or disrupted attachment with caregivers (Masson, 2019; Booth, 2020). Doka (1989, cited in Roberts, 2012), and Minson (2018) refer to prisoners' families feeling 'disenfranchised grief', because they may feel they cannot openly acknowledge that the person is gone due to the stigma and embarrassment attached to this.

Schools have opportunities to tackle the stigma associated with having a family member in prison and can 'actively seek to reduce [this] by incorporating issues around prison, crime, blame and punishment into the curriculum' (Roberts, 2012, p 25). In addition, Roberts (2012) believes that schools can play a key role in supporting the maintenance of family relationships, by continuing to include and engage parents who are in prison in their child's education. She argues that 'in order for any relationship with a child to be truly meaningful it must include his or her school life … [as that is] so much of who they are' (Roberts, 2012, p 7).

For most children, having the ability, and support, to maintain a relationship with their parent in prison will be important and will have an impact on their emotional wellbeing. However, it should also be noted that there will be some children for whom contact with their imprisoned parent is not beneficial '…if the parent has been particularly anti-social, violent or disruptive in the home' (Murray et al, 2012, p 179). In some circumstances, the nature of their parent's crime/s and behaviour prior to imprisonment could compromise the child's safety and emotional wellbeing, and maintaining relationships in this instance may be detrimental. In addition, it may not be possible for the child to visit their imprisoned parent due to the logistical and financial implications involved in prison visits; this is particularly so for a child whose mother is in prison, as there are only 12 women's prisons located in England and none in Wales (Beresford, 2018; Booth, 2020). If visits are possible, these may not be wholly positive experiences for the child; Moran (2013) highlights how the 'liminal' space of prison visits draws in the children and families of prisoners, temporarily making them not quite a prisoner, but not quite free either. Moran (2013) suggests that 'secondary prisonisation' occurs and thus visitors, including children, experience the same shame and stigma felt by the prisoner.

While it can be argued that it is not having a parent in prison per se that may cause the child to be vulnerable, the children who are affected by imprisonment are often vulnerable due to a range of factors existing before, during and after their parent's imprisonment. Furthermore, children with a close relative in prison are susceptible to bullying and associated stigma in school (Baldwin and Epstein, 2017; Beresford, 2018; Masson, 2019). Therefore, it is for these reasons that schools should be aware of these learners and do all they can to support them.

Research methodology

Despite the rise in attention that children of people in prison are now receiving, there is still a relatively small amount of research that focuses on the impact of familial imprisonment on *school* outcomes and experience and also on what schools can do, or are doing, to support this group (Roberts, 2012). In order to develop a better understanding of some of the challenges and opportunities schools face in supporting children of people in prison, a small-scale research project was carried out in 2018.

Semi-structured interviews were conducted with members of the senior leadership team (SLT) from three different school contexts, all of whom had some teaching responsibility alongside their strategic leadership roles. School leaders were chosen as research participants, in order to explore the issue with those who had an oversight of the policy and practice in the setting as a whole, rather than from the perspective of class teachers who may have had a narrower view of how things are. The participants were secured via volunteer sampling and responded to a request from the researcher to take part. Volunteer sampling was necessary, as it was not possible to access schools (and its senior leaders) easily due to safeguarding. Safeguarding is statutory guidance for schools, which seeks to prevent maltreatment or harm to children and means that all adults entering schools for work or research purposes must have a Disclosure and Barring Service (DBS) check and, where possible, be known to the school.

From those who responded to the research call, research participants who held leadership positions in different educational contexts/ locations were selected with a view to providing a broad picture of the issue across the range of education settings for pupils of statutory school age. The participants were: the early years phase leader from school A – a state-maintained mainstream primary school in London; the head teacher and deputy head teacher from school B – an independent special secondary school for students experiencing social, emotional and behavioural difficulties in London; and the special educational needs coordinator from school C – a mainstream secondary school within a multi academy trust in Brighton.

It is important to note that the findings from this research cannot be generalised due to the small-scale nature of the study; however, it could be argued that the opinions of the small sample of school leaders may be indicative of the experiences of school leaders in other similar contexts. The interviews were analysed using thematic data analysis (Braun and Clarke, 2006, cited in Silverman, 2006), transcribed, then coded with the use of the computer software Nvivo, in order to organise the data into the challenges and opportunities that the participants identified.

Research findings: challenges for schools

What follows is a discussion of some of the findings from this research in relation to wider literature in the field.

Raising awareness and knowing which pupils are affected by familial imprisonment

Since there is a limited (but growing) body of research into children of people in prison and limited reference to this group in education policy, inevitably 'children of prisoners all too often constitute a hidden population in schools too' (Morgan et al, 2013b, p 201). This presents an issue; if schools are unaware of the children affected, then it is likely that they are also unaware of the issues they face, and the right kind of support to mitigate for these issues may not be on offer. In fact, many of the teachers who took part in research with Morgan et al (2013b) and Pact (2018) said that they did not know if they had any children affected by familial imprisonment in their schools and they were unaware of their needs and how to support them effectively.

There could be a number of reasons why schools are unaware of the number of pupils in their community who are affected by familial imprisonment. As previously mentioned, children of prisoners are 'not recorded in any official statistic' (Scharff Smith, 2014, p 43) and prisoners report inconsistencies regarding whether the prison asks if they have children when they are received into custody (Baldwin and Epstein, 2017, p 31). It has been widely reported that prisoners' families may face stigma, embarrassment and bullying when others in the school (and wider) community find out that they have a family member in prison (Murray et al, 2008; Dallaire et al, 2010; Scharff Smith, 2014; Baldwin and Epstein, 2017; Pact, 2018; Masson, 2019). Such concerns about this may prevent parents and caregivers from reporting this information to schools, in order to protect the child and family. Schools generally rely on the parent or carer who is not in prison to inform them of the imprisonment of a parent. However, 'imprisonment can be perceived as "unacceptable" within communities (including schools)' (Roberts, 2012, p 4), so families may feel it is best to keep this information to themselves.

Children may feel or be told that they cannot or should not talk about what has happened and how they feel, and may become withdrawn or 'act in' presenting behaviour that may be a barrier to their learning. In some cases, parents or carers may feel it best not to tell the child the truth about where their parent has gone, which can cause issues later on, if their peers are aware of this and/or they find out they have not been told the truth.

In O'Keeffe's (2013) research interviewing primary head teachers regarding working with children of people in prison, all of the head teachers stated that getting information from parents was a challenge. The head teachers also noted the effect that communities can have on the willingness of a parent to share information, due to perceptions that they are 'guilty by association' or 'contaminated' (O'Keeffe, 2012). The school may also find out about imprisonment through the community itself rather than through the families' choice, if the case is high profile, in the local media or simply because the person in prison is known in the community. Equally, if the case is known in the community, this may cause the family not to disclose any information to the school for fear of judgement by the school or others. The head teachers in the current study emphasised the importance of good lines of communication between parents and the school, so that all parents and carers felt they could share information that was necessary for school staff to work with their child effectively (O'Keeffe, 2012).

In addition to possibly facing judgement and perceptions from the school community as a whole, Dallaire et al (2010) found that teachers may have lower expectations of what children of people in prison can achieve compared to other children. Pact (2018, p 21) also found that some schools thought that 'openly supporting a pupil with a parent in prison would represent a reputational risk to the school'. These kinds of attitudes and judgements clearly present a challenge not only for children and families of prisoners but also for school leaders in ensuring that they create an inclusive learning community where everyone has the opportunity to thrive without judgement.

What became apparent from the current research interviews was that communication between the parent/carers and school is key in knowing whether pupils had a parent in prison. The participants in this research felt that they were relying on the remaining parent/carer to be willing to provide this information. Of the children in their settings who they knew had a parent in prison, the participants said that for the most part, they were made aware of this because the remaining parent or caregiver had shared this information with them. This is in contrast to other studies suggesting that parents and carers may not wish to disclose this information. This might suggest that the parents/carers discussed in this study had a positive, trusting relationship with the school and felt able to disclose this information.

All the research participants in this study did, however, raise concerns that they felt they did not have the full picture about the pupils with a parent or other family member/s in prison. The head teacher in school B, the special school, gave particular emphasis to the fact that no other agencies had informed them if a pupil had a parent in prison and that it was through other means – and often by chance – that they discovered this information. The head teacher stated:

> 'Sometimes we find out about it if you go to a "child in need"[1] meeting or something. I'm thinking of one of our boys at the moment he isn't and his mum or dad aren't [in prison] but his brother is. And that became apparent at a child in need meeting that his brother wasn't at home. His brother is now gone, had a custodial and that was it.'

The participants from each school also discussed the wide range of opportunities parents had to communicate with the school, and it was clear that in all three school settings, these lines of communication were very much open. It would be of great value for all schools to replicate the practice of the schools in this study, which give clear examples of good practice, especially in terms of developing positive home/school relationships. Although the specifics of how these positive, trusting relationships were achieved varied for each school, the participants each gave examples of parent meetings or home visits as being vital for information sharing. These meetings were valued by the school leaders, because it was where they were able to establish a relationship with the family and develop an understanding of the child and their pre-existing needs. Home visits for children entering the school in the Early Years Foundation Stage (Reception class) seemed especially useful for the participant in school A:

> 'So I've taught two children that I'm aware of who have had, both of them have had their Dads in prison and the only way that I actually found out was through the parent telling me, the parent openly telling me on a home visit … had Mum not shared that information with me, I wouldn't have known anything, no other agency got into contact with the school, nobody. So it was only through her own need of support and wanting her child to get the right support that she shared that with me. The other child who I didn't teach but was in a parallel class to me, his dad is in prison, and again the only reason we found out was because his Nan told us on the home visit.'

This example suggests that it would be beneficial for all schools to ask a question relating to family incarceration during home visits or pre-entry meetings; however, this would not be relevant to a child who experiences family incarceration at a later stage of their school journey. To support families in feeling able to share this information when relevant, schools should create an environment that encourages positive relationships and open discussions within its community.

All participants said that their school did not keep specific records for 'children of people in prison' as a distinct group in the same way they would have a register of pupils with special educational needs, for example. However, they did discuss the ways they kept and circulated information on their pupils in general. For example, at school A there was a 'vulnerable book', which is a place staff can record any concerns they may have about specific children. This is monitored by the special educational needs coordinator (SENCO) and discussed at weekly senior leadership meetings. At school B there were 'pen portraits', which are created for every child on joining the school and shared with staff; these include, for example, family background, how the child learns best, and triggers for challenging behaviour. Likewise, at school C there is a data tracking system for pupils' attainment and pastoral care, linked to the school information management system (SIMs). The participant from school C stated that if they were aware a child had a parent in prison, this would be recorded on the child's file on SIMs. If schools are able to find ways to ask for and encourage information sharing in a more systematic way (such as those discussed here), then it is also necessary that they record this information in a systematic way. This is so that school staff can access this information and use it to support their pupils to make progress and reach their potential.

However, the participants in this study had differing opinions on which people in school should have access to information about children affected by parental imprisonment. The participant in school A discussed a situation which arose as a result of not sharing information about the incarceration of a child's father. The child's father had been released from prison and: "suddenly I remember being out on play duty one day and the Dad stood at the gate with a dog and adults were saying who is that? And there's nobody in the school knew who it was and for that child that could have been very upsetting." In that situation, the participant felt that school did not have the right support in place "because only limited people know. And I think the problem is in school sometimes the inclusion manager can feel only the teacher should know this. And it's not fair for the child to not share information when actually you're doing a disservice for that child."

On the other hand, the participant from school C felt quite strongly about:

> 'how and who that information was shared and obviously where you have a disclosure from a parent or carer it's okay because you can talk about you know what mechanisms you would use to communicate that ... I don't think it is imperative just because a child's got a family member in prison that everyone has to know. I guess it's kind of well child protection kind of considerations I would employ about that. That piece of knowledge would be communicated on a need to know basis.'

As with any sensitive information about a child or their family, it is important for schools to respect confidentiality and consider who needs to know this information and for what purpose, in order that the best interests of the child are met.

Impact on educational outcomes – behaviour and social, emotional and mental health issues

Kincaid et al (2019, p12) state that 'a substantial body of research highlights the negative effects parental incarceration has on children. Children with a parent in prison are twice as likely compared to other children to experience conduct and mental health problems [and are] less likely to do well at school'. They go on to describe parental incarceration as an 'adverse childhood experience', a traumatic and stressful event which can have a significant negative impact in the child's later life. It is therefore not unreasonable to expect that the negative impact on a child's emotional wellbeing will have an impact on their behaviour in school.

In two UK studies carried out by Morgan et al (2013a) and O'Keeffe (2013), it was reported by school staff that there was a noticeable change in behaviour when a parent was imprisoned. Head teachers interviewed recounted that "[a child] becomes aggressive, verbally … and physically … with the other children, non-cooperative and angry, generally angry about everything and everybody" (Morgan et al, 2013a, p 273) and "it could be that they are withdrawn or weep or fall out with their friends" (O'Keeffe, 2012, p 25). A view shared by O'Keeffe (2013), Morgan (2013a) and their research participants is that the behaviour will often change, but how that manifests will vary from child to child. Similarly, caregivers to children of people in prison interviewed in Minson's (2018, p 6) research all described the children they cared for as having "intense emotional needs, far beyond that of a 'normal' child of the same age".

When the participants in this study were asked about their experience of the potential impact of parental imprisonment on the children they have worked with, recurring factors mentioned were: behaviour; social, emotional and mental health; and insecure attachment. All those interviewed discussed several incidents of unusual, challenging or concerning behaviour displayed by the children of people in prison they had taught in their schools.

The participant from school A gave an example of a child in reception whose father was in prison when she described behaviour that would be classed as 'acting in'. That is, the child inwardly reacts to their experience, often becoming withdrawn and reluctant to communicate. In the case of the child at school A, the participant explained that "Mum let me know all about the background because the boy had become a mute because of [his father's arrest and subsequent incarceration]. He wasn't speaking because he'd been attacked." However, once the child started speaking again, the mother seemed to be satisfied that her son was making good progress, when in fact the child was not meeting the expected levels of attainment in the Early Years Foundation Stage. The participant from school A went on to explain that "at the time her [mum's] biggest concern of the whole experience was about his language needs, was the fact that he had stopped talking. And I think once he regained his speech again and was talking it was almost as if her concerns went." The participant from school A also highlighted that the child's social and developmental skills had fallen behind and felt this was because:

> 'the family had to move areas and I think they were naturally quite untrusting. I think the child wasn't able to socialise with the other children too much. She [mum] didn't really ever have friends around to play so he found it quite difficult to socialise ... I think through protecting him she almost then didn't enable him to kind of have the same freedoms.'

Likewise, the deputy head teacher from school B commented on examples of children becoming withdrawn:

> 'Particularly with if the [family] member has gone into prison recently. Then you've got underlying trauma for both the mother and the child and usually the child's quite reactive to that. They're walking around closed down and you think why are they so closed? And it's because they can't take anymore.'

The participant from school B went on to say that she felt that for some of their pupils, it was easier for them to shut down and ignore the issues at school, because in that way they could keep school and home completely separate. She felt that this was a strategy they used in order to be able to function; however, she said that "maybe it's good in many ways if it allows them to thrive but I'm not sure it does really because in many cases they're not thriving, are they? In terms of emotional and mental health."

These examples highlight the fact that it is imperative for school staff to get to know their pupils, in order that they can understand and respond to their needs with empathy and compassion.

Attachment theory developed by Bowlby (1969, cited in Murray and Murray, 2010) states that children who have securely attached relationships with their caregivers will generally have a secure base from which to operate and therefore will function well in their environment. In contrast, those children who have insecure or disrupted attachments caused by separation from a caregiver, children of people in prison for example, are more likely to experience negative effects and will find it more of a challenge to function well in their environment. Insecure attachments experienced by children of people in prison may happen between the imprisoned parent as well as the remaining caregiver due to the varied stresses placed on the family during this time (Masson, 2019).

Knudsen (2016) maintains that the way a child experiences and reacts to the imprisonment of their parent will heavily depend on the pre-imprisonment experiences of family life for that child. She recommends careful thought before assuming that family life prior to imprisonment will have comprised child/ren living with both parents in a secure and stable unit with no financial concerns and without being witness to any violent or traumatic events, including their parent's arrest. What is known is that insecure attachment generally has detrimental psychological effects on the child. However, Scharff Smith (2014) makes a similar argument to Knudsen (2016), when he says that the scale of the effects on the child will be dependent on the relationship between the child and parent before the separation due to imprisonment. Assuming that the child has had a relationship with their parent before they were imprisoned, it is important to understand that this separation can be 'particularly traumatic, often leading to a mistrust of authority and feelings of anger that can make engaging in education challenging' (Roberts, 2012, p 8).

Knowing the negative impact of insecure attachment and relational trauma on children of people in prison presents school staff with a clear obligation to address this. Bombèr and Hughes (2013, p 9) advocate that the way schools should seek to address these issues is to ensure that they focus on forming quality staff:child relationships: 'we know that developing safe and meaningful relationships with a few key adults is central to emotional growth. The same is true for learning ... quality relationships provide the necessary vehicles for adaption and recovery'. Bombèr (2020) is a firm believer that educationalists, who will all at some point work with a child suffering insecure attachment and relational trauma, must be 'attachment aware and trauma responsive'. This means that school staff should seek to develop an environment for all pupils which is relationally rich, provides nurture and gentle challenge, provides sensory interventions and offers relentless care (Bombèr, 2020).

Bombèr and Hughes (2013, p 5) state that of the 8,000 permanent UK school exclusions in 2010, 'the majority of these pupils will have experienced or are experiencing significant relational traumas and losses in their own homes'. As previously mentioned, there is a well-established link between school exclusion and subsequent criminal behaviour and imprisonment; statistics show that 43 per cent of males in the current prison population were excluded from school (Prison Reform Trust, 2018). It is conceivable, then, that 'a result of parental imprisonment, according to several studies, is an increased risk of later antisocial behaviour and criminalisation among the children' (Scharff Smith, 2014, p 74).

While parental imprisonment is not necessarily the cause for intergenerational offending, there is certainly a correlation; for example, children of people in prison are overrepresented in young offenders' institutions (Scharff Smith, 2014). In this research, the participants from school B talked about the fragile nature of children of people in prison's emotions, and stated that staff had to think carefully about any triggers which may cause the child to lose their temper or become upset. They felt that it was sometimes difficult to predict when a child's behaviour may become explosive in school, and it was often after the event through talking to the child that it became clear that what was going on at home had had an impact. The deputy head teacher from school B said:

> 'I think with all the trauma and the changes and the different things that happen to them. You never know when it's going to be coming out. It could be in a major meeting, it could be one to one, it could be talking about something really minor and they have a big blow up. You take them away then you can and massage the problem out. And also say they are having a PSHE [Personal, Social, Health and Economic Education] lesson or when they're studying these kind of subject areas, it can be upsetting so the staff have to be told, must be warned about all of these issues.'

The participant from school B clearly demonstrates that in their school, staff take the time to understand and mitigate for situations that may trigger a pupil's challenging behaviour. They work with the child on ways to move forward, rather than chastising. It is not to say that school staff should merely accept unwanted behaviour but, as is the case in school B, take the time to understand why that behaviour may be occurring. All schools have a duty to ensure that the needs of all pupils are met. Pupils' unmet needs can often be expressed through challenging behaviours; hence the most vulnerable learners are the ones who may face school exclusion.

While Bombèr and Hughes (2013) refer to the cultivation of positive relationships between staff and children of prisoners in school as being beneficial, there has been much research to show that supporting the maintenance of the relationship between the imprisoned parent and the child has benefits for both as well. As the Farmer review (2017) outlines, maintaining family ties can help to reduce reoffending rates for the prisoner and can potentially provide the child with a way to rebuild the insecure attachment they may have experienced.

There are a number of programmes within the prison system which seek to support prisoners to maintain and build – or rebuild – family relationships, such as family days and homework clubs (Pact, 2020). In addition, schools have an opportunity to provide support in this area through the way they communicate with, and report to, parents in prison about their child's education. School staff can also provide support for the families of people in prison through allowing and encouraging attendance at prison visits (if appropriate) and through reducing the stigma around familial imprisonment, so that children feel able to talk about their parent in prison in a safe space, if they wish to do so. As Farmer (2017, p 18) states: 'access to organisations and services that have proven expertise in helping families with members inside prison is vital for guarding children's future life chances'.

While a school's primary purpose is to provide an education and they may not have expertise in helping prisoners' families, they can seek advice from and/or provide access to those who do offer this, including charities such as Children Heard and Seen; Pact; and Families Outside. Roberts (2012, p 8) also believes that if a school is able to help foster the child/imprisoned parent relationship, 'this can go a long way to restoring a child's trust in authorities as well as reinforcing their belief that their parent can still have important input in their life'. Schools must consider ways in which they can support all pupils to develop and maintain relationships within families, but even more so for those children who are experiencing relational trauma and loss.

All the participants in this study were quite clear that they felt the biggest impact on the educational outcomes of children of people in prisons was caused by the emotional and psychological distress and trauma they appeared to have experienced. Participants from school B talked about particular trauma, such as domestic violence, they knew their pupils had experienced before their parent was taken into prison. They also talked about behaviour becoming 'turbulent' when a parent was due to be released from prison, disrupting their somewhat calm, more ordered life than the one they had before the parent was imprisoned. All participants recognised the trauma caused by separation to some of their pupils when a parent was imprisoned. They all discussed the inevitable difficulties children would have in focusing on their schoolwork, while going through these emotional struggles.

Access to appropriate resources

The National Education Union (2019) states that '83% of schools will be worse off next year than they were in 2015... 16,523 schools will have cuts in April 2020 compared to 2015'. So, it is perhaps not surprising that the issue of a lack of appropriate resources and training to support children of people in prison has been raised in this research. Ultimately, schools are inspected and measured on the academic attainment of their pupils, so priorities of leadership teams often lie within subject-specific areas. It could be claimed though, that for schools to overlook the importance of good emotional health to learning is a huge oversight. Barnardo's (2013) highlighted some of these pressures in its handbook for schools working with children of offenders: 'Educational priorities such as an emphasis on pupil attainment, school performance and student attendance may also result in staff feeling under pressure and pulled in many directions with not enough time to focus on other issues' (p 8). Bombèr and Hughes (2013, p 9) highlight the same issue:

> the systems we are trying to work within are often traumatised too, because of the extraordinary stress around in schools at this time. Competencies are being questioned. Resources are being cut. Different education agendas are being delivered at a fast pace. Troubled pupils are present in all our classes. Staff to pupil ratios are decreasing.

The school leaders interviewed each mentioned the importance of having the right resources to support children of people in prison, in particular empathic members of staff to whom the children could relate well. However, the leaders from the mainstream schools noted some organisational, structural and systemic challenges to providing this. Participants from the mainstream schools were firm in their belief that children of people in prison needed to build good relationships with key adults in school; that they needed to trust those adults; and they needed a consistent person/s to go to when they were having issues. They also emphasised that these adults should have the relevant skill set and training to help support the child to make progress in school.

Both participants from the mainstream schools discussed the somewhat limited availability of this in their schools. The participant from the mainstream primary school A said:

> 'We've got limited resources in school. Because when he [child of person in prison] was with me in reception all I really had to offer was we have a sports coach comes into school. And he takes out groups to do work around team skills and social interaction. And that's really all I have beyond myself and my teaching assistant. But again he's trained in doing team sports and that, but he's not necessarily trained you know in supporting children with these backgrounds.'

The school leader from the mainstream secondary school C identified the need for time – time to spend with children who have experienced (and/or are experiencing) trauma and emotional difficulties. She said it was important that there was someone in the school with:

> 'a skill set in house that could actually you know have positive or identifiable impact for that person in the sense of you know a key worker or mentor because it will all be about establishing relationships with that young person. Staff retention could be an issue that I'm very familiar with at the moment.'

The participant from school A agreed with this and discussed some of the cuts to staffing made in her school in recent years:

> 'Even our work with families has really been reduced which I think is sad. Before we used to have three learning mentors and one of the learning mentor's roles was purely to work with the families. She would be able to do much more, sort of be the middle person to say to us right now the family are going through this and this is what you can do. And now we've lost her; that link has gone. I think it's very hard and sadly you only hear about, you only have meetings with families when things are going really wrong.'

The participant from school C also discussed the fact that provision and budgets for training in this area would be dependent on what the priorities identified for the whole school were. She said that provision to support children of prisoners would not be improved specifically, because "it's not identified as a school priority – emotional health and wellbeing". Therefore, organisational constraints would prevent this from being developed.

Whereas the leaders from school B, the special school, did not cite these organisational, structural and systemic challenges as being a particular challenge for them. They made several distinctions between what they were able to provide as a specialist provision compared to what mainstream schools were able to offer. The leaders from school B, through their work in this specialist provision, have developed a level of experience and expertise that staff in mainstream schools will not have been privy to. They work with a range of agencies and draw on a wide range of resources, such as police liaison officers and therapists, to support their pupils. They were firm in their belief that to support children with behavioural issues is to "really surround it and do the whole package. Because in fact in the mainstream school you can't be the whole package unless you get a therapist in, police liaison, etc – it's a lot to ask". Support from specialist external agencies such as those described by the special school leaders would be of benefit to pupils in all schools, and should therefore be a priority for funding at a national level.

In relation to the findings from this research, it seems that these pressures were considerably more noticeable in the mainstream settings. Staff to pupil ratio in the special school is 1:4 and every child has a key worker. What is interesting is the fact that children attending the special school have been excluded from mainstream schools. To look at this crudely, one could argue that if mainstream schools were able to offer the full complement of intervention and provision that the special school can, there would be no need for special schools at all. Vulnerable learners would be accessing the support they needed in a mainstream school, and exclusion would be a thing of the past. Of course, this is a somewhat utopian vision, but the contrasts between what is on offer in the different settings do seem quite stark.

Conclusion and summary

It was apparent from the current research that there is no consistent approach from local authorities and other agencies in reporting to schools about whether their pupils have a parent in prison. This continues to be identified as an issue in recent reports by the House of Commons and House of Lords Joint Committee on Human Rights (2019) and Kincaid et al (2019).

The three schools taking part in this research all had experience of working with children of people in prison and, in contrast to the existing literature, the majority had known about this via the remaining parent/carer. It was clear that the senior leaders interviewed in this research had a secure understanding of the importance of, and a well-established system for, building good relationships with the children and their families. It could be argued that it was because of the time and trouble the schools took to get to know not just their pupils but their families as well, that parents felt confident in telling them about their partner's imprisonment.

However, this may not be the case for all parents in the sample schools or, indeed, for parents in all schools. Given that we know around 300,000 children are affected by parental imprisonment every year (Kincaid et al, 2019), it is important that schools are factored into the support that should be available to children of people in prison. It is clear, even from this small-scale study, that current support is offered on an ad hoc basis, if and when schools become aware of children in their school being affected in this way. Therefore, with an issue of this magnitude and complexity, schools need to be supported and guided in how to provide appropriate, reflective and responsive care to children affected by parental imprisonment.

The examples the research sample shared regarding the behaviour of children of prisoners was comparable to findings in other studies by Morgan et al (2013b) and O'Keeffe (2013). Changes in behaviour were consistently noted in the interviews for this study as a barrier to learning for children of prisoners. All of the research participants had an awareness of the implications of parental separation on children's emotional and mental health. It also appeared that the sample were aware of attachment-informed practice and already seemed to have specific, albeit different, interventions in place in their schools to address the needs of all children who may have been struggling in this area. Returning to the fact that this is a very small sample, it is difficult to know whether school leaders in all schools would have this awareness and offer this provision, and this is something that further research could explore.

Despite constraints the school leaders were working within, they all emphasised the importance of schools taking opportunities to develop strong relationships between vulnerable children, staff and families. They were all very positive when talking about ways of working which focused on building relationships, and felt that it was something they would like to continue to develop in order to address the needs of children with a parent in prison. They also talked about the fact that a relationships-based approach would benefit all children, not just those with a parent in prison.

These findings show that the school leaders in the sample had some concerns over the provision they could offer to children of people in prison – or in fact to any child who may be experiencing social, emotional or mental health difficulties. This was particularly apparent in the interviews with leaders from the mainstream schools, although all participants were in agreement that key workers or mentors were of benefit to children of prisoners. The importance of positive relationships was present throughout all the interviews. The need for specialist training to support children of people in prison was mentioned by the participants. All participants felt that schools could improve provision for these children if they looked at opportunities for more specialised training.

Therefore, it can be argued that local authorities and school improvement leads have a responsibility to respond to this unmet need, as not doing so will potentially have a profound effect on a large number of pupils. While it is always necessary to bear in mind that children will be affected differently by parental imprisonment, the anecdotes shared as part of this research show that the impact of parental imprisonment is often far reaching. It certainly can, and does, affect children's educational experiences, and impacts on their academic, emotional, social and personal progress. Therefore, it is important that sensitive, appropriate support is made available to those families and children who will – and do – require support, and schools arguably have an important role to play in what that support could or should look like.

Recommendations and reflections

- Recommendation: Information about children of people in prison should be shared across agencies and with schools.
- Reflection: What might be the negative implications associated with this and how might these be addressed?
- Recommendation: Schools should prioritise developing positive, empathic relationships with all pupils and their families. They should be willing to try to understand the reasons for pupils' challenging behaviour and look to attachment-aware, trauma-informed models to support them in their response.

- Reflection: What are some of the wider societal barriers to tackling negative behaviour in schools and reducing exclusions? How might these be addressed?
- Recommendation: Responsibility for developing specialist training and improving resources for schools to support children of people in prison should lie with national agencies and local authorities.
- Reflection: What recommendations would you make to develop policy both nationally and locally to support children of people in prison at school?

Note

[1] A child in need is defined under the Children Act 1989 as a child who is unlikely to reach or maintain a satisfactory level of health or development, or their health or development will be significantly impaired without the provision of services, or the child is disabled (Department for Education, 2019).

References

Baldwin, L. and Epstein, R. (2017) *Short But Not Sweet: A Study of the Impact of Short Custodial Sentences on Mothers and their Children*. Available at: https://www.dora.dmu.ac.uk/bitstream/handle/2086/14301. Accessed: 11 December 2020.

Barnardo's (2013) *Children Affected by the Imprisonment of a Family Member: A Handbook for Schools Developing Good Practice*. Available at: https://www.nicco.org.uk/userfiles/downloads/453%20-%20Welsh%20Schools%20Handbook_English.pdf. Accessed: 12 June 2020.

Beresford, S. (2018) *What About Me? The Impact on Children when Mothers are Involved in the Criminal Justice System*, Prison Reform Trust.

Bombèr, L. M. (2020) *Mindful Teaching*. Available at: https://touchbase.org.uk/therapy/mindful-parenting-teaching/. Accessed: 12 June 2020.

Bombèr, L. M. and Hughes, D. A. (2013) *Settling to Learn: Settling Troubled Pupils to Learn: Why Relationships Matter in School*, London: Worth Publishing.

Booth, N. (2020) *Maternal Imprisonment and Family Life: From the Caregiver's Perspective*, Bristol: Policy Press.

Dallaire, D., Ciccone, A. and Wilson, L. (2010) 'Teachers' experiences with and expectations of children with incarcerated parents', *Journal of Applied Developmental Psychology*, 31: 281–90.

Department for Children, Schools and Families (DCFS) and Ministry of Justice (MoJ) (2007) *Children of Offenders Review – A Joint Department for Children Schools and Families/Ministry of Justice Review to Consider How to Support Children of Prisoners to Achieve Better Outcomes.*

Department for Education (2019) *Characteristics of Children in Need: 2018 to 2019*, England.

Farmer, M. (2017) *The Importance of Strengthening Prisoners' Family Ties to Prevent Reoffending and Reduce Intergenerational Crime*, Ministry of Justice.

House of Commons and House of Lords Joint Committee on Human Rights (2019) *The Right to Family Life: Children Whose Mothers are in Prison*, HC 2017–19 (1610) HL 2017–19 (411), London: The Stationery Office.

Kincaid, S., Roberts, M. and Kane, E. (2019) *Children of Prisoners: Fixing a Broken System*, Crest Advisory. Available at: https://www.crestadvisory.com/post/children-of-prisoners-fixing-a-broken-system. Accessed: 1 April 2021.

Knudsen, E. (2016) 'Avoiding the pathologizing of children of prisoners', *Probation Journal*, 63(3): 362–70.

Masson, I. (2019) *Incarcerating Motherhood: The Enduring Harms of First Short Periods of Imprisonment on Mothers*, Oxford: Routledge.

Minson, S. (2018) 'Direct harms and social consequences: an analysis of the impact of maternal imprisonment on dependent children in England and Wales', *Criminology and Criminal Justice*, 19(5): 1–18.

Moran, D. (2013) 'Between outside and inside? Prison visiting rooms as liminal carceral spaces', *GeoJournal*, 78(2): 339–51.

Morgan, J., Leeson, C., Carter Dillon, R., Wirgman, A. and Needham, M. (2013a) 'A hidden group of children: Support in schools for children who experience parental imprisonment', *Children and Society*, 28(4): 269–79.

Morgan, J., Leeson, C. and Carter Dillon, R. (2013b) 'How can schools support children with a parent in prison?', *Pastoral Care in Education*, 31(3): 199–210.

Murray, J. and Farrington, D. (2008) 'The effects of parental imprisonment on children', *Crime and Justice: A Review of Research*, 37: 133–206.

Murray, J. and Murray, L. (2010) 'Parental incarceration, attachment and child psychopathology', *Attachment and Human Development*, 12(4): 289–309.

National Education Union (2019) *School Cuts Updated Funding Figures.* Available at: https://neu.org.uk/press-releases/school-cuts-updated-funding-figures. Accessed: 5 January 2021.

O'Keeffe, H. (2013) 'The invisible child: perspectives of head teachers about the role of primary schools in working with the children of male prisoners', *Prison Service Journal*, 209: 24–8.

Prison Advice and Care Trust (Pact) with support from the Children's Rights Alliance for England (2018) *Hear Our Voice – Recommendations for Action to Safeguard Children Affected by the Arrest and Imprisonment of Family members.*

Prison Advice and Care Trust (Pact) (2020) *Visitor Support Services.* Available at: https://www.prisonadvice.org.uk/Pages/Category/visitor-support-services. Accessed: 11 June 2020.

Prison Reform Trust (2018) *Bromley Briefings Prison Fact File Autumn 2018*, Prison Reform Trust.

Roberts, S. (2012) *The Role of Schools in Supporting Families Affected by Imprisonment*, Winston Churchill Memorial Trust and Families Outside. Available at: https://www.wcmt.org.uk/sites/default/files/migrated-reports/1073_1.pdf. Accessed: 1 April 2021.

Scharff Smith, P. (2014) *When the Innocent are Punished: The Children of Imprisoned Parents*, Basingstoke: Palgrave Macmillan.

Silverman, D. (2006) *Interpreting Qualitative Data: Methods for Analyzing Talk, Text and Interaction*, London: Sage.

8

Impact and engagement work in the context of families of people in prison

Anna Kotova

Introduction

Research on families and children impacted by imprisonment is a rich and growing field of research (for example Kotova, 2019; Booth, 2020). Despite the fact that families of people in prison were described as the 'forgotten victims' as recently as 2007 (Light and Campbell, 2007), their experiences are now receiving a great amount of scholarly attention. For example, a recent collection of chapters edited by Condry and Scharff Smith (2018), examined a wide range of experiences of families of people in prison across the world and discussed the ways in which imprisonment shapes their lives and identities. The numerous consequences for families include grief, practical difficulties associated with maintaining the relationship in question, financial challenges, and stigma (see Condry et al, 2016 for an overview).

At policy level, there is also an emerging awareness of the importance of family ties for men and women in prison, as demonstrated by recent government reports on the family ties of men (Farmer, 2017) and of women (Farmer, 2019) in prison. As a response to the first Farmer Review (Farmer, 2017), Her Majesty's Prison and Probation Service (HMPPS) has obliged each prison to develop a Families and Significant Others Strategy, focusing on how visits, extended family visits for eligible people in prison and family support are maintained and reinforced. These strategies have been conveniently archived on the National Information Centre on Children of Offenders website[1]. This recent focus on the importance of family and family ties in relation to rehabilitation has led to a number of significant and positive developments – not least, the implementation of the HMPPS Families group, which has been tasked with overseeing additional family-focused developments and family-related policies.

The Families and Significant Others Strategy encompasses activities such as visits and other aspects of prison policy that involve families directly. Although these are undoubtedly important, arguably *every* facet of prison may have some impact on families outside. Historically, families have not been the central focus when making prison policy. For instance, when Chris Grayling, the then Justice Minister, limited the sending in of books to people in prison in 2013, some relatives noted that this, in effect, limited their ability to connect with their relative in prison via sharing books they enjoyed (see overview in Prison Reform Trust, 2014). The policy very much focused on people in prison, with no recognition of the knock-on impact on families and the emotional connectedness that the sending in of books could facilitate.

More recently, the government has proposed changes to how people convicted of terrorist offences are released, in effect proposing that they should only be released if deemed safe to do so by the Parole Board. The impact assessment mentions family ties very briefly, but not, for example, the practical and financial impact on families of having a relative in prison for, potentially, much longer than they would have been previously (Ministry of Justice, 2020).

These are but two examples of policies that were introduced without, it appears, careful discussion of the impact they could have on families. This suggests that family relationships are yet to become something that is routinely discussed when developing penal policy, regardless of whether a given policy affects families directly or not. It remains to be seen whether the Farmer Reviews will lead to a greater policy recognition of the impact that all prison policies can have on families outside.

In the wider society, families of people in prison are often portrayed in crudely and negatively stereotypical ways. Although programmes such as *Prisoners' Wives* (BBC, 2012) attempted to portray a range of women (working class, middle class, and so on), media reporting is often bereft of such nuance. For instance, Laurie Fine, the wife of a sports coach accused of molesting young boys, was accused (by ESPN, a TV channel) of facilitating and condoning her husband's actions (O'Brien, 2012). Relatedly, Hutton (2018), in her work on relatives visiting people in prison, noted that families were stereotyped by staff as being untrustworthy and thus posing a risk to the institution. Much has been written about the stigmatisation that families of people in prison experience (for example Condry, 2007; Hutton, 2018; Booth, 2018; Masson, 2019), and it is important to acknowledge stigma as being critical to how we disseminate our research and engage with policy makers and practitioners in this context. This is discussed later in this chapter.

Therefore, there remains much to be done, if families' experiences become truly engrained within penal policy. Lord Farmer (2017) described family ties as a 'golden thread' that ought to run throughout the penal system (see Chapter 5), but their importance is not yet recognised habitually when decisions about people in prison are made. Although this report marked a recognition of the importance of family ties at a policy level, it still defined family rather narrowly as a heterosexual nuclear family – often as a man in prison with a wife/partner and children. Families, and modern families especially, are diverse, and can include same-sex families, families with stepchildren and adoptive families (see Masson and Booth, 2018). A marked minority of people in prison may have no 'traditional' family, having been in care or in abusive relationships (Masson and Booth, 2018). Definitions matter, because policies are then developed using terms like 'family', so how particular relatives are treated will depend on how these terms are defined. More work is therefore needed to ensure that family is defined flexibly and subjectively. In fact, one useful model is that of the HM Prison and Probation Service in Wales (2019), which recently defined family as anyone who is important to the individual – a much broader and inclusive definition. Other family ties might not be positive – such as if the person in prison were abusive towards their family – but the family themselves might still require formal support, such as information about the individual in prison, and emotional and financial support.

In order to promote a more cohesive approach, researchers should engage with policy makers and key stakeholders. These include charities such as Families Outside, Partners of Prisoners (POPS) and Children Heard and Seen, all of which support families of people in prison. The growing research evidence (Baldwin and Epstein, 2017; Booth, 2018; Masson, 2019; Kotova, 2019; Booth, 2020), based on the experiences of families, can inform the practice of the prison system and the development of penal policy, and effective engagement with policy makers and stakeholders can facilitate this.

Drawing on the lessons learned from a funded engagement project, this chapter argues: first, for a creative approach to policy and stakeholder engagement; and second, that such an approach makes it easier to humanise stigmatised groups such as families of people in prison, by foregrounding their voices and presenting their experiences in a more authentic manner. Ensuring that the experiences of hidden and often voiceless families are heard goes beyond simply doing ethical research and is a matter of social justice – an issue unpacked in more detail in this chapter.

Methodology

This chapter discusses a recent engagement project undertaken by the author, funded by a British Academy Rising Star Engagement Award (BARSEA).[2] Two events were organised as part of this project and involved around 40 different people/representatives of organisations. The first event brought together early career researchers working on family experiences of people in prison, senior academics, and stakeholder organisations such as Himaya Haven and POPS. First, the discussion focused on helpful ideas and advice from academics whose work on families has had significant policy impact. Second, the researchers and representatives of third-sector organisations discussed how best to work alongside each other, to maximise the practical and policy impact of research in this area.

The second event took place in London (to enable policy makers to attend easily), and brought together the same early career researchers and Lord Farmer, as well as representatives from the House of Commons Justice Committee, to discuss what can be done to better engage with policy makers. Lord Farmer opened the event with a keynote, and policy impact was then discussed with representatives of campaigning organisations such as the Prison Reform Trust and the Howard League for Penal Reform. The BARSEA funding was used to cover the travel costs of the attendees, which was especially important as most of the academics attending were early career researchers. Furthermore, the grant covered the costs of catering for the events. The remainder was used to commission an artist to turn the work of three of the early career researchers – including the author – into two graphics on families of people in prison. These graphics are discussed later.

Working with stakeholders

Stakeholder organisations are often extremely important for the work we do as researchers in this context due to the mutual benefits of collaboration (discussed later). The author's PhD on partners of men serving long sentences (Kotova, 2019) would not have been possible without the help and publicising of charities such as Pact and POPS. Likewise, Condry (2007) accessed her participants via a charity that supported families of people with convictions for serious offences, Aftermath (this charity no longer operates). She not only interviewed the members, but also took part in their meetings. Since there is no simple way of accessing the families of people in prison, researchers will thus often rely on the help of these third-sector organisations. During the author's doctoral project on the experiences of partners of people serving long sentences, numerous charities emailed out my call for research volunteers, allowed me to attend meetings, and otherwise helped and assisted me with the recruitment of research participants.

Moreover, the charities and campaigning organisations that work with families are also useful allies when it comes to dissemination and policy engagement. First of all, the larger charities often have good links to politicians and civil servants. They could therefore set up meetings, help disseminate research findings and raise awareness of research. Second, they can also use their social media and other online presence to publicise research on Twitter and other social media platforms. For example, the author's professional relationship with a major Scottish organisation, Families Outside, meant that both her MSc thesis on stigma and shame experienced by wives of men who committed sexual offences (Kotova, 2017a) and a policy-focused overview of the author's doctoral thesis were published on their website (Kotova, 2017b) and publicised using their official Twitter and Facebook accounts.

During the BARSEA meetings, we discussed the need to maintain cooperative and meaningful professional relationships with stakeholder organisations from early on in the research process. Too often, researchers only see the organisations in question as gatekeepers to research participants. In order to maximise impact, however, we can co-develop research with stakeholders, discussing it with them at the proposal stage. Preliminary meetings with representatives of stakeholder organisations could be useful to develop the research proposal and dissemination strategies that would make the research outputs useful to those who we might want to use the research in their practice.

One important question we, as researchers, can ask during such meetings would be: 'What kind of dissemination approach would you as an organisation most engage with?' Different options of disseminating findings could be discussed, such as a roundtable, a brief report, a podcast, visual outputs, and others. Ensuring that stakeholder organisations are involved in this way could mean that they feel a degree of investment in the research and therefore, by the time the research is completed, they would be ready to implement it into their practice. Developing a close professional relationship with them would also ensure that charities, which are often small and poorly funded, are more motivated to engage with the research. Developing these relationships will also help researchers to enhance their professional profile, which is in itself helpful in attracting additional research funding.

Organisations are, of course, not the only stakeholders in this context. Families of people in prison themselves are stakeholders, too, and the importance of engaging service users has been recognised in other areas of public work. The need to engage service users in the process of providing public services more broadly, and within the criminal justice context specifically, has been increasingly recognised in the last decade. NHS INVOLVE,[3] for instance, is an advisory group that allows NHS users to have a say in developing, designing and disseminating research. The Prison Reform Trust now has a Head of Prisoner Engagement (who co-wrote Chapter 10 of this edited collection) – a post specifically designed to ensure that people with experiences of prison are heard during the development of policy and research. The Prison Reform Trust also host the Prison Policy Network,[4] which aims to enable prisoners, former prisoners and stakeholder organisations to share their expertise and experiences in the context of policy. The network has succeeded in engaging a large number of men and women in prison, and this engagement has resulted in well-received reports in the last few years. It should be noted that the latest report, entitled 'What do you need to make the best use of your time in prison?', was based on over 1,250 responses from people in prison and their families across the county. This shows that many stakeholders are engaged and wish to be heard. Similarly, voices of families of people in prison should also be magnified.

Research has shown that involving people with lived experiences from the outset can be immensely beneficial in a number of ways, for both the individual themselves because they are able to make their voices heard and share their stories, and in terms of the quality of the research. Certainly, the women the author interviewed for her PhD study (Kotova, 2019) often mentioned that they enjoyed telling their story to a non-judgemental researcher.

In another context, Staniszewska et al (2007) discussed this in the context of research on people whose babies were born prematurely. Staniszewska involved service users from the outset, accessing them via a support group (highlighting the importance of organisational stakeholders described earlier). Users were involved in the process of developing the research questions and formed a part of the research advisory group. She found that this resulted in research that was more informed by the experiences of the people whose experiences she was studying, and that their input helped to ensure that the project was tapping into a topical issue that needed more research. (For further work looking at the involvement of service users, see Chapter 9 and Chapter 10.)

It is thus important to ensure that relationships are maintained well after a particular research project has ended – since most researchers work on particular areas, we are very likely to need the help and support of organisations and service users repeatedly during our academic careers. During the Birmingham BARSEA meeting, the ways in which we can maintain good professional relationships after the end of a particular project were discussed. Some suggestions included attending AGMs and other events, endorsing relevant organisations' reports or other publications, and inviting representatives of organisations to speak to students (where the researcher also teaches). In other words, and as endorsed in later chapters, stakeholder relationships should not be one-off or transient.

Creative engagement: thinking beyond academic outputs

One of the key themes to arise out of the discussions that took place as part of this project was the need to think creatively and to engage in a way that goes beyond traditional academic outputs such as reports, books and journal articles. Academic outputs are often inaccessible to anyone outside of academia due to paywalls and high access fees, and may not be written in a manner that is accessible to people outside of academia. Russell and Diaz (2011, pp 425–36) rightly argued, in the context of the use of photography in research, that the use of art to complement research findings can be 'a way of bringing conflicting social problems to the surface'. Photography and other creative means of presenting research findings are more accessible and can help foreground important social issues. This is because creative outputs can focus the social issue at hand, rather than focusing on the academic argument, and are often accessible to a wider audience (see also Chapter 9 for further discussion).

Policy makers are often time-poor and have numerous tasks to navigate, and therefore researchers need to think of alternative attention-grabbing (but not time-consuming) methods of communicating research with them. They may not have the time to read a lengthy academic article, and/or may not, as lay people, engage with academic language and style of presentation. They may be disengaged because part of the day-to-day job is to consume large volumes of written materials. At the current project's London event, a Scottish attendee discussed the use of posters as part of a mental health campaign. He noted that the visual output was found to be highly engaging by policy makers, precisely because it was something different (Smith and Dean, 2009).

This was taken as inspiration, and the BARSEA funds were used to commission Dr Penelope Mendonça to produce two graphics on the issues faced by children and families of people in prison (see Figure 8.1 and Figure 8.2). Drawing on three research studies (Booth, 2017; Deacon, 2019; Kotova, 2019) with families of people in prison in Britain, Mendonça depicted the key themes of the research as graphic narrative, anonymising and fictionalising contributors. These are colourful, detailed images that grab attention immediately, and use the 'voices' of the participants in an undiluted manner. As a result, they have garnered interest from prisons, charities and policy makers, have been widely shared on social media, and are now used within prison staff training and displayed in a range of prison visiting rooms. In order to ensure that the lessons learned from these events were disseminated beyond those who were able to attend, a write-up was produced by three of the attendees and is available online.[5]

Penelope Mendonça's approach to her work is that of values-based cartooning.[6] The key values of this approach are 'diversity, equality and inclusion', requiring an engagement with multiple lived experiences of the issues being explored (Mendonça, 2018a, 2018b, 2020). She thus points out that such an approach is particularly suited to examining social issues. Since families of people are often portrayed in highly negative and stereotyped ways, value-laden cartooning (Mendonça, 2018a, 2018b) provides an excellent way to provide a more nuanced narrative about their experiences, including the experiences of families from different ethnic background, social classes, ages and relationship types (parents, partners, distant relatives, and so on).

It is perhaps not surprising that Mendonça has produced other graphics on the experiences of a range of excluded and vulnerable populations,[7] such as the Windrush generation and people with disabilities. Her work shows that participant engagement methods and academic outputs can – and should – go beyond simply traditional written ones. There is, in fact, an emerging discipline that theorises creative academic work. This type of work is not simply art or cartoons; rather, it is theoretically underpinned by relevant literature, as discussed by Mendonça (2018a, 2018b). We, as social sciences researchers, should be cognisant of this emerging field of scholarship and can benefit from, and make alliances with, scholar-artists and other creative individuals working in this field.

Values-based cartooning is just one method of disseminating research, and broadening understanding, that academics could consider. Another

Figure 8.1: 350,000 children affected by imprisonment

This graphic includes fictionalised characters based on the research of Dr Anna Kotova, Dr Natalie Booth and Kirsty Deacon. It is an output of the British Academy Rising Star Engagement Award funded by the British Academy (EN170063). For further details about the project and for links to the research, please visit: https://tinyurl.net/barisea2018.

Graphic by Dr Pen Mendonça
www.penmendonca.com

Source: https://ethos.bl.uk/OrderDetails.do?uin=uk.bl.ethos.782016

Figure 8.2: Separation and stigma

Source: https://ethos.bl.uk/OrderDetails.do?uin=uk.bl.ethos.782016

popular method that is gaining traction is podcasting. A number of influential podcasts with a focus on the criminal justice system now exist, including The Secret Life of Prisons.[8] Dr Shona Minson has successfully used short films to disseminate her research on children of women in prison to the legal profession and to policy makers.[9] This shows that academics have a range of engagement approaches to choose from in order to supplement traditional outputs such as reports, articles and books.

Social justice and making the voices of the stigmatised heard

It goes without saying that it is important to many researchers that their work is seen, heard, and engaged with. In this context, as well as other contexts where research involves stigmatised populations, the issue is one of social justice. As the author and her colleagues have analysed in detail elsewhere (Condry et al, 2016), social justice – broadly defined – goes well beyond redistribution of resources. Young (1990, p 15) defined social justice broadly as 'the elimination of institutional domination and oppression'. This includes distribution of resources, but also wider political and cultural oppression. Condry et al (2016) showed that families of people in prison experience a range of social injustices, but the one this chapter focuses on is stigmatisation and silencing.

It is relatively rare for the voices of these families to be heard within the media, the political arena or society more generally. They may fear telling people about their circumstances due to the fear of stigma, as research has found to be the case with some families (for example Condry, 2007). In fact, silence or hiding the truth are common strategies that families use in order to cope with their situations (Condry, 2007). Silencing, as Hallsworth and Young (2008) discuss in their paper on the topic, often occurs in the context of power inequality, with those who are less powerful often being effectively silenced when wanting to talk about their experiences. Silence and invisibility serve to reinforce feelings of shame and fear of stigma (see Taket et al, 2009). Culturally, we know that families of people in prison tend to be stigmatised as deviant, feckless or collusive (see Condry (2007) for examples of this happening to families of people convicted of serious offences).

We also know that when members of the public are presented with more detailed information about people who have offended, they are less likely to be punitive, arguably because the person who offended is humanised to them (Hough and Roberts, 2017). Research has found that public attitudes tended to be less punitive towards, for example, young people who offended and people with no prior convictions (Zamble and Kalm, 1990). Thus, portraying stigmatised groups of people (such as people who offend and their families) in a way that goes beyond crude stereotypes could be very important, if we are to begin to break down punitive, stigmatising public attitudes. Creative research outputs can help portray the experiences of stigmatised populations in more nuanced ways and help engage stakeholders, the public and other parties using accessible, non-academic methods of research dissemination.

Hallsworth and Young (2008) point out that silence serves the purpose of reinforcing the status quo. As such, making the negative consequences of imprisonment on families more widely known would potentially force policy makers to face, head on, the need to improve penal policy. This could have financial and political implications for governments, because it could stimulate discussion about the need to invest in improving penal institutions, which runs counter to the punitive narrative prevalent within politics today. This means that policy makers may be reluctant to talk about the issues this chapter is concerned with, which in turn means that researchers have an important role in ensuring that the problems faced by these families are made visible.

Consequently, researchers working in this area need to ensure that the voices of families are heard beyond academic publications. We need to promote engagement with the media, the public and policy makers – not simply because, as researchers, we want our research to have positive impact, but also because it is a matter of social justice. This is especially important when research involves populations that otherwise are comparatively silenced and less able to discuss their own experiences in the open without fear of stigma or exclusion. We, as researchers, can do much to help share their experiences without putting our participants under the limelight and thus risking them being stigmatised further.

Nonetheless, where families are themselves willing to discuss their experiences publicly, we ought to facilitate this as researchers and not presume we always need to protect the families concerned by speaking for them. We could invite families to attend media interviews with us, for example. Another excellent output, and a further example of creative means of generating understanding, was that of researchers Lucy Baldwin and Ben Raikes, who edited a book (2019) of poems produced by parents and children affected by imprisonment. This was a non-academic output that allowed the unfiltered voices of the children to be heard, while at the same time generating knowledge and understanding about their experiences (see Chapter 9 for more information about this project). In 2019, a conference called Our Time to be Heard took place in London, during which children of people in prison spoke openly about their experiences and read their own poems from the collection. This was another example of the way in which we, as researchers, can facilitate the voices of stigmatised groups to be heard. The children were given the option of being photographed for social media, and many seemed extremely empowered and proud of having been given the opportunity to speak to academics and policy makers

Research should be conducted in an ethical manner that recognises the agency of the participants, especially when they share deeply personal stories with the researcher. As discussed earlier, we can involve service users from very early stages of developing research, and therefore allow them the space to have their voices heard and to share their experiences. The process of taking part in research development can also be empowering for service users, since it does not simply treat them as research subjects but as more equal research partners (Staniszewska et al, 2007, in the context of health research) (see also Chapter 9 and Chapter 10).

When academic outputs are produced, unless there is extensive co-production with the participants engaging in writing and editing outputs, the data is analysed by the researcher and the conclusions are those of the researcher alone. Although participants could be involved in analysing the data, and even as co-authors of publications, this might not be practically possible due to temporal constraints, or because the participants might not want to engage in extensive and protracted communication with the researchers. After all, data analysis and academic publication are very lengthy processes. Creative dissemination strategies, however, can allow the experienced to be shared without an academic filter, such as demonstrated in the book edited by Baldwin and Raikes (2019). Participants could also be filmed talking about their experiences in their own voices, could participate in recording podcasts, or could contribute to blogs – all of which may be empowering and, indeed, may help to counter the invisibility that they might have experienced previously.

It is important to note that we, as researchers, need to be aware that individuals are different and have different preferences. Some participants might want to be more visible; others might want to remain anonymous. Audio, visual and graphic outputs offer the opportunity for a more 'real-life' method of engaging with politicians, stakeholders and the public, without identifying people who might not want to be identified. Some individuals may be vulnerable and at risk if identified – this can, and should, be taken into account, for example by using people's testimonies read out by actors. It is also important to note that anonymity is often dictated by ethical guidelines. As such, regardless of dissemination methods chosen, research should, of course, still be conducted ethically, and participants should not be forced to become visible against their wishes.

Summary

Academics working on research that explores the experiences of stigmatised and socially hidden groups might find it helpful to see their work as being an exercise in enhancing and promoting social justice. Many researchers working with excluded and stigmatised groups might already see their work as being politically important in ways that go far beyond simply having an impact in the strict Research Excellence Framework definition, or as a way towards career progression. However, conceptualising it in the context of social justice can help us to frame dissemination strategies when applying for grants and writing research proposals. The concept of social justice also highlights the need to make the experiences of stigmatised and marginalised groups visible, whether we do this ourselves as researchers, or facilitate this by making the space for individuals to speak directly about their experiences.

Creative outputs can humanise populations that are often presented in highly stereotypical and negative ways. They can help society to see people with these experiences as individuals with their own stories and not as simplistic, stereotypical images portrayed in the media. Value-laden cartooning, as one method, is specifically focused on portraying a range of experiences, including those of people of different ethnicities, genders, social classes and ages. This takes the discourse beyond highly stereotypical discourses (such as those prevalent in the popular media in the context of offending and families of people in prison). Penelope Mendonça, when producing the graphics as part of the BARSEA project discussed in this chapter, specifically included people with a range of different characteristics, such as people from different ethnic backgrounds, people with disabilities, people of different ages, and so on. This can be an exercise in promoting social justice because it enhances the cultural visibility of socially marginalised groups.

One of the key practical lessons learned from undertaking this project is the importance of research support staff who might be very well placed to help researchers develop creative approaches to outputs. The author would not have come across Dr Mendonça's work were it not for a member of the research team at my institution. These teams can develop a set of examples of good practice, such as visual, audio and dramatised outputs of research. When developing research proposals, they can specifically discuss these types of outputs with academics and show them a range of examples of outputs from previous projects.

I found the issues discussed here to be an important part of my development as an early career researcher. I have now involved service users in developing my future research, and have written a range of non-traditional research dissemination strategies into research grant applications. Doing this has allowed me to build a network of connections, including with theatre groups working on penal issues, individuals who had been in prison who are doing excellent outreach work, and organisations and policy makers with interest in the type of research I do. The opportunities for future engagement are exciting indeed. This has been discussed in the context of foregrounding the experiences and voices of people in prison authentically (see Aresti et al, 2016), and is also important in the context of families.

Researchers are increasingly using a range of research engagement strategies that go beyond the usual journal articles and academic books. Perhaps this has been motivated by the need to consider the Research Excellence Framework and the fact it has highlighted impact and engagement. Research training needs to routinely discuss creative methods of engagement and enable research to elect, and put into practice effectively, appropriate output methods. It is of note that the Social Research Association does not currently offer training courses on non-traditional dissemination strategies, which is a gap that could be filled to enhance their range of courses.

It is also notable that there is a growing body of funding for engagement and impact activities. The grant that funded the project described in this chapter is one such. Another good example is the Economic and Social Research Council's Impact Acceleration Accounts. These are given to research organisations, such as universities, to fund engagement and impact activities. They can provide funding for training and other activities, such as symposiums with stakeholders and policy makers, as well as funds for commissioning creative research outputs. It is therefore clear that effective engagement is now receiving more attention and funding, allowing researchers to put time and energy into developing innovative engagement strategies.

Reflection points

- What other creative methods of engagement can researchers use?
- Can you recall any non-traditional outputs that have grabbed your attention and made you engage with the research findings?

- What other type of research might such approaches to disseminating research be especially suitable for?
- What are some of the main risks and benefits of user involvement in research?

Acknowledgements

The project described in this chapter was funded by the British Academy, Grant reference number: EN-170063. I would like to thank everyone who contributed to the discussions during the two roundtables and who kindly shared their thoughts, ideas and experiences.

Notes

1   nicco.org.uk
2   Details of the funding scheme can be found at: https://www.thebritishacademy. ac.uk/funding/british-academy-rising-star-engagement-awards.
3   The website for the NHS Involve scheme: https://www.invo.org.uk
4   The following article provides an overview of the work the Prisoner Policy Network aims to do and how it operates: https://insidetime.org/ listening-to-prisoners-the-launch-of-the-prisoner-policy-network/
5   The link to a write-up of the lessons learned during the BARSEA project: https:// 9b93f97b-1317-41c7-b9c8-a7afc14b351d.filesusr.com/ugd/749b01_dde3f4510e db4080b4d7a8cbc4317d20.pdf
6   Other images can be found at: http://www.penmendonca.com/?LMCL=oCFfoH
7   For more examples of Dr Mendonça's work, visit: http://www.penmendonca. com/
8   The link to the Secret Lives of Prisons podcast: https://prison.radio/ the-secret-life-of-prisons/
9   The link to Shona Minson's short film on maternal imprisonment: http://www. russellwebster.com/mothersprison/

References

Aresti, A., Darke, S. and Manlow, D. (2016) '"Bridging the gap": giving public voice to prisoners and former prisoners through research activism', *Prison Service Journal*, 22: 3–13.

Baldwin, L. and Epstein, R. (2017) *Short But Not Sweet: A Study of the Impact of Short Custodial Sentences on Mothers and their Children*, De Montfort University with Oakdale Trust. Available at: https:// www.nicco.org.uk/userfiles/downloads/5bc45012612b4-short-but-not-sweet.pdf. Accessed: 18 December 2020.

Baldwin, L. and Raikes, B. (2019) *Seen & Heard: 100 Poems by Parents & Children Affected by Imprisonment*, Hook: Waterside Press.

Booth, N. (2017) *Prison and the Family: An Exploration of Maternal Imprisonment from a Family-centred Perspective* (PhD), University of Bath.

Booth, N. (2018) 'Disconnected: exploring provisions for mother–child contact in female prisons serving England and Wales', *Criminology and Criminal Justice*, 20(2): 150–68.

Booth, N. (2020) *Maternal Imprisonment and Family Life: From the Caregiver's Perspective*, Bristol: Policy Press.

Condry, R. (2007) *Families Shamed: The Consequences of Crime for Relatives of Serious Offenders*, Abingdon: Willan.

Condry, R. and Scharff Smith, P. (eds) (2018) *Prisons, Punishment and the Family: Towards a New Sociology of Punishment*, Oxford: Oxford University Press.

Condry, R., Kotova, A. and Minson, S. (2016) 'Social injustice and collateral damage: the families and children of prisoners', in Y. Jewkes, B. Crewe and J. Bennett (eds) *Handbook on Prisons* (2nd edn), Abingdon: Routledge, pp 622–40.

Deacon, K. (2019) *Families – Inside Prison and Out: Young People's Experiences of Having a Family Member in Prison* (PhD thesis), University of Glasgow.

Farmer, Lord M. (2017) *The Importance of Strengthening Prisoners' Family Ties to Prevent Reoffending and Reduce Intergenerational Crime*. Available at: https://assets.publishing.service.gov.uk/government/uploads/system/uploads/attachment_data/file/642244/farmer-review-report.pdf. Accessed: 12 February 2020.

Farmer, Lord M. (2019) *The Importance of Strengthening Female Offenders' Families and Other Relationships to Prevent Reoffending and Reduce Intergenerational Crime*. Available at: https://assets.publishing.service.gov.uk/government/uploads/system/uploads/attachment_data/file/809467/farmer-review-women.PDF. Accessed: 12 February 2020.

Hallsworth, S. and Young, T. (2008) 'Crime and silence', *Theoretical Criminology*, 12(2): 131–52.

HM Prison and Probation Service in Wales (2019) *HMPPS in Wales Family and Significant Other Strategy*. Available at: 5d8d9a2f7b50-cym-hmpps-in-Wales-families-strategy-2019.docx. Accessed: 12 March 2020.

Hough, M. and Roberts, J. (2017) 'Public opinion, crime, and criminal justice', in A. Liebling, S. Maruna and L. McAra (eds) *Oxford Handbook of Criminology* (6th edn), Oxford: Oxford University Press, pp 239–59.

Hutton, M. (2018) 'The legally sanctioned stigmatisation of prisoners' families', in R. Condry and P. Scharff Smith (eds) *Prisons, Punishment and the Family: Towards a New Sociology of Punishment*, Oxford: Oxford University Press.

Kotova, A. (2017a) *Blaming and Stigmatising Female Partners of Male Child Sex Offenders. Families Outside*. Available at: https://www.familiesoutside.org.uk/content/uploads/2019/03/Kotova-Report.pdf. Accessed: 12 February 2020.

Kotova, A. (2017b) *Lost Time, Stigma, and Adaptation: The Experiences of Long-term Prisoners' Partners*. Available at: https://www.familiesoutside.org.uk/content/uploads/2017/11/families-outside-in-brief-12.pdf. Accessed: 12 February 2020.

Kotova, A. (2019) '"Time … lost time": exploring how partners of long-term prisoners experience the temporal pains of imprisonment', *Time and Society*, 28(2): 478–98.

Light, R. and Campbell, B. (2011) 'Prisoners' families: still forgotten victims?', *Journal of Social Welfare and Family Law*, 28(3–4): 297–308.

Masson, I. (2019) *Incarcerating Motherhood: The Enduring Harms of First Short Periods of Imprisonment on Mothers*, Abingdon: Routledge.

Masson, I. and Booth, N. (2018) *Examining Prisoners' Families: Definitions, Developments and Difficulties*, Howard League ECAN.

Mendonça, P. (2018a) 'Situating single mothers through values-based cartooning', *Women: A Cultural Review*, 29(1): 19–38.

Mendonça, P. (2018b) 'Values-based cartooning: mothers storying the absent father (a case study)' (PhD thesis), University of the Arts London. Available at: https://ethos.bl.uk/OrderDetails.do?uin=uk.bl.ethos.782016. Accessed: 7 July 2020.

Mendonça, P. (2020) *Pen Mendonça – Echoing Inequalities and Picturing Possibilities: Values-Based Cartooning in the 21st Century*, University of the Arts London. Available at: https://doi.org/10.25441/arts.12582929.v2. Accessed: 8 July 2020.

Ministry of Justice (2020) *Impact Assessment*. Available at: https://assets.publishing.service.gov.uk/government/uploads/system/uploads/attachment_data/file/864910/to-signed-impact-assessment.pdf. Accessed: 12 February 2020.

Russell, A. C. and Diaz, N. D. (2011) 'Photography in social work research: using visual image to humanise findings', *Qualitative Social Work*, 12(4): 433–53.

Smith, H. and Dean, R. T. (eds) (2009) *Practice Led Research, Research-led Practice in the Creative Arts*, Edinburgh: Edinburgh University Press.

Staniszewska, S., Jones, N. and Newburn, M. (2007) 'User involvement in the development of a research bid: barriers, enablers and impacts', *Health Expectations*, 10(2): 173–83.

O'Brien, J. (2012) 'Laurie Fine to sue ESPN for libel, says the network "spitefully destroyed" her reputation'. Available at: https://www.syracuse.com/news/2012/05/laurie_fine_to_sue_espn_for_li.html. Accessed: 12 February 2020.

Prison Reform Trust (2014) *Punishment Without Purpose*. Available at: http://www.prisonreformtrust.org.uk/Portals/0/Documents/punishment%20without%20purpose%20FINAL2941007.pdf. Accessed: 12 February 2020.

Taket, A., Foster, N. and Cook, K. (2009) 'Understanding processes of social exclusion: silence, silencing and shame', in A. Taket, B. R. Crisp, A. N. G. Lamaro, M. Graham and S. Barter-Godfrey (eds) *Theorising Social Exclusion*, London: Routledge, pp 173–83.

Wainwright, L. Harriott, P. and Saajedi, S. (2019) *What Prisoners Need to Make the Best Use of Time in Prison*. Available at: http://www.prisonreformtrust.org.uk/Portals/0/Documents/PPN/What_do_you_need_to_make_best_use_of_your_time_in_prisonlo.pdf. Accessed: 12 December 2020.

Young, M. I. (1990) *Justice and the Politics of Difference*, Princeton: Princeton University Press.

Zamble, E. and Kalm, K. L. (1990) 'General and specific measures of public attitudes toward sentencing', *Canadian Journal of Behavioural Science*, 22(3): 327–37.

9

Presence, voice and reflexivity in feminist and creative research: a personal and professional reflection

Lucy Baldwin

Introduction

This chapter extends a presentation given by the author during the 2019 Women, Family, Crime and Justice seminar series. This was a reflexive presentation incorporating both personal and professional reflection and experience. Exploring reflexivity and creative research through a personal and professional lens, the chapter alternates between the first person and the third person, where appropriate.

The chapter first sets out what is understood by feminist research, emphasising that it is more than simply research undertaken by researchers who consider themselves feminist, but research informed by broader feminist principles via its topic, design, process, analysis and researcher reflexivity. Critically, feminist research advocates for the presence and voice of participants, and the reflexivity of the researcher to be visible in the final products of research (Maynard and Purvis, 1994; Oakley, 2016).

Thereafter, there is a reflective discussion about my doctoral research (Baldwin, forthcoming) and research process, notably how mothers themselves assisted in shaping the research decisions, research tools and the methodology (for example, where the interviews took place). It then explores the researcher/research relationship and its significance. The final section presents the author's recent research project (jointly undertaken with Ben Raikes), which sought to generate knowledge and understanding about parental imprisonment. The project concluded with the production of a published collection of poetry.[1] We posit that the collection constitutes a form of research that has produced a significant body of knowledge (see later discussion), and one which reveals much about the impact of parental imprisonment. Importantly, and in line with feminist principles (Doucet and Mauthner, 2006), the project saw the participants' words presented undiluted, in an accessible format, and via an inclusive project in which the participants/poets were able to retain power and control in the research process.

What is meant by 'feminist research'?

Historically, defining 'feminist research' has proved challenging, even to the point of reaching a consensus that feminist research has a distinct and separate identity (Gelsthorpe, 1990; Letherby, 2004). Gelsthorpe (1990, p 105) suggests it is often difficult to differentiate between feminist research and 'good' research, asking if feminist research is simply 'old wine in new bottles?'. Merriam (1988) similarly argued that feminist researchers simply employed good practice concerning their research design and methodology. However, Doucet and Mauthner (2006) state that while it may be difficult to argue that methods and methodology can be particularly and uniquely feminist, there are central and key underlying principles which should *always* be present in feminist research – precisely, that feminist research ought to concern itself with giving voice to women who have traditionally been neglected in research and who may lack social power.

Oakley (1981) has presented a convincing and long-standing argument that interaction between the researched and the researcher is imperative in feminist research, suggesting that an objective standardised and detached approach to interviewing is not the most effective means of finding out about people or, specifically, their thoughts and feelings. Rather, this is 'best achieved when the relationship of interviewer and interviewee is non-hierarchical and when the interviewer is prepared to invest his or her own personal identity in the relationship', thereby facilitating mutuality and reciprocity (Oakley 1981, p 41). Oakley further suggests that where both share the same role identity and critical life-experiences, social distance can be minimal.

Furthermore, when membership of the same minority group is shared, for example single motherhood, the basis for equality may impress itself even more urgently on the interviewer's consciousness (Oakley, 1981, p 55; see also Stanley and Wise, 1983; Finch, 1984; Reinharz, 1993).

Maynard and Purvis (1994, p 2) suggest that although there is 'no clear consensus as to what feminist research definitionally might comprise', feminist research is undoubtedly, or ought to be, adaptive, flexible, interactive and reflexive. Thus, feminist research incorporates principles widely regarded as good ethical practice in research generally, but *also* includes an increased awareness of the significance of power, agency, reflexivity and the facilitation of voice, specifically in relation to women (Maynard and Purvis, 1994; Letherby, 2004).

As suggested by Nencel (2014, p 75), a substantial group of feminist researchers, particularly those with an anthropological leaning, will expect to be reflexive throughout their research, and thus, 'writing oneself into the text comes virtually as second nature'. Indeed, Finch (1984, p 81) posits that the 'only morally defensible way to conduct research with women is to invest some of one's own identity'. However, striking a balance is vital (Doucet, 1998). Pillow (2003) cautions against reflexivity for reflexivity's sake, but nonetheless accepts reflexivity as an essential component of good feminist research. Philip and Bell (2017, p 72), argue that the 'complexities' surrounding reflexivity and the researcher/researched relationship are 'all too often' left out of the process of writing and the final products of research, and should be more visible.

Doing feminist research

In keeping with my feminist, matricentric (that is, mother-focused (O'Reilly, 2006, 2016)), ontological and epistemological standpoint, the aforementioned underlying principles and considerations were central to my doctoral study, thus informing the research study in its methodology, analysis, design and presentation, as now discussed.

My doctoral research: shaping the methodology

My doctoral research investigates the lasting harm of maternal imprisonment, particularly in relation to maternal identity and role. It is a matricentric feminist study, which reflects my ontological and epistemological position.

From the outset, I was clear that the study would be guided by the aforementioned feminist research principles, which were central to my decision making and design of the study. For example, I had initially intended to interview mothers while they were still in custody. I wrote to the head of research at the National Offender Management Service (NOMS), and the Scottish Prison Service, informing them about the study and enquiring as to the likelihood of being accepted to proceed. However, despite replies from both to say that my application would be 'very likely' to be accepted (on the basis that it would have 'fed nicely' into the then forthcoming reviews of female offender management), I had concerns. After reflection, my instincts were telling me that interviewing mothers, arguably at their most vulnerable and at a point of often great pain – that is, separation from their children – and without unrestricted access to support, and importantly comfort, was not without risks to the participants. I was concerned about adding to mothers' trauma when they were perhaps already struggling with their maternal emotions. In the interests of making as informed a decision as possible, I therefore decided to seek the views of mothers who were so affected.

At that time, I was working with mothers in and after prison in a voluntary capacity, so with the permission of the relevant authorities, and after ethical approval,[2] I ran several focus groups,[3] both in and outside of prison with mothers known to me, and who I knew had access to both formal and informal support. Importantly, the mothers in the in-prison focus group were serving their sentence in an open[4] prison and were, therefore, free to leave the group at any time because of their 'free movement' status.[5] The purpose of the focus groups was to 'test' out my concerns and to seek the women's views about interviewing mothers in prison. The groups confirmed my concerns, and felt it would be 'safer' to interview mothers post-release. However, they suggested that mothers in prison could still be involved by letter, giving them more individual control over their participation. This, we (the group) decided, would facilitate a greater degree of control, and fewer risks for the in-prison mothers.

Our collective concerns (mine and the mothers'), were multiple, not least that in an interview situation in prison, women may not necessarily be permitted the freedom to leave an interview should they become upset, thus meaning they may feel compelled to stay and continue. Furthermore, many of the women admitted they 'avoided' talking about their children to each other at all while in prison, because it was 'too painful'. Additionally, "because we don't always know who has care of their children or not" (Diane). As such, mothers in prison can be wary of triggering painful and negative feelings in others, thus they stated they often didn't even speak to each other about their mothering routinely. The mothers were concerned that although mothers might seize the opportunity to talk about their children in an interview, "because as mothers, of course, we *want* to speak about children really, we often just choose not to" (Natacha), they were concerned that this might 'spiral'. Meaning the mothers may be left in a highly emotional and vulnerable state, which because of the nature of the institutions, might mean them having to deal with the 'fall out' on their own later in their rooms/cells.

Given that over 46 per cent of women in custody have previously attempted suicide (Walker and Towl, 2016), and the continued high level of self-harm in women's prisons (MoJ, 2020), this caused me great concern. I therefore decided, based on principles of ethical care, not to interview mothers in prison and to interview mothers post-release only. Thus, the mothers contributed to the design and decision making about the study – something that Aresti et al (2016) suggest occurs all too infrequently with 'convict' research participants, but which is an important part of feminist research (Oakley, 2016), and which significantly also reflected my commitment to undertake a feminist approach.

Further, I had intended simply to open the interview with one narrative-inducing question, at the outset of unstructured interviews (Creswell, 1998). However, the mothers (in the focus group) felt this would be too much, and 'too hard', stating they would feel more comfortable being asked questions. We worked together to devise a set of appropriate 'prompt' questions to use, should the participants need more structure.

Therefore, in several ways, and in line with feminist principles, as outlined by feminist research advocates (Maynard and Purvis, 1994; Renzetti, 2013), mothers and their views assisted in the shaping of the research methodology, design and its processes. Mothers in the focus groups described appreciating the opportunity to be in involved in research at an early stage, and they valued having input or 'a say' in the shape of the project. Burgess-Proctor (2015, p 125) suggests that this can be 'empowering' and so illustrating the preferred feminist 'collaborative' approach to research design. Two of the in-prison focus group members later contributed to the study by letter, and four of the community focus group members became interviewee participants. The mothers would later refer to the study as 'our' project, indicating they felt a sense of equality and ownership over the study, which again is a valued aspect of feminist research (Renzetti, 2013).

Aresti et al (2016) suggested that participants often have no presence in the final products of research, but instead are reduced to isolated quotes framed by the researchers' interpretations and analysis. However, it was important to me that the participants in my study were present in the final thesis in a more whole and visible way than merely a series of disembodied quotes, or thanks in the acknowledgements, or a table in the methodology chapter or, worse still, in the appendix. Thus, I successfully argued for the mothers to be 'introduced' prior to the findings chapters, via 'pen portraits' for each mother. These portraits, although brief, captured the essence of the women as mothers, as people, and not merely a pseudonym and a couple of static facts.

Pseudonyms were something of a contentious issue for some of the women in my study, as also found by Lockwood (2013), and discussed in Chapter 10. Several participants specifically requested to use their real names and not pseudonyms; as one mother put it, "I'm not ashamed to be me" (Kady). This presented a dilemma to me and my feminist standpoint, as someone passionate about ensuring that women's 'voices' are heard via research and, wherever possible, allowing participants to influence the research (Maynard and Purvis, 1994). However, my ethical approval clearly stated that the study would be anonymised, and that pseudonyms would be used, so on this occasion this was non-negotiable (although something I will bear in mind for future ethical applications). Clarification and reassurance were given to the participants that anonymity was not intended to render them invisible, or to silence or hide them (they were free to disclose to whomsoever they wished that they had participated in this research), but was more about protection from any adverse consequences and/or exploitation. I was clear that explicit confidentiality was a requirement/condition of my University Ethics Committee. However, to facilitate participants in feeling heard and respected, participants were given the opportunity to choose their pseudonym. One participant who had questioned the requirement for anonymity was appeased, stating: "well at least if I've chose it, it's still *my* name, and I will know it's me if I see this written anywhere won't I?" (Kady).

Other researchers, interestingly in a similar field, have described facing a similar issue and call for additional consideration of this in future research, particularly in feminist research (Lockwood, 2013). Lockwood described the use of pseudonyms, particularly for women in prison, as potentially akin to 'being heard, but remaining silent' (2013, p 120). Burgess-Proctor (2015, p 125), suggests, and I concur, that 'conventional' ethics boards and their 'conventional orientation' are often unfamiliar with the nuances of feminist research, and as such 'may actually serve to reinforce participants disempowerment'. Further, she suggests:

> 'Thus, feminist interview strategies that go beyond simply protecting participants and that instead create opportunities for participant empowerment may be especially welcome, especially for participants who are survivors of violent victimisation.' (2015, p 125)

All the interviewed participants were offered a copy of their transcripts and will be alerted to the final publication of the thesis. I would have liked to have been able to hold a dissemination event to which the participants would have been invited; however, due to the wide geographical area of my participants, this would not be practical – although again, something I will bear in mind for future research projects. I have co-presented findings and recommendations from the research with some participants at academic, practitioner and user forums, and have plans to co-write with two mothers from the study. I have maintained and demonstrated a feminist standpoint throughout the analysis and in the presentation of the thesis, and will continue to do so beyond submission.

Reflexivity and my doctoral research

As a qualified social worker and probation officer prior to becoming an academic in 2004, I had many years of experience working with mothers in social and criminal justice settings. Thus, when I chose to undertake doctoral study, I declared my chosen topic as 'obvious'. However, it was only on reading a paper written by Alison Liebling (1999), in which she stated her observation that *any* research is often driven by personal curiosity, conscious or unconscious interests, that I realised just how 'obvious'. I have described this moment as a 'light bulb' moment in my thesis. It was the exact point I recognised that my relationship with my research was much closer than I had realised. Like many mothers, motherhood is central to my world (Oakley, 1979; Rich, 1976; O'Reilly, 2006, 2016), not least because I have been a mother since I was 16. Moreover, my own childhood experience of being mothered was not a terribly positive one. So almost without noticing mothers, motherhood and mothering have been an ever-present and dominant factor in my psyche and my physical reality. Motherhood, in many ways, consumes me, so in that context, it is perhaps not surprising that it became the focus of my doctoral research. I recognised that honest, open reflexive examination would be all the more critical because of this.

There is often a discomfort about detailed reflexivity. However, feminist researchers like Burgess-Proctor (2015) argue that often that discomfort is informed by conventional and boundaried views on the researcher/researched relationship, and arguably the accepted and expected inevitable power imbalance this can assist to prevail, and that detailed reflexivity is, in fact, essential. Nonetheless, Philip and Bell (2017, p 72) have suggested that the in-depth, honest reflexivity encouraged by feminist researchers can feel 'unsettling' to some researchers and wider audiences.

Indeed, when I shared some of my lived experiences of physical and sexual abuse, violence and rape (which are also known to be common life experiences of criminalised women) as part of the live presentation session which informs this chapter, I sensed an element of that discomfort in the room. But whose discomfort was it and why? Was it out of concern for me, even though I have long since come to terms with my abusive past and was relatively comfortable disclosing this as part of my reflexivity discussion? Or was it because the 'audience' was uncomfortable, due to concerns about the appropriateness of 'professionals' being so candid about lived experiences and shared characteristics with participants? Or was it about the sharing of lived experience per se, particularly from someone not specifically commissioned to do so – that is, not a recognised 'speaker' with lived experience, but rather an academic speaking about her life?

Perhaps reflexively pushing through and examining that discomfort can contribute to positive change. It is essential, as researchers and more generally, to think about and question our feelings around disclosure and the reactions of others. I, like many (if not most) other survivors (Moor 2007), have experienced years of shame and self-blame, so the reactions of others are always important.

It is essential to consider how the reactions of others can perpetuate silence, especially to survivors of abuse, and importantly, how do we enable voice and choice instead? Why is it sometimes differently 'unsettling' or uncomfortable to hear about such experiences from 'professionals', compared with service users, invited lived experience 'speakers' or participants? The experience of sharing my experiences publicly, and perhaps especially to professional peers, made me feel vulnerable. It reminded me of my deeply embedded, long-held internal shame at having experienced them, which in turn reminded me of the inequalities and blame culture in broader society towards women as victims of all forms of abuse (why didn't she just leave, why didn't she fight, why did she wear that?). (See Chapter 4 for further discussion of shame.) It also powerfully reminded me of the vulnerability and bravery of participants who volunteer to speak about traumatic and painful events in the name of 'research'. It made me think about what a huge ask it is and what an honour it is to hear people's stories – stories that, however sensitively they are responded to, will in their telling leave participants at the least with resurfaced feelings and potentially difficult emotions that they must quash after the interview.

It also reminded me how important our immediate reactions are, how vital compassion, genuineness and kindness are, which somehow seems at odds with the often-encouraged stance of 'professional distance'. After my disclosures, I *needed* someone at that meeting to say something positive to me, to acknowledge the pain of my story and my experience, to say it was okay. Although it felt as though people present were not sure how to respond to my disclosures, thankfully that affirmation did come, and it helped. Interestingly, it came mainly from others in the room with similar lived experience (that is, those who were also 'othered'). I am very aware of how awful and empty I would have felt if no one in that room had acknowledged what a painful and risky experience it had felt to me to share my story.

From my reflections, I draw obvious comparisons with research interviews and the importance of explicitly and immediately acknowledging participants' contributions and emotions following research interviews. These were all-powerful lessons for me that I will ensure I take into my future research. I hope that by sharing them here, they will inform others pursuing similar research.

Feminist researchers suggest that unconscious 'othering' is often a feature of researcher/researched relationships, and that somehow there is perceived distance, on both 'sides', that goes beyond merely their individual roles. Yet I was very conscious throughout my research of the higher number of similarities between my participants and me than the differences, and I remember thinking that was about more than just shared experiences. Maxey (1999, p 203) regards 'critical reflexivity' as an essential process by which we, as researchers, examine not only our relationship to the research (as is a standard requirement of all research) but a deeper more nuanced and honest critical reflection of our thoughts and feelings about all aspects of the research – the topic we chose, the participants, our research relationships, power, identity and the purpose of our research.

Philip and Bell (2017, p 71) encourage the acceptance of the 'messy boundaries of research relationships' and challenge binary thinking about the researcher/researched relationship. It is, of course, always important to consider (not only in feminist research) potential harm to participants and how to mitigate any such harms that may occur, and furthermore to ensure that decisions are made sensitively and ethically.

There must be an honourable mindfulness applied to research and working with people who may be vulnerable, but also a recognition and acknowledgement of individual strength. It must be an honest, open, non-oppressive relationship, where our own and the participants' expectations are understood and spoken about. As researchers, particularly in feminist research, we need to be less afraid of sharing aspects of ourselves in the research exchange, and shying away from 'doing' out of fear of crossing boundaries (Renzetti, 2013). For example, in my research, I connected several participants with potential volunteering opportunities (one of which led eventually to employment in prison in a therapeutic peer support role). Furthermore, my work around my research expanded to the point where I became actively engaged in the pursuit of positive change, parallel to my research.

Maxey (1999) recognises this as 'research activism', which he feels is often feared and underexplored in academia, resulting in a maintenance of an academic/activist binary. Aligning himself to feminist methodology, Maxey (1999) advocates for research to become an 'ongoing process of reflection, action and reaction', thereby encouraging both reflexivity and activism in research, at individual and macro levels. Nonetheless, given that reflexivity is an essential aspect of feminist research – and arguably, all research – it remains crucial to be mindful of researcher welfare and appropriate boundaries, however flexible those boundaries may be.

Given that the focus of my study was to facilitate the voices of the mothers, not my own, it would not have been appropriate to share in-depth deeply personal details of my abusive experiences in the interviews with the mothers. However, I did share my personal self (as opposed to only my professional self) and spoke about mothering and my children and my excitement at being a new grandmother. I also answered any personal questions openly and honestly if asked, recognising that this is what I was asking of my participants. One of my supervisors commented that on listening to one recorded transcript, it felt very much "more like a conversation than an interview". My supervisor meant this as a negative, but I viewed it as a positive. I laughed, and I cried with the mothers from the research and have remained in touch with many of them. It is their stories that continue to drive me for the positive change that I have been actively seeking alongside my study.

Oakley (1979, 2016) and Abbott and Scott (2019) warn against creating 'false' friendships or making promises of ongoing contact that cannot or will not be kept. Therefore it is vital to be reflexive and genuine about our position and what we are prepared and able to commit to concerning contact after the study has completed. Nevertheless, Abbott and Scott (2019) reiterate the importance of withdrawing from research relationships which needs to be given careful and compassionate consideration. It was important to be fully open, honest and reflexive in the final product of the research. Hence, in my final thesis, I have included a chapter which situates myself to the study and the mothers, and explores the relationship between my lived experience and my feminist methodology and my relationship to the mothers themselves as participants; this is presented alongside the chapter containing the mothers' pen portraits.

My research was undertaken in the context of me having a multilayered identity as a social worker, probation officer and academic; but also as a mother and a grandmother. Furthermore, I shared many lived experiences and characteristics with my participants; all of which bore some relationship to the research. By way of illustration, I remember only too well what it feels like to be judged and othered, especially concerning motherhood. As a single teenage mother, living in poverty and on benefits, in the 1980s, Margaret Thatcher and her 'Tory' followers saw single mothers as the 'scourge' of society[6] (Kiernan et al, 1998). The media of the time was very often full of how single mothers were 'breeding' a generation of delinquents and deeming our very existence to be undermining 'traditional family values'. In true patriarchal, misogynistic style, the fault was laid squarely at the feet of the mothers, with little attention paid to the role of fathers.

This period of my life had a profound effect on me. I had been married at the time of my son's birth, but unable to wear my wedding ring due to pregnancy swelling. On admission to the labour ward, aged 16, I was offered a wedding ring by a nurse who told me "we keep a box of spare rings on the ward for girls like you"! As a new mother, I vividly remember trying to look older, to escape the judgement I felt surround me, and later wearing a wedding ring long after my divorce with the same aim in mind. I remember all too well the comments, the stares and the assumptions which accompanied my single teenage mother status. Moreover, I was embarrassed the next time I became pregnant (at 18), despite it being a planned pregnancy, and hid my pregnancy for as long as I was able.

With the benefit of hindsight, wisdom and maturity, I now recognise that I was feeling 'stigmatised', also a key finding in previous research with mothers in and after prison (Baldwin, 2017; Booth, 2017; Masson, 2019) – just one of many feelings I had in common with the mothers in the research. It was vital for me to enter into reflexive discussions with colleagues and supervisors about my relationship with the research and the mother participants; to explore my thoughts and feelings honestly in a research journal, and importantly also in the thesis, as a product of research. These conversations did not relate to methodology necessarily, but to my own lived experiences and how undertaking this research had brought many past experiences to the fore, particularly my complicated relationship with my mother, which involved separation and emotional and physical absence. I was also troubled by parallels between the mothers in prison being 'unavailable' to their children and my guilt at sometimes being 'unavailable' to my own children and grandchildren, because I was consumed by the doctorate.

This raises important questions regarding researcher welfare, which I discussed with colleagues and my fellow editors as something we don't feel is given enough consideration by the supervising institutions and perhaps by researchers themselves, when they embark on studies around potentially painful topics (or perhaps any study). Although perhaps not always directly related to the study itself, these conversations were important, not least to ensure that, as far as possible, my own beliefs and experiences did not unconsciously influence or shape my interviews, responses and analysis – and if they did, that I would be able to recognise and acknowledge this.

The reflexive discussions I held with friends, colleagues (including my fellow editors) and my supervisors were important in assisting the 'critical reflexivity' encouraged by Maxey (1999). However, also significant was the public presentation of my research and aspects of my personal reflexive journey at the Women, Family, Crime and Justice seminar. Together, they facilitated a much more comprehensive understanding and appreciation of the importance of reflexivity, especially in qualitative research. I would encourage all researchers, but especially feminist researchers, to engage in such activities and conversations (formally and informally), not only to hone and shape their reflexive skills, but also to appreciate more fully what we are asking of our participants.

Feminist principles, creative research and the Children Seen and Heard Book Project

Understanding more about the thoughts, feelings and experiences of participants is a key element of qualitative research. Traditionally, qualitative research is undertaken via a range of widely accepted data collection methodologies, for example interviews, ethnography, action research, which is then interpreted and analysed accordingly (Braun and Clarke, 2006; Bryman, 2012). However, there are many more creative and diverse means of conducting research and producing knowledge that increases understanding of an issue or experience. For example, the work of the Koestler Trust,[7] who in nurturing and producing the creative outputs of criminalised people in a variety of forms (for example poetry, pictures and sculptures), generates a level of understanding of the experiences of those in the criminal justice system to a broad audience, through galleries and exhibitions open to the public. Smith and Dean (2009, p 1) suggest that adopting creative methodologies in research can 'revolutionise academic research'.

Smith and Dean also state that in the humanities, theory, critique and traditional forms of investigation have been prioritised. However, they posit that in recent decades exploring more creative, arts or practice-based means of generating knowledge and understanding has become more acceptable to universities, arguing: 'they are as important to the generation of knowledge as more theoretically, critically or empirically based methods' (Smith and Dean, 2009, p 2). Further, they argue that what is traditionally considered 'research' is boundaried by conventional definitions about what constitutes 'research' and what constitutes 'knowledge'. It is certainly clear that anyone reading the poetry presented in 'Seen and Heard' (discussed shortly) would gain insight, knowledge and understanding about what it feels like to experience imprisonment as a parent or as a child with a parent in prison, even if only vicariously. Thus, Smith and Dean (2009, p 3) argue simply that research 'is a process which generates knowledge', and further that 'research needs to be treated, not monolithically, but as an activity which can appear in a variety of guises across the spectrum of practice and research' (Smith and Dean, 2009, p 3).

Utilising creative research can often involve broader 'audiences' in both the research experience and the dissemination of knowledge. Traditionally, academic research seeks to explore and theoretically analyse the significance of experiences and to contextualise this in broader society. However, different kinds of 'knowledge' can be produced or co-produced with research 'participants' or contributors, such as the collection described later in this chapter, which is just as valuable and effective, sometimes more so, and which can often be shared with a broader, not necessarily academic, 'audience', for example the general public, practitioners and service users.

Through a joint project with Ben Raikes,[8] underpinned by the aforementioned feminist standpoint and principles, we sought to creatively explore and understand more about the experiences of parents and children affected by imprisonment. Rather than investigating this via traditional research methods, we decided to produce a collection of poetry. The rationale behind this collection and its methodology was that we wanted the voices of the children and parents affected by imprisonment to be loud and undiluted. As Diane Curry OBE stated in the foreword of the final product of the research, a published book:

> This book is important because it gives voice to those who so often go unheard. Voices that are muffled or disguised in academic papers, policy documents or reports. Whereas this book provides a rare opportunity for voices to be heard in their purest form, untampered, raw and powerful. (Curry in Baldwin and Raikes, 2019, p xi)

We wanted to ensure that parents who were currently incarcerated as well as post-release parents were represented in the final collection. We were able to capture such experiences, and they are presented alongside poetry written by children who were experiencing – or had experienced – the imprisonment of a parent. In order to achieve this, we utilised our contacts in the United Kingdom (UK) and internationally, and were able to invite contributors directly to contribute to the collection from several prisons from England, Wales, Scotland, Ireland, the US and Canada. Submissions were also received via post/email, following poster invitations to contribute in a range of settings such as prison visiting places, prison wings and education sites, and probation offices. Our only criteria were that contributors were either a parent who was experiencing or had experienced imprisonment; and, in relation to the children, that they were experiencing or had experienced a parent in prison. We also placed advertisements inviting contributions in prison newspapers (*Inside Time* and *Jail Mail*).

We felt it was important to be physically present during the poetry collection where possible, so one or both of us travelled to several UK-based prisons, women's centres, and children's support groups to run poetry workshops. In line with good ethical and feminist practice (Maynard and Purvis, 1994), we created a safe learning space, by taking time to explain the purpose of the project and to get to know our poets. We described the publication that would result from the project, and how it had come about.[9] Group members signed release forms for their poetry, which gave permission for the poems to be published in the book and/or other resources in the future.[10] The group members were free to leave at any point or were welcome to attend but not contribute. We asked all contributors if they would prefer to use their own names (first name only), or choose a pseudonym to be published against their poem in the final publication.[11] Concerning the child contributors, we sought confirmation from parents if the children chose their own first names. Most contributors chose to use their own names (see earlier discussion and note 11). We had a prepared 'script' (slightly adapted to each group), which we went through prior to the poets signing their release forms. This script explained the project and its aims and goals and the deadlines for withdrawal of poems.

Each session evolved organically according to its context and we were responsive to this. Thus, each poetry collection session was unique but followed an essentially similar structure. We did not stipulate the age of the 'child', and so we had several submissions from young adults who were writing retrospectively through the lens of their childhood self. Poetry was collected from children under 16 during sessions also attended by staff and volunteers of the two organisations supporting them (Children Heard and Seen[12] and My Time[13]). The staff were well known to the children, and as such, the children felt comfortable with them. Contributors were encouraged to write individual poems, either alone or with one-to-one support. Group poems were created by asking contributors to supply 'one line each' under a given heading, for example 'what does it feel like to be a father in prison?'. The lines were then collated and arranged into a poem, importantly without any further words being added or deleted. Thus, all the poems are the pure, undiluted words of the poets.

Collectively, the poetry reveals much about what it feels like to experience imprisonment either from the perspective of a child at home or a parent in prison. The 'voices' and 'presence' of the contributors are presented 'centre-stage', not embedded in a research report, where they may have been reduced to a series of extracted and disembodied quotes. That is not to say that other more traditional forms of data/knowledge presentation are not valuable sources of knowledge and understanding; of course they are. Still, this project simply demonstrates that there are also alternative and creative means of generating knowledge, awareness and understanding.

The finished book or 'product of research' is now an adopted text on a number of undergraduate criminology programmes and vocational professional programmes (for example social work, midwifery, and probation) and is therefore used as a means of illustrating the impact of parental imprisonment, importantly through the direct lens of those most deeply affected. An additional, important but not necessarily expected use of the publication, is that it is now being used in prisons in group settings, as a way of encouraging other prisoners to express their feelings and emotions via poetry and/or storytelling. Some examples of the poetry collection are as follows.[14]

Poems by children affected by parental imprisonment and by parents with experience of prison

Prison I hate you (by Conrad aged 8)
Prison you keep my mum from me
You stop her from being free
I need her home I miss her so
Why can't you just let her go
I hate you prison with all your bars
I'd like to blow you up to Mars

So, tell me prison what I want to know
When oh when will you let my mum go?

Alone (by Millie aged 11)
I don't know if I love him
He made my mummy very very sad
He made me cry a lot
I was worried he would come back again
So, I didn't want to leave my mum
I couldn't do my work at school
I didn't want to go out
I was upset I was worried
I was worried all the time
I didn't like to speak to my friends
Because they didn't know how I felt
I felt very very alone.

I Miss My Mum (by Annie aged 5)
I miss my mum
that's it
The End.

That Dreaded Night (by Inistar, a post-prison mum)
The night I was arrested you bounced up and down on
my knee
With my fingers ticking your belly you laughed in glee
That wonderful moment was brought abruptly to a halt
And I now I can't blame anyone because it's all my fault
They knew you were there, but they broke down the door
Snatching you from my arms and throwing me to the floor
I was helpless when you cried and screamed in fear
They ransacked the house and did nothing but shout and sneer.

The Key (by Neil, a dad in prison)
I arrive at a wall
Walls that hold my future and the future of missing
Of missing my little girl
A little girl whose smile I will never forget.
To never forgetting the key to unlock my loving memories.
For all that is now all that I have within these walls.
A future of remembered pasts, but with a key.
A truly special key, my little girl's smile.

Rainbows and Unicorns (first verse of a group poem written by children aged 5–16)
My mind is carefree and fun
Filled with rainbows and unicorns
And wonderful things
No worrying just playing and dreaming
Of what life will bring
What could change this
And make it so bad?
Well I'll tell you
The imprisonment of my mum and dad!

Finally, one extracted verse (on being a mum in prison) of a group poem (by the MIO[15] group mums from HMP Downview). The group contributors were asked to write one line each under the verse heading, and these were then collated into a poetic order, with no words being added or removed:

Time
I'm broken, I'm helpless, I have no control
I'm sad
Desperately trying to be part of their lives
There's pain, there's worry
I feel lost, I feel I've lost my heart
I feel I've failed, I feel alone
I'm broken, I'm fighting, I realise my family is important
I'm working hard, I'm improving
I'm wiser, I'm forgiving
I'll think twice

The poems reveal so much about what it feels like to experience parental imprisonment. Arguably, the contributors have more power and control over the creation of their own poems than perhaps they might in an interview led by the researcher. The contributors all described feeling positive after the sessions, despite the sensitivity of the topic. Many described it as 'cathartic', 'a release', 'a good thing' or as something they 'needed' to do; but especially as something that had made them feel 'heard'. Such comments illustrate the success in achieving core principles of feminist research, which is to 'cause no harm' to its research participants, and to ensure wherever possible that participants also actually benefit from taking part (McCormick, 2012, p 24).

Several studies have demonstrated that arts-based projects can have a positive impact on criminalised individuals, especially in relation to mental health and empowerment, and can be a useful and innovative way to explore their experiences. Taking part in such projects can be a means of building social capital, something widely accepted as a factor in the process of desistance from crime (Maruna and Toch, 2005). Similarly, Nellis (2010) found in his arts-based research with women in prison that the women found it liberating to allow their imaginations to run free, even for a short space of time, and found that while engaged in the research one women refrained from her usual prolific self-harm. It makes sense that the evidence for the usefulness and effectiveness of arts-based activities in prison can be transferred to arts-based research. This was perfectly illustrated by one woman in Caulfield and Wilson's (2010, cited in Nugent and Loucks, 2011, p 365) music-based study, who stated: "it might not help many people long term, but for me, it was one of the best experiences of my life, and I have not had many of them".

In our project, the mothers and fathers made similar comments during and after the workshop, with several saying they had 'loved' the experience of writing and producing poetry, and that they 'couldn't wait' to share them with their children. Where possible and permitted, poets and contributors were offered a copy of the finished book, sometimes given personally by us. Seeing their poems published in the final product was a source of great pride and promoted a sense of accomplishment, as illustrated by one young woman, who had written retrospectively about her experience of parental imprisonment when she was a child: "Who would have thought it, me? A published author, I'm so proud of myself" (Toni).

Hughes (2005) suggests that arts-based projects can help disaffected young people to re-engage with education and facilitate emotional and psychological development. This was something borne out in our research project. Indeed, feedback from the poetry workshops with the children who took part was extremely positive, for example:

> 'Daniel and James found the poetry workshop extremely helpful, they both said it was a good way to get their emotions out and they have continued to write poems since that day, in fact Daniel used one for his school assignment and got an A★, he never normally even does his homework!' (Grandparent carer of boys with parents in prison)

We had the honour and pleasure of seeing some of the poets reading their own published poems, sometimes privately just between us, but also at public events. For example, some of the child poets were latterly involved in a Children's Voice event at Westminster, hosted jointly by the charity Children Heard and Seen and the My Time organisation. As part of the conference, children read out their own published poems from the book and spoke about what this meant to them. Alongside generating knowledge and understanding about their situation, the children felt 'listened to'. This gave them a sense of accomplishment and pride at their involvement in the project, and importantly in the finished product. Feedback from other organisations and individuals who had supported service users to send in poetry, informed us and shared on social media just how pleased and gratified poets were, not only to have contributed to the book but to see it published and to have the opportunity to read their words to an invited audience. Similarly, we had letters from contributors who had used their poems and the book to open conversations with their children about the experience. One mother and daughter who had never spoken about the mother's imprisonment when the daughter was a young child, yet each wrote a poem for the collection and shared their poems with each other. They both attended the launch of the book and both now speak at user forums about the harmful effects of maternal imprisonment. The examples described here illustrate our feminist research principles in action (Renzetti, 2013), which when combined with the commitment of feminist colleagues to involve service users, participants and contributors in the active pursuit of change, was extremely powerful – not least for the individuals themselves.

Recommendations

It is clear from the examples provided, again in harmony with feminist principles (Oakley, 2016), that striving to reduce power imbalance ensures that voices are present and heard in the processes and products of research, alongside creativity and reflexivity. This can not only generate knowledge and understanding, but can also facilitate inclusion and be of benefit to participants, often beyond the originally intended scope of the research.

Therefore, recommendations for undertaking ethical feminist research globally, as a minimum, would include the following:

- Consider risks to participants, by actively seeking ways to mitigate these, being mindful of the research principle of 'do no harm'.
- Consider for whose benefit you are undertaking the research – actively consider how your research will benefit your participants and/or those with shared characteristics.

- Wherever possible, involve your participants in the process and design of the research.
- Ensure that your participants are 'visible' in the final product of research and are considered in its dissemination (for example conferences and co-presenting/co-publishing).
- Engage in honest critical reflection that involves questioning your motivations for undertaking the research. Practise reflexivity throughout the process, demonstrating this in the final product of research.
- Consider creative means of generating knowledge and understanding, and how your work can reach wider and different audiences.
- Reflexively explore your positionality and privilege, and explore opportunities for research activism both within and beyond your study.

Summary and conclusion

This chapter has argued that, broadly speaking, feminist research perspectives advocate that research, particularly into women's lives, but also with other vulnerable populations (for example, prisoners and children) should only be undertaken with mindfulness of reflexivity, power imbalance, recognition, acknowledgement of differences and similarities. Further, it is argued that attention be paid to the relationship between the research(er) and the research(ed), any insider/outsider status, and the potential for activism (Maxey, 1999). The chapter echoes the arguments of Finch (1984), Letherby (2004) and Oakley (2016), who maintain that the presence of the 'personal' story of the researcher is an essential factor to consider in the accurate understanding and viewing of research, particularly in research with women. Moreover, in good feminist research, participants should be as involved as possible in the design and process of research, with full access to, and visibility in, the final products of research.

The chapter's arguments have international reach and application. It is advocated herein that knowledge, insight and understanding of a particular topic, especially those around thoughts, feelings and emotions, can be gained internationally (across cultures and language barriers) by utilising creative research.

Traditional qualitative research methods, such as interviews and questionnaires, are not the only means of gaining insight into the experiences of others. The poetry highlighted in this chapter is only one form of creative research, but one which revealed much about the experiences of children and parents affected by imprisonment.

Other creative research outputs – such as pictorial art, sculpture and music, and theatre – can equally generate insight, understanding and new knowledge about human experiences, arguably often in a more accessible way, and to a broader audience, than traditional academic research reports. Thus, this chapter advocates for increased acceptance in academia universally for more creative research methodologies and for a move to broader definitions of what constitutes knowledge.

Reflection points

- As a researcher and/or practitioner, how can you facilitate greater involvement of participants and service users, particularly in dissemination and processes of change?
- As a researcher/practitioner, how could you actively seek to reduce power imbalance with your participants/service users?
- As a researcher/practitioner, how do you demonstrate reflexivity?
- What creative means could you utilise to find out more about your particular areas of interest or practice?

Notes

[1] See reference Baldwin and Raikes (2019).
[2] Ethical approval was given from De Montfort University Faculty Research Ethics Committee and also from Women's Breakout, the umbrella organisation that oversaw 53 women's centres in the UK at that time.
[3] There were six participants in each focus group. The community focus group was recorded; the in-prison group was not, but copious notes were taken during and after the session. The participants were (in prison) Natacha, Diane, Adrienne, Zoe, Charlie and Fran; the community members were Dee, Cynthia, Tamika, Jaspreet, Connie and Jenny.
[4] Women's prisons are not categorised in the same way as the male estate, but they are simply 'open' or 'closed'. Women's movement is much freer in open establishments, with some prisons having free unescorted movement between blocks at certain times of day.
[5] In many (closed) prisons, women are escorted round the prison by officers and would not be allowed simply to return to their cells/rooms independently.
[6] For example, see http://news.bbc.co.uk/1/hi/uk/197963.stm:'Mrs Thatcher said: "It is far better to put these children in the hands of a very good religious organisation, and the mother as well, so that they will be brought up with family values"'. She told an audience in the Commonwealth Convention Centre in Louisville that the spread of illegitimacy "devalues our values, our community".
[7] The Koestler Trust, a UK-based charity working with those in the criminal justice system to produce art with a view to supporting those affected by the criminal justice system to lead more positive lives and to generate understanding of their experiences: https://www.koestlerarts.org.uk/
[8] Senior Lecturer in Social Work at the University of Huddersfield.

[9]   The project was kindly part-funded by Lady Edwina Grosvenor and Waterside Publications, following a request made by Lucy Baldwin.

[10] We were advised that ethical approval was not required for a 'poetry' book, but Ben and I are both qualified social workers and so are bound by social work codes of ethics and consider ourselves to be ethical researchers/practitioners.

[11] As we were not bound by an ethics board, we were able to facilitate the use of first names only (in line with our social work and feminist ethical principles). We ensured that there would be 'no harm' caused by using own names and that confidentiality was still preserved with no additional identifying factors present.

[12] Children Heard and Seen, a charity supporting children and families affected by parental imprisonment: https://childrenheardandseen.co.uk/

[13] My Time, a Liverpool-based organisation supporting children with a parent in prison: https://www.themytimeproject.com/ (for support, email info@ themytimeproject.com)

[14] Permission to reproduce the poems from the original publication was sought and granted by Waterside Press (see also note 1).

[15] Mothers Inside Out, a prison-based mothers programme, designed to support maternal identity and emotion and to help prepare for release; developed by the author, now delivered by Pact across the female estate (see also Chapter 6).

References

Abbott, L. and Scott, T. (2019) 'Reflections on researcher departure: closure of prison relationships in ethnographic research', *Nursing Ethics*, 26(5): 1424–41.

Aresti, A., Darke, S. and Manlow, D. (2016) 'Bridging the gap: giving public voice to prisoners and former prisoners through research activism', *Prison Service Journal*, 224: 3–13.

Baldwin, L. (2015) *Mothering Justice: Working with Mothers in Social & Criminal Justice Settings*, Sherfield on Lodden: Waterside Press.

Baldwin, L. (2017) 'Tainted love: the impact of prison on mothering identity explored via mothers' post-prison reflections', *Prison Service Journal*, September, 233: 28–34.

Baldwin, L. (forthcoming) 'Motherhood challenged; a study exploring the persistent pains of maternal imprisonment' (ongoing PhD thesis), De Montfort University, Leicester.

Baldwin, L. and Raikes, B. (2019) *Seen and Heard: 100 Poems by Parents and Children Affected by Imprisonment*, Sherfield on Lodden, Hampshire: Waterside Press.

Booth, N. (2017) 'Maternal imprisonment: a family sentence', in J. Hudson, C. Needham and E. Heins (eds) *Social Policy Review 29: Analysis and Debate in Social Policy*, Bristol: Policy Press and Social Policy Association, pp 105–26.

Bozkurt, S. and Aresti, A. (2018) 'Absent voices: experiencing prison life from both sides of the fence – a Turkish female's perspective', *Journal of Prisoners on Prisons*, 27: 17–26.

Braun, V. and Clarke, V. (2006) 'Using thematic analysis in psychology', *Qualitative Research in Psychology*, 3(2): 77–101.

Bryman, A. (2012) *Social Research Methods* (4th edn), Oxford: Open University Press.

Burgess-Proctor A. (2015) 'Methodological and ethical issues in feminist research with abused women: reflections on participants' vulnerability and empowerment', *Women's Studies International Forum*, 48: 124–34.

Creswell, J. W. (1998) *Qualitative Inquiry and Research Design: Choosing Among Five Traditions*, London: Sage.

Doucet, A. (1998) 'Interpreting mother-work: linking ontology, theory, methodology and personal biography', *Canadian Woman Studies*, 18: 52–58.

Doucet, A. and Mauthner, N. (2006) 'Feminist methodologies and epistemologies', in C. D. Bryant and D. L. Peck (eds) *Handbook of 21st Century Sociology*, Thousand Oaks, CA: Sage, pp 26–32.

Finch, J. (1984) '"It's great to have someone to talk to": the ethics and politics of interviewing women', in C. Bell and H. Roberts (eds) *Social Researching: Politics, Problems, Practice*, London: Routledge and Kegan Paul, pp 70–87.

Gelsthorpe, L. (1990) 'Feminist methodologies in criminology: a new approach or old wine in new bottles?', in L. Gelsthorpe and A. Morris (eds) *Feminist Perspectives in Criminology*, Buckingham: Open University Press, pp 89–106.

Harding, S. (1987) 'Is there a feminist method?', in S. Harding (ed) *Feminism and Methodology: Social Science Issues*, Bloomington: Indiana University Press, pp 1–14.

Hughes, J. (2005) *Doing the Arts Justice: A Review of Research Literature, Practice and Theory*, London: Department for Culture, Media and Sport.

Kiernan, K., Land, H. and Lewis, J. E. (1998) *Lone Motherhood in Twentieth-Century Britain: From Footnote to Front Page*, Oxford: Oxford University Press.

Landsdown, G. (2010) 'The realisation of children's participation rights: critical reflections', in B. Percy-Smith, N. P. Thomas, C. O'Kane and A. T-D. Imoh (eds) *A Handbook of Children and Young People's Participation*, London: Routledge, pp 11–24.

Letherby, G. (2004) 'Quoting and counting: an autobiographical response to Oakley', *Sociology*, 38(1): 175–89.

Liebling, A. (1999) 'Doing prison research: breaking the silence', *Theoretical Criminology* 3(2): 147–173.

Lockwood, K. (2013) *Mothering from the Inside: Narratives of Motherhood and Imprisonment*, (doctoral dissertation) University of Huddersfield.

Maruna, S. and Toch, H. (2005) 'The impact of imprisonment on the desistance process', in J. Travis and C. Visher (eds) *Prisoner Reentry and Crime in America*, Cambridge: Cambridge University Press, pp 139–78.

Masson, I. (2019) *Incarcerating Motherhood: The Enduring Harms of First Short Prison Sentences on Mothers*, Abingdon: Routledge.

Maynard, M. and Purvis, J. (1994) *Researching Women's Lives from a Feminist Perspective*, London: Taylor & Francis.

Maxey, I. (1999) *Beyond Boundaries? Activism, Academia, Reflexivity and Research*, The Royal Geographical Society, JSTOR, 31(3): 199–208.

McCormick, M. (2012) 'Feminist research ethics, informed consent, and potential harms,' *The Hilltop Review*, 6(1), Article 5.

Merriam, S. B. (1988) *Case Study Research in Education: A Qualitative Approach*, San Francisco: Jossey-Bass.

Minkler, M. and Wallerstein, N. (2003) *Community-Based Participatory Research for Health*, San Francisco: Jossey-Bass.

Ministry of Justice (2020) Safety in Custody Statistics: Self-harm Annual Tables, 2004–2019, London: Ministry of Justice.

Moor, A. (2007) 'When recounting the traumatic memories is not enough: treating persistent self-devaluation associated with rape and victim-blaming rape myths', *Women & Therapy*, 30(1–2): 19–33.

Nellis, M. (2010) 'Creative arts and the cultural politics of penal reform: the early years of the Barlinnie Special Unit, 1973–1981', *Journal of Scottish Criminal Justice Studies*, 20: 1–19.

Nencel, L. (2014) 'Situating reflexivity: voices, positionalities and representations in feminist ethnographic texts', *Women's Studies International Forum*, 43: 75–83.

Nugent, B. and Louks, N. (2011) 'The arts and prisoners; experiences of creative rehabilitation', *The Howard Journal*, 50(4): 356–70.

Oakley, A. (1979) *Becoming a Mother*, London: Martin Robertson.

Oakley, A. (1981) 'Interviewing women: a contradiction in terms', in H. Roberts (ed) *Doing Feminist Research*, London: Routledge and Kegan Paul, pp 30–61.

Oakley, A. (2016) 'Interviewing women again: power, time and the gift', *Sociology*, 50(1): 195–213.

O'Reilly, A. (2006) *Rocking the Cradle: Thoughts on Motherhood, Feminism and the Possibility of Empowered Mothering*, Ontario: Demeter Press.

O'Reilly, A. (2016) *Matricentric Feminism, Theory, Activism and Practice*, Ontario: Demeter Press.

Philip, G. and Bell, L. (2017) 'Thinking critically about rapport and collusion in feminist research: relationships, contexts and ethical practice', *Women's Studies International Forum*, 61: 71–74.

Pillow, W. (2003) 'Confession, catharsis, or cure? Rethinking the uses of reflexivity as methodological power in qualitative research', *International Journal of Qualitative Studies in Education*, 16(2): 175–196.

Reinharz, S. (1993) 'Neglected voices and excessive demands in feminist research', *Qualitative Sociology*, 16(1): 69–76.

Renzetti, C. M. (2013) *Feminist Criminology*, Abingdon: Routledge.

Rich, A. (1995 [1976]) *Of Woman Born: Motherhood as Experience and Institution*, London: Virago.

Smith, H. and Dean, R. T. (eds) (2009) *Practice Led Research, Research-led Practice in the Creative Arts*, Edinburgh: Edinburgh University Press.

Stanley, L. and Wise, S. (1983) *Breaking Out: Feminist Consciousness and Feminist Research*, Boston, MA: Routledge & Kegan Paul.

Wahidin, A. (2004) *Older Women in the Criminal Justice System: Running Out of Time*, London: Jessica Kingsley.

Walker, T. and Towl, G. (2016) *Preventing Self Injury and Suicide in Women's Prisons*, Sherfield on Lodden: Waterside Press.

10

Service users being used: thoughts to the research community

Michaela Booth and Paula Harriott

Introduction

The pains of imprisonment are well documented by researchers. As far back as 1862, depictions of women in prison were dominated by portrayals of weak and vulnerable individuals such as Mayhew's (in Zedner, 1998, p 298): 'In them one sees the most hideous picture of all human weakness'.

The pains of women's imprisonment, looking at the contemporaneous and longitudinal (through the lens of largely negative) impact on their health and wellbeing, their family life, their mothering identity, stigma and relationships are rich areas of academic research. Thus, women who have experienced the criminal justice system are much sought after as research participants. We start this contribution with a direct question to the research community. Where are the authored pieces of research by those who have lived it? Indeed, where are the co-authored pieces with you? We would ask you to pause and reflect before reading on.

As two women with the lived experience of being both in prison, and being former participants in various research projects, four times respectively, we intend in this contribution to shine a light on the lived experience of being researched, examining researcher–participant relationships, power, purpose, ownership and ethics. In doing so, we raise questions over the equity and ethicality of research with criminalised women. This contribution delves into our concerns that women's collective and personal experiences of pain are often subjected to being used, manipulated and repackaged – often without our direct knowledge and indeed without actual real consent – mostly leaving marginal benefit and minimal impact on the actual lives of the criminalised women themselves nor on the wider structural conditions under which we labour.

The intention for this contribution is to lean back into our positions as research subjects and to reflect on the impact of these experiences, on our lived, living and real lives. It is through reflection, collectively and individually, that we continue to develop our understanding about the radical and humanistic changes needed to ensure safe, reciprocal and useful participation – participation which more often than not positions us (the community of the researched) as 'useful' for a limited time, and results in reputational development for academic institutions and individual validity for the researcher. As part of this process, the researched are left behind as a footnote; 'with thanks to our participants'.

We are mindful of contributing our experiences with integrity, which requires us to remain sensitive to researcher experiences and practice. We must also bear in mind the changes we want to establish in researcher/subject dynamics. This requires a truthful and in-depth recollection of our involvement in research, as criminalised women subjects. However, the intention here is not calling out researchers for individual failings. If we are to change the frameworks underpinning research production, delivery and evaluation, we must unite, reflect and learn together. As such, we are committed to remaining truthful but sensitive in our approach to reflecting on our experiences as the researched.

We seek to understand what and whose endeavour are we actually participating in, and what control do we exert over the final product? Who owns and profits from the knowledge that is co-produced through user involvement in research? Whose voices and views are privileged in the discourse? How can researchers act with personal integrity when considering research proposals that attend to questions of impact for social change and social good? How honest, or thoughtful, are researchers, about the assumptions that underpin their work and any theory of change that may exist or not, to justify the research in the first place? How is this conveyed to women being researched?

In all of our experiences as research participants, we have only twice had a conversation with a researcher about how they have considered this piece of work to be fundamental to our social emancipation, and the role the research will play in ameliorating and challenging our social conditions, setting out a theoretical basis for our proposed relationship. In fact, except on these two occasions, that critical component – that ought surely to form part of 'informed consent' – has not been communicated to us. Importantly, too, we also did not ask. Why was that? As participants at that time, we too could not identify any connection between research and tangible social change.

For there to be such an odd disconnect between research and change, in our experience as activists and as the researched, is now very worrying. It is a weird vacuum to uncover that is symptomatic of a depoliticisation of the research process and its engagement with participants broadly. We acknowledge the existence of gatekeepers, however we would argue that this apolitical vacuum is even more concerning when looking at women's issues, by women researchers who undoubtedly must have been exposed in their lives to the impact of patriarchy. Why is this, especially in work with communities of women led by women researchers? Have we all forgotten, or not been taught, that the 'personal is political'? In the need to stay within the parameters of the research process, to satisfy the gatekeepers, have researchers constrained themselves to the role of mere bystanders in the process of meaningful social change?

Maybe the writings of Audre Lorde (1984), and her speech 'The Master's Tools will never dismantle the Masters House', ought to be essential pre-reading for all researchers seeking to do research with women in the criminal justice system:

> Those of us who stand outside the circle of this society's definition of acceptable women; those of us who have been forged in the crucibles of difference; those of us who are poor, who are Black, who are lesbians, who are older, know that survival is not an academic skill. It is learning how to stand alone, unpopular and sometimes reviled, and how to make common cause with those identified as outside the structures in order to define and seek a world in which we can all flourish. It is learning to take our differences and make them strengths. For the masters tools will never dismantle the master's house. (Lorde, 1984, p 112)

As early as 1967, Martin Luther King addressed the Conference on Social Change and the role of behavioural scientists, calling for the involvement of social scientists in social issues (American Psychological Association, 2020):

> 'We do not ask you to march by our sides, though as citizens you are free to do so. Rather we ask you to focus on the fresh social issues of our day, to move from observation of operant learning, the psychology of risk, to the test tubes of Watts, Harlem, Selma and Bogalusa. We ask you to make society's problems your laboratory. We ask you to translate

your data into direction, – direction for action.' (cited in Noffke, 1997, p 305)

Ethics and informed consent

Ethics are central to the research process. As professionals now, we know that you have written in your ethics submissions about how you, the researchers, intend to safeguard us, research participants, in the process. You would not 'get through' ethics unless you had. You accept the potential for harm and write, as standard, in your ethics application about how support for any potential retraumatisation is in place. However, do you write about the continued trauma of leaving us where you find us without a plan of how your research will aid us by radically changing our material conditions or wider societal conditions?

We would argue that research cannot – and should not – exist without ethical consideration of how any change in our lives more widely, as a consequence of the research, is considered to occur. You accept there is a risk of retraumatisation, yet do you give space to the risk of your non-action, of intellectual stagnation, of trauma tourism? Our position is this: unless researchers consider why they want to investigate our lives for our benefit – and if they cannot be sure that it is because, beyond the research, they can see a strategy for bringing about change in our communities for good – then do not do it. Instead, if you are concerned, focus on activism, become an activist-scholar and leave your voyeurism at the gates of the prison. Or, as Martin Luther King says, join us as allies and march side by side, cite our writings, invite us into your spaces, privilege our voices, refuse to sit on panels without us, if we are to be discussed. Write to us, send your research reports to us, share with us, and support us to learn and to lead. Campaign with us, be prepared to feel with us.

Paula Harriott (co-author of this chapter) recollects a positive experience with a researcher:

> 'I went to her house to do the interview, she did not present as a researcher, just as a curious person. And caring. We ate food, she told me about the research and why she wanted to write it. I met her family, I met her daughter, I saw her as a genuine person. I felt comfortable, I think she assumed I didn't want to be named, but suggested I use a name I chose. I chose my second name. I came to the launch of the research, I have co-presented about the research at conferences. I have stayed in touch with her.'

As co-author of this thought piece, Michaela Booth leans into her experience as a researcher for her undergraduate degree, in which criminalised women were research subjects, including Paula. Extracted from her study, Michaela (2019) evidenced how she created a study framework that enabled a reciprocal relationship with the participants, showing authenticity in her understanding of the consequences of their lived experiences:

> In the research project design, purposeful attention was paid to ensuring a damaging narrative of women who have experienced imprisonment was absent from the proposal. As Tuck (2009) notes, research that focuses on deficits and vulnerability help to reinforce and sustain helplessness. Further, in the creation of a pre-screen questionnaire and interview schedule, participants were not asked to disclose their convictions. The nature of conviction was considered irrelevant for this project as the research is underpinned by relational desistance theory (Nugent and Schinkel, 2016) whereby recognition of identity change is accepted and reinforced by others. Moreover, the absence of mandatory offence disclosure for participation was to mitigate participant harm and consequential maladaptive coping mechanisms due to perceived stigma. As Winnick and Bodkin (2008) assert, individuals who have ascribed stigmatised labels may self-isolate or withdraw as a form of protection against stigmatisation from others.

In her attempt to move away from research which positions criminalised women's lives as by-products of law, order and control, Michaela's research was designed to explore how women with histories of state punishment and patriarchal oppression navigate their lived experiences to assert their power and identity as organisational leaders of change. As such, it focused on female strength, resilience and professional identity, as opposed to a study regurgitating the prescribed rhetoric of criminalised woman as damaged and vulnerable.

As a research participant in Michaela's (2019) study, Paula wrote:

> A great afternoon, pure joy. She asked clever probing knowledgeable questions that pushed me deep inside because she had thought about it too and was living it too. We pushed each other. It wasn't about damage; it was about desire for change. It was about what was before us not behind us, still

acknowledging what was behind us, but with a vision for what we can do and have done. It was about our strength. She smiled, she engaged, she encouraged. She wrote to me several times afterwards telling what an immense session it had been. I felt strong as I left her company after the session. I knew she knew the foundations, so we could go deep, I felt safe to be me and I found more of me in the research process. We discussed what the research was finding out and what we could do with it and discussed plans for maximising impact. It was always we.

We do not doubt that many research programmes are well intentioned, but we wonder why ethics applications do not, as a central concern, discuss the tension between examining misery and damage (the misery memoirs) and its juxtaposition with healing and social justice. We seriously question why some researchers seem not to consider the impact of labelling us as disadvantaged and vulnerable in their writings about us, and how that might also act to retraumatise us. How many times have we sat on panels, in meetings and heard our community discussed with this overarching label that reduces us to a singular identity? How can we manage to escape this labelling to move to agency when we too live in society and absorb this label (Boppre and Reed, 2020) which forms the public discourse about us? Do you not discuss this risk in your ethics applications? As participants in various research endeavours, and as criminalised women, not only do we *know* *and understand* the negative impact of our prescribed deviant labels. We *feel* that impact, sometimes forever.

Research studies have wider implications than a final grade of a master's or doctorate. Those wider implications, however, are directed at us, your subjects. So, when your next proposal is being drafted or you are packing up your office to move on to a promoted role, we are fighting for equality in the workplace, trying to prove that your vulnerable and damaged portrayal of us, is one dimensional and not the full picture. When you are taking your well-deserved holiday after submission, we are still undeserving of visas to travel to the US, or restricted through licence conditions from travel, or having to fight for acceptance as a student at the very universities where you work. When your study is over, our lives are still real – the real lives that you failed to capture in your data analysis and conclusion, because knowing that reality (and founding the research in understanding of systemic inequality and patriarchy, and intersectionality), requires you to see it and feel it too, and amend your work to reflect this in its fullness.

We wonder how and why, especially when it is well intentioned and with a view to reducing marginality, do research and academia reserve their position as guardians of thought, and place research participants in the margins, replicating the very marginalisation that they seek to shine a spotlight on? As researchers, we respect you as co-constructors of knowledge production (Finlay, 2002). However, the marked absence of space and recognition for criminalised women to actively and visibly contribute to knowledge production within the discipline is an issue worthy of debate, as Belknap (2015) suggests: 'A significant part of Criminology activism is broadening the diversity of criminologists to provide a lens that more accurately reflects what we study'. In the majority of our experience, our support and involvement in the co-construction of knowledge through research participation have been mostly invisible. Only twice in the experiences of being researched have we been sent a copy of the final report, or invited to a launch event, or even invited to co-present the research we have undertaken with a research team. This dissonance is not lost in translation for the researched, even if it is for the researcher. Paula recollects:

> 'I thought it was weird at the time that they were talking about how they wanted to raise up our voices, but then years later I read on the internet the research and I appeared in the final paper as Participant A, they might as well have used my prison number, and I was equally powerless in the end.'

We want, in this thought piece, as women activists, to let you know that reliance on process alone can obfuscate feeling. It is delving into feelings and deep personal reflection on lived experiences of power, privilege and oppression that will add to, not detract from, process. The 'rigour' of your research process feels often like the emperor's new clothes; you are naked to us in your bias, your privilege, your extraction and your ignorance of our actual emancipatory needs. You see us as 'others' and examine us as such, when we are women living in oppression and patriarchy, just like you, yet you cannot feel that. We ask you to recognise our absence, which is not really absence. See our invisibility within the academy, which is not really invisibility. We wonder whether, with your own grants, do you make space for criminalised women to co-construct knowledge alongside you? Do you question and challenge the lack of opportunity and funding for criminalised women to enter into the spaces where their data and lives are under analysis? We endorse Belknap's (2015, p 4) assertion that 'criminologists have a heightened responsibility for activism', given the attribution earned personally and institutionally from research conducted with those who face a multitude of oppression and lack opportunity for visibility, in your co-construction of knowledge.

We see our lack of visibility as violent practice. Research on violence has already identified that the act of imprisonment leads us to direct victimisation of systemically violent practices (Zizek, 2009). As researchers in academia, have your ethics applications ever identified how you will negate systemically violent practices in data collection, analysis and dissemination? The World Health Organization (2002, p 4) defines violence as:

> The intentional use of force or power, threatened or actual, against oneself, another person, or against a group or community, that either results in or has a high likelihood of resulting in injury, death, psychological harm, maldevelopment, or deprivation.

If you are using your positions of *power* as a research community, against a *group or community that results in deprivation*, then your approach adopts a systemically violent approach. If your language is oppressive, you are depriving us through the consequences of stigma. How many times have you referred to us as 'female offenders'? If your ethical permissions rely on participant anonymity without choice, you are depriving us of contributing to knowledge production. Furthermore, as you identify the need to 'give voice to' under-researched groups in your project pursuit, and use pseudonyms and letters in place of our names, the only person benefiting from voice in your project is yourself. If your data collection practices rely on utilising 'lived experience teams' through organisations who make a living through their damaged-centred lens (Tuck, 2009), you are contributing to our deprivation from the labour market, as many of the participants who attend will be paid a minimal fee or given Love2shop vouchers, while the organisers will be drawing a salary.

Power in the research relationship

One of the first acts of the Cuban Revolution was the literacy campaign, which subsequently developed into a global adult literacy campaign, known by its Spanish name, Yo, Sí Puedo (Yes, I Can). Castro and the Communist revolutionaries understood clearly that the challenge the revolution would face was immense, and political education of the citizenship was the first line of defence. For Castro, education was the gateway to understanding, to critical analysis, to liberation from dominant ideologies, to creating new understandings, social emancipation, challenge and resistance to power and its misuse (Kozol, 1978). This sat alongside his commitment to universal literacy as a fundamental human right (Gonzalez et al, 2012). Castro was not alone in this belief in mass literacy as a liberationist act; it was shared by many anti-colonialist leaders of the 20th century, who believed that mass adult education was essential to develop the values and skills base needed to chart an alternative development path to capitalism (Youngman, 1986). For those (un)educated researchers, let us teach you. Exclusion from mass literacy, anti-oppressive teaching and experiences of anti-oppressive research practice, are simply another means of maintenance of oppression.

Speaking from our experiences as women in the criminal justice system, our interaction with academia has not been, in the main (leaving British convict criminology and feminist-informed experiences to one side) as co-recipients of knowledge sharing, as recipients of an approach that understands the need to lend us space to learn as a means to social emancipation, as co-investigators, of academia in assistance as allies in the endeavour to support us to self-educate and to teach and lead. Our experiences have not been of support to build, via the research process and outcomes, the capacity to self-advocate, to self-organise, to drive forward the debate about the vision for criminal justice. Our interaction with academia, as individuals within the system, has, in the first instance, been about pure and power-laden 'expert' extraction of knowledge. You ask us, we tell you; our identity and role as mere lived experience of the topic under review, our lives reduced to snippets of anonymous quotes used to build a premise, a position. It acts as an assertion of the researcher's 'expert' view. Our experiences are not foreign to us, they constitute our norm; it is academia that is educated through extraction of our experience, and it is academia that mainly benefits from it. Researchers do not teach us through these interactions of being researched, that which we do not know. Mostly they do not even deign to inform us of what they have concluded from what they have extracted from us. Reflecting on the two times we have been sent copies of the research to which we have contributed, we now know that we have been slighted when we have not received copies, and that is being polite. We have actually been exploited. This, then, clearly was not a relationship based in mutuality and reciprocity; and we would ask the research community to deeply reflect on this point in their 'ethics' applications and future practice.

To reinforce: it is academia that learns that which it did not know from us. Researchers reinforce the gulf between us, merely by asking us to respond to questions which demonstrate the gaping holes in understanding. We are reduced through this to being cogs in the wheel that turns extraction into polished research papers from 'experts' in our experience. Researchers turn up in prison with preconceived research agendas, methodologies, ethics permissions, information sheets, consent forms, interview templates; they extract from us and disappear. We disappear too in their writings, turning up only as Participant A, or Participant B, or as Lived Experience teams, or Lived Experience participants. Academia, in its processes of research and research behaviours, does not liberate us. It constrains us, anonymises us, magnifies our misery and generally fails to have any significant emancipatory and anti-oppressive impact on us, neither as individuals nor as communities.

As women who have been researched, we have come to understand that it is we who must learn to navigate and contend with the hidden discussion about power – power in society and its connection to our condition, and power as exercised in the relationship with the researchers who come to us seeking our involvement. We know this from years of lived and real oppression, from observation about power, with experiences in the misuse of power, in infringements of our community, individual and embodied spaces by those systems and individuals who hold power over us. From the moment you (we), as a prisoner, are told to submit to a full body search, there is a reality to conversations about how power manifests. We are frustrated with approaches that focus on individual deficits and avoid discussion with us about systemic power and inequality. We learn this in prison, with its focus on individual culpability, with no reference to the societal conditions that drive many of us into the system. In this sense, education is liberation, just as Freire (1970, p 30) said: 'only as they (the oppressed) discover themselves to be "hosts" of the oppressor can they themselves contribute to the midwifery of their liberating pedagogy'.

Your questions are almost always about us as individuals, and rarely about how the system affects us. If you asked us (taught us) to think about systems and how they affect us, then that, at least, would be a contribution to our liberation. (What is it about the jam jar that makes it difficult to open? Not why can you not open the jam jar?) If researchers feel comfortable doing this individualised and misery-memoir research in the flawed belief that those in power will feel empathy and shift thinking and resources as a consequence, then they themselves need educating about systemic economic inequality and the casualties of the class system. The system is not broken, it is working perfectly fine for those for whom it works. Waiting on power to concede power feels like a Disney fantasy. As in *The Matrix* films, you need to take the blue pill and wake up. These are the dreams of those who have not experienced the full force of judgement and malevolence handed down to those with criminal convictions, reduced as we are to numbers not names in our journey through the criminal justice system. Do not continue to think we do not resist, we do not fight for our space in all of our interactions. Our resistance is sometimes subtle, nuanced, often barely visible, and sometimes clear to see in our activism, sometimes in our non-engagement, but there nonetheless.

We have learned that we can assume a degree of power within the research process in both overt and covert ways. People often label our behaviours as manipulative, when we try to claim power. Sometimes we subvert the research process through fantasy responses, untruths or duplicity, seeking either to please or exploit, and sometimes we use the time offered within the research interview to speak, to enjoy ourselves, to explore ourselves:

> Participating in a research project mitigated that. The reason for this is that the research relationship, when done properly (with concern, humanity, interest, honesty), *requires* you to be the person you are. Not what the prison wants you to be, not the person you were, but the person you are. The researcher wants to know what *you* think, what *you* feel, what *you* have to say. They do not want the simulacrum. They want the honest you. This is what I, and other prisoners, got out of participating in that study: a return to some semblance of personhood – even if only for a fragment of our time. That was precious. (Warr, 2018)

Failure on the part of the researcher to craft the conditions of concern, humanity, interest and honesty will leave the research interview prone to emptiness. We speak different languages, learned through different life experiences. We live daily the inequalities of the class division that are often neatly sidestepped in the researcher–participant relationship by the researcher who shares little of themselves while expecting and urging soul-bearing, heart-wrenching exploration of damage. The pretence at objectivity by researchers is rapidly understood by us as disdain or, even worse, a blatant ignorance hidden but permeating through the façade of academic objectivity. Paula recollects participating previously in research about the experiences of women in prison, where she took part to educate the researcher about the assumptions and correct language throughout: "I started and then I couldn't continue, as I witnessed her naivety and youth; I didn't need to use the space to talk about me, so I converted that space to teach her about her". Michaela, too, recollects a recent experience, in which she was sought to help direct various research projects aimed at 'helping' prisoners:

'I attended under the pretence of using my professional and lived experience to support the direction of new policies and projects aimed at improving prison conditions. As I began conversing with researchers it seems obvious to me that the projects had already been signed and sealed, just not delivered. It quickly became apparent that I was not there to help the direction of the projects, but simply to tick a box to say that a person with lived experience had been consulted. Although, I wasn't consulted, I was just read a pre-existing proposal. A proposal, which for the main, was not up for amendment because any amendments were, "outside of the researchers remit". I remember being asked if I thought prisoners learned helplessness through the prison environment not offering choice, and if so, did I think that a proposal promoting digital technology would help to reinstate personal ownership in prison. I shudder as I think about this, and my response to the question was simply a reiteration that the previous year a mother had given birth in a cell on her own, and her baby died in her arms. Let's be very clear, a tablet in a cell which lets someone choose their meals and book a visit, is not a systemic change that will positively impact on a woman's life when she is calling for assistance from a cell bell whilst in labour, and being ignored. Learned helplessness as a theory is reliant on individuals not seeking help due to past experiences in which they have learned that help will not come. The women who gave birth alone, was seeking help. Her help seeking was ignored. Therefore, if learned helplessness is a result of the prison environment, then the issue is with services and resources not providing help. And, if the issue is with services and resources not providing help then I cannot fathom at all how a proposal underpinned by views of prisoners as "learned helpless" would suggest that in-cell technology offering "choice" could support prisoners to move away from their helpless state. For me, this was an issue of blindness and ignorance to wider and systemic issues of health inequality, austerity, and theories of retributive punishment prioritised over a rehabilitative culture, where support is offered to those who seek it. My observations about the flawed understanding of the theory underpinning the proposal was met with disinterest, and my explanation about wider issues was met with blank stares.'

Researchers must take part in the relationship with participants with a deep consideration of the self; the self they are bringing to the relationship. If you want real from us, then you must lead with real: who are you, how many children do you have, what do you feel about imprisonment, what are your views on drugs? How ready are you to learn from us and change your practice and thought process? How will this aid us? In healthy relationships, would we not share of ourselves freely, if we did not have an idea of the person to whom we are speaking? Paula recollects a good experience in prison, taking part in a study on health inequalities:

'I remember the kindness of the researcher, I witnessed it in the extra steps she took to go beyond the scope of the research, She told me about her life, why she was involved in the work. I was worried about my weight; she weighed me, she looked through my medical records and she came to find me in my cell and let me have my weight on arrival in the prison so I could track it. She responded to my needs, not just me hers. She bought in biscuits and cake, she asked us what we wanted her to bring in and brought it. I don't really remember the actual research, but I remember her authenticity, her commitment to acknowledging us. She gave me her contact details to stay in touch afterwards. When I saw her again in my professional work ten years later I was pleased to see her. When in prison as invisible, you always remember those that saw you, who acted with humanity and circumvented process to reach you.'

Please do not confuse our readiness to take part with a real notion of informed consent. What do we know of consent under the conditions we are experiencing in prison? Imprisoned women are conditioned/ coerced to share the most demeaning experiences as a matter of norm in sentence planning, parole reports, meetings with 'helping' professionals. So, if a researcher wants to demonstrate anti-oppressive practice, then please acknowledge the need to present with a critical awareness of these conditions in the relationship and to acknowledge them with us.

Learning the language to speak of oppression, to the oppressor as the oppressed is not easy. How many times have we heard talk of 'offender health' of 'female offenders', of 'manipulation', of 'drug addicts' – our lives described with loaded assumptions that can either drive sympathy or disdain. Casual conversations where you *lead* with our offence; but deep down, believe us, we are nothing but incredibly offended and sometimes diminished. We know the wealth and depth of our life histories, but we are reduced to a singular identity through use of language such as this. And you harm us now and in the future by so doing. As eloquently explained by Tran et al (2018, p 1), your words matter to our lives:

> stigma can be enacted and reinforced through labelling. Such labelling can drive the stereotyping, prejudice, and discrimination of groups of people, such as individuals involved in the criminal justice system who are often denounced as being responsible for their incarceration. As a result, those in the criminal justice system are excluded from social and economic resources and services that ultimately affect their health and wellbeing. Therefore, language used to describe individuals and populations, either respectful or stigmatizing, matters and shapes people's views and understanding of past and present events, as well as future possibilities.

From our experience, wresting back control of the process and exerting influence on the outcomes, lies in command of the language of the oppressor. It is the first rule of the 'game': understanding how the oppressor communicates and controls. Without command of this language we can only intuit, but we cannot influence nor lead a movement. Language opens up the will to reformulating lived experience into a coherent and communicable wisdom that acts to bolster resistance and open up both desire and vision for change. How can we ever break the chains of damage-focused research, if we cannot find a way to vocalise its impact, in a language and an environment where our voices will be heard and understood? Simply, we cannot.

The purpose of research: damage or desire?

We query the notion of damage-based research acting to liberate communities from subjugation to inequalities in power, whether that is political, social or economic. What do we mean by damage-based research? We mean research that examines mainly pain and marginalisation (Tuck, 2009). Researchers, if they are even thinking of the purpose of the research at the macro level, operate, we assume, from the presumption that by raising awareness of the pain, those in power will act to remedy the inequity, pain and trauma. However, in this instance, from our perspective, this appears to advance from distorted presumptions about how real, sustainable social change occurs.

If we look back over the history of social change, we see the galvanising of lived experience leadership and the building of social movements that aid, assist and create momentum for the wider movement of social change. The Civil Rights movement led by black leaders, the right for women to vote led by women, the rights of the LGBTQ+ movement led by the LGBTQ+ community. Resistance from the frontline is critical in this process. These critical resistances of the frontline are embodied by those with the actual lived experience, who come to see that power needs to be directly challenged and thus lead as active agents/actors of change. This power to act comes not from an identity of damage, but one that harnesses the deep wisdom that emerges from reflection on the multiple learnings that emerge from experiences of oppression. With survival comes strength, and the acknowledgement of these strengths is the prerequisite for personal and social change. But often, within research parameters, researchers focus on damage at the expense of strength, connecting us – as women with the lived experience – with a label of pain, distress and vulnerability that compounds the structural and institutional damage already excercised against us.

Michaela's personal experience of research participation depicts how her criminalised identity dominated her involvement in a research project:

> 'I was involved in a research project which involved the being filmed. A family member was participating in the project and when filming, the family member was asked to drive a member of the research team's car as opposed to their own car. This was due to "perceptions" of criminalised women and their family, as the car the family member owned did not fit with the preconceived perceptions of the research audience. As told by the researcher when the request was made.'

Michaela's ability to lean back into her lived experience of participation, enables her to provide a reflective account of how the experience enhanced her learning and understanding of damage-centred research. On reflection, she asserts:

'at the time, the request from the research team was granted and the family member was filmed in the research team member's car. My position as a participant in the project was voluntary and I was informed of my right to withdraw at any time. If I had of known then what I know now, I wouldn't have withdrawn from participation in the study. I would have utilised the experience to talk about why and how, that request is damaging and oppressive practice. However, at that time I didn't know it was damaging and I didn't know it was oppressive. What I now know, through academic study, professional experience and personal development is that by granting the car swap request, both the research team and I fed into the rhetoric of criminalised women and their families as undeserving. We undermined and ignored the family member's hard work in obtaining the capital to purchase a nice car and told them, they can't be seen to have that capital in this research project. Because, families of criminalised women don't have those things. Moreover, the research audience wouldn't have been as susceptible to influence of criminalised women's hardship, if they witnessed a family member driving a nice car. Can women who have been criminalised and imprisoned, not still face a multitude of hardship, oppression and victimisation if a family member has a nice car? In this instance, the views of the research team and anticipated views of the research audience were prioritised over a truthful account of my lived and living experience. I had the opportunity to resist this but I lacked the knowledge in understanding the wider harm and impact, at that time. As such, the research team owned and exerted the power in the researcher/researched dynamic. That power was harmfully displayed, positioning my family member as an underserving owner of a nice car. Due to their relationship to me, as a criminalised women. This led to my participation in the research being controlled to fit the narrative of criminalised women and their families as vulnerable, poor and undeserving.'

Stepping into our identities as research subjects, recalling experiences which have been dominated by expressing our pain, misery and brokenness to fit a preconceived narrative is painful for us, and reduces our duality of strength and fragility to a prewritten script that fits, but does not challenge. Surely all research needs to be ground-breaking, not replication of pre-existing knowledge repackaged to look new. For both of us, living as criminalised women in the system, we know that 'if we always do what we always did, we will always get what we always got!' Understanding that deeply is what has pushed us forward as we seek both personal and systemic change. Reliving painful experiences is not helpful, in the main, to anyone who has lived it, other than within a therapeutic and caring relationship of duration. We can only examine these experiences in such settings and conditions, as we move through them to positions of synthesis and freshly connected positions of strength. In this way, we lean into our lived experiences, to extrapolate that which heals and activates change. Sandhu (2017) calls this activation of lived experience for social purpose.

Researchers seeking to understand women in the system ought themselves to have a deep and self-connected sense of social purpose – a vision of what works to create change – and be able to demonstrate that theory of change both in their ethics applications and, equally importantly, to their chosen communities of interest, before commencing research activities with such communities. Imagine how collaborative such work might be – and how the notion of 'informed consent' is deepened, strengthened and authenticated – by such a mutual and reciprocal deliberation. Herein lies allyship. Without this being clearly understood and emerging in anti-oppressive practice and methodologies, sadly most research continues to reflect the institutional oppression of our community, without even acknowledging it. Your fascination with damage, even well intentioned, hurts us more, disconnecting us even more from an identity as worthy, respected leaders of change with vision and desire for change, to helpless and vulnerable. Even in our darkest moments we never saw nor believed in our own survival as evidence of our vulnerability. Our fragility was always laced with strength.

For those who are the researched communities, we must begin with asserting our positions as autonomous agents, with ownership over our lives, our deficits, our strengths. We must learn to resist research that is not founded in liberation ideologies, but here is a thought: ethics applications to research us are decided on through the National Research Council by the very system that imprisons us. The prisons decide, as our gatekeepers, the nature of the research to which we are invited as anonymous participants. We wonder why that conundrum does not exist as an ethical conflict in ethics applications. Yet, more importantly, we need to take ownership of our life experiences (you call them stories as if they are fantasy), and explore them in the words, and using methodologies, that we choose to tell them. As our history tells us, participating in research has often ended in our experiences being negated, or assimilated to fulfil political, professional and personal endeavours which research subjects are often not aware of – endeavours that detail and sustain our outsider status.

Importantly, our contribution to this debate is not solely about surrendering to or resisting that status. We seek a vital role in examining the practices and procedures which would end the production and sustaining of invisibility and voicelessness through participation. In doing so, we aim to build an allyship and collective movement – a movement that can inclusively and collaboratively re-envision co-production, participation and research that is framed through an alternative lens. A lens which does not *only* position criminalised women as helpless, as vulnerable, as broken, but which also supports our liberation to lead our community away from such patriarchal and oppressive labelling and experiences.

Conclusion

Sharing this thought piece is a plea from our hearts and from our hard-won human wisdom as those who have lived the experiences about which you are curious. We exhort you to dwell on the points we have made and move forward in learning, as we have done and continue to do so. We honour the elders in learning who have gone before and we build on their contribution, looking to a future where our capacity to lead change, our opportunities to write for ourselves about ourselves are maximised and through true allyship with research – a time when we are no longer the 'sister outsiders'.

To that end, we cordially invite you to reflect critically on the paradigmatic, prescriptive and casual assumptions that inform how you practice (Brookfield, 2009). We offer you room in our space to learn, as together we seek to rectify our one-dimensional depiction in research and together develop a more sophisticated, innovative and ground-breaking analysis of the conditions we find ourselves experiencing and the way to challenge them.

Reflection points

- Why are you interested in research with criminalised women?
- What impact do you envisage your work might have?

- How will this happen? Does this link to a theory of change?
- Are you an impartial observer of social injustice, or are you working as a researcher activist?

References

American Psychological Association (2020) *King's Challenge to the Nation's Social Scientists.* Available at: https://www.apa.org/monitor/features/king-challenge. Accessed: 3 April 2020.

Belknap, J. (2015) 'Activist criminology: criminologists' responsibility to advocate for social and legal justice', *American Society of Criminology*, 53(1): 1–22, doi: 11.1111/1754–9125.12063.

Booth, M. (2019) *Exploring the Experiences of Criminalised Women in Leadership Roles Within the Criminal Justice Sector: Are the Bars Ever Truly Removed?* (Unpublished BA, independent study), University of Worcester.

Boppre, B. and Reed, M. S. (2020) '"I'm not a number, I'm a human being": a phenomenological study of women's responses to labeling', *Feminist Criminology*, 1(25), doi:10.1177/1557085120953488.

Brookfield, S. D. (2009) 'Engaging critical reflection in corporate America', in J. Mezirow, E. W. Taylor and associates (eds), *Transforming Learning in Practice: Insights from Community, Workplace and Higher Education*, San Francisco: Jossey Bass, pp 125–36.

Finlay, L. (2002) 'Negotiating the swamp: the opportunity and challenges of reflexivity in research practice', *Qualitative Research*, 2(2): 209–30.

Freire, P. (1970) *Pedagogy of the Oppressed.* Available at: https://www.transcend.org/tms/wp-content/uploads/2018/05/Paulo-Freire-pedagogy-of-the-oppressed.pdf. Accessed: 4 April 2020.

Gonzalez, J. C., Hickling-Hudson, A. and Lehr, S. (2012) 'Challenging educational underdevelopment: the Cuban solidarity approach as a model of south-south cooperation', in A. Hickling-Hudson, J. C. Gonzalez and R. Preston (eds), *The Capacity to Share: A study of Cuba's International Cooperation in Educational Development*, New York: Palgrave Macmillan, pp 35–52.

Kozol, J. (1978) *Children of the Revolution: A Yankee Teacher in the Cuban Schools*, New York: Dell.

Lorde, A. (1984) 'The master's tools will never dismantle the master's house', *Sister Outsider: Essays and Speeches*, Berkeley, CA: Crossing Press, pp 110–14. Available at: https://collectiveliberation.org/wp-content/uploads/2013/01/Lorde_The_Masters_Tools.pdf. Accessed: 3 April 2020.

Noffke, S. E. (1997) 'Professional, personal, and political dimensions of action research', *Review of Research in Education*, 22: 305–43. Available at: www.jstor.org/stable/1167378. Accessed: 7 April 2020.

Nugent, B. and Schinkel, M. (2016) 'The pains of desistance', *Criminology and Criminal Justice*, 16(5): 568–84 Available at: https://doi.org/10.1177/1748895816634812. Accessed: 7 April 2020.

Sandhu, B. (2017) *The Value of Lived Experience in Social Change: The Need for Leadership and Organizational Development in the Social Sector.* Available at: https://scottishrecoveryconsortium.org/wp-content/uploads/2020/04/the-lived-experience-baljeet-sandhu-vle-full-report-1.pdf. Accessed: 1 April 2021.

Tran, N. T., Baggio, S., Dawson, A., O'Moore, É., Williams, B., Bedell, P., Simon, O., Scholten, W., Getaz, L. and Wolff, H. (2018) 'Words matter: a call for humanizing and respectful language to describe people who experience incarceration', *BMC International Health and Human Rights*, 18(41), doi:10.1186/s12914-018-0180-4.

Tuck, E. (2009) 'Suspending damage: a letter to communities', *Harvard Educational Review*, 79(3): 409–28.

Warr, J. (2018) *Quid Pro Quo in Prison Research.* Available at: https://www.compen.crim.cam.ac.uk/Blog/blog-pages-full-versions/blog-18-jasonwarr. Accessed: 4 April 2020.

Winnick, T. A. and Bodkin, M. (2008) 'Anticipated stigma and stigma management among those to be labeled "ex-con"', *Deviant Behavior*, 29(4): 295–333, doi:10.1080/01639620701588081.

World Health Organization (2002) *World Report on Violence and Health.* Available at: https://www.who.int/violence_injury_prevention/violence/world_report/en/summary_en.pdf. Accessed: 4 April 2020.

Youngman, F. (1986) *Adult Education and Socialist Pedagogy*, London: Routledge.

Zedner, L. (1998) 'Wayward sisters', in N. Morris and D. Rothman (eds) *The Oxford History of the Prison*, Oxford: Oxford University Press, pp 295–325.

Zizek, S. (2009) *Violence*, London: Profile Books.

11

Continuing the conversation: reflections from the Women, Family, Crime and Justice network

Lucy Baldwin, Isla Masson and Natalie Booth

Women and families have diverse experiences of criminal and social justice. We are proud that the Women, Family, Crime and Justice (WFCJ) research network has provided a platform to share knowledge and experiences towards tackling some of the enduring challenges associated with this. The collection of works presented powerfully symbolises the original aims of the network, when launched in 2018 to bring together practitioners, those with lived experience, external agencies, service users, academics and researchers, in a safe, supportive, non-judgemental, egalitarian forum. We sought to facilitate the coming together of similarly focused individuals, all connected in one way or another by a shared passion for criminal and social injustice. We hope that the discussions presented in this text provide a valuable point of reference to inspire action for all these communities.

Since our launch, we have hosted a veritable plethora of amazing speakers in our quarterly seminar series sessions. All of the speakers have shared their work and experiences to audiences eager to hear and to learn. The conversations, debates and discussions in the seminars, much like the chapters in this collection, have been stimulating, fascinating, sometimes challenging and/or painful, but always informative. This critical collection seeks to broaden the reach of the network by sharing some of the presentations in written form with a wider audience.

The introduction reiterated the WFCJ research network's commitment to facilitating and influencing positive change via sharing of knowledge, critically exploring and informing research and policy, informing and collaborating with practitioners, and dissemination and publication. This collection contributes to meeting those commitments.

Additionally, we share a commitment to feminist principles of equality and reflexivity, and this is also returned in the chapters present herein. Notwithstanding the diversity of the chapters, there were a number of recurring themes across the chapters. These included: stigma and shame; power, equality and agency; access to appropriate services and failure to meet needs; and family and relationships.

Stigma and shame

Most of the chapters alluded in some way to the importance of shame and/or stigma. Nicola (Chapter 2) spoke of how the women in her research became labelled, tainted and criminalised from the moment they were deemed 'deviant' or law breakers. Similarly, Isla (Chapter 5), Erin (Chapter 6), Anna J (Chapter 7) and Anna K (Chapter 8) highlighted how the shadow of stigma and shame often felt by criminalised people, but especially prisoners, also falls onto families. This is taken further by Anna J (Chapter 7), Anna K (Chapter 8) and Lucy (Chapter 9), who detailed how children of prisoners can become stigmatised and where and how this can manifest. Erin's chapter (Chapter 6) explored how the vital work of family engagement workers can help to mitigate some of the secondary harms experienced by children and families of prisoners, and joins Isla (Chapter 5) in examining the ways in which prisons can actively seek to reduce this secondary stigma; for example, by ensuring that visits are as open and child and family friendly as it is possible to be inside a prison.

Other chapters, like Zinthiya and Isla's (Chapter 3), Alex, Kirsty and Rose's (Chapter 4), Lucy's (Chapter 9) and Michaela and Paula's (Chapter 10) highlighted the relationship between lived experience and shame, exploring how women, who are victims of abuse and trauma, are often 'othered', and sometimes feel somehow responsible for the negative and abusive experiences meted out to them (whether that abuse and trauma originates from cultural, societal, individual or criminal justice sources).

Together these chapters gave a convincing account of how a perceived sense of shame, often alongside external judgement, creates additional barriers to seeking appropriate and positive support. Common to all of the chapters in the collection was a sense that any deviation from the 'norm' and/or contact with criminal and social justice systems can result in painful feelings of shame and stigma, which has a 'knock-on' effect in terms of individual or collective agency and power. As such, this collection of work as a whole provides a convincing argument for the importance of considering the role of shame in all of our own work, and how it is vital that practitioners make steps to eradicate shame, if they want to provide appropriate and meaningful support.

Power, equality and agency

Many of the chapters described situations where a lack of equality, agency or power was a feature, whether that be in relationships, in access to goods and services, or in experiences. The issue of power – or rather women's' lack of power – featured heavily in many of the chapters. Through the incredibly painful and powerful accounts of the women in their research, Zinthiya and Isla (Chapter 3) highlighted the ongoing challenges for South Asian women to navigate through a cultural heritage in which they have traditionally had little by way of equality and power, while also living in contemporary British society (supposedly more equitable). A recurring feature in the edited collection was how little power many of the participants in the research perceived themselves to hold. Chapter 3 explored the internal and external barriers women face in accessing support, highlighting alongside other chapters, the limited access to appropriate and tailored resources, necessary to address some of the issues raised, which was mirrored in other chapters.

What is clear across these and other chapters, and again in line with existing literature, is the significance of gender, power and equality in relation to agency (McNay, 2013), especially for people affected by criminal and social justice systems (Howe, 1994). Several chapters highlighted how negative life experiences can contribute to a perceived or very real reduction in agency. This in turn serves as a great reminder of the importance of informed, gender-specific responses and services, such as those highlighted across many chapters, for example in Nicola's (Chapter 2), Alex, Kirsty and Rose's (Chapter 4), Isla's (Chapter 5) and Erin's (Chapter 6).

Lucy's chapter (Chapter 9) and Michaela and Paula's chapter (Chapter 10) are almost two sides of the same coin, with Lucy exploring reflexively her experience of feminist research, and Michaela and Paula exploring their experiences of being researched. Both chapters highlighted the importance of the relationship between the researcher and the researched; incidentally also mirroring Nicola's (Chapter 2), Zinthiya and Isla's (Chapter 3) and Alex, Kirsty and Rose's (Chapter 4) chapters, which also highlighted the importance of the relationship between service user and practitioner.

Access to appropriate services and failure to meet needs

All of the chapters herein, in one way or another, identified ways in which some of the harms of imprisonment and/or criminalisation can be mitigated. Erin (Chapter 6), Anna J (Chapter 7) and Anna K (Chapter 8) focused specifically on the impact of imprisonment on families, often children, separated from loved ones. They collectively revealed current gaps in services and missed opportunities to support families more effectively (Beresford, 2018; Booth, 2020). Isla (Chapter 5) reiterated the significant impact of maternal imprisonment and highlighted that had women been more appropriately responded to on reception into the criminal justice system, they may have avoided custody and the subsequent pains of their imprisonment altogether.

Many of these chapters echo previous research, which has argued that appropriate 'wrap around' tailored support for women who do end up in custody is essential in the post-release period (Leverentz, 2014). Nicola (Chapter 2), however, questions the appropriateness of some existing community resources, and explores innovative, responsive and flexible means of engaging with women serving a community sentence. Nicola (Chapter 2), Alex, Kirsty and Rose (Chapter 4) and Zinthiya and Isla (Chapter 3) all emphasised the importance of really understanding the women's experiences and needs, in order to provide appropriate and effective support.

Furthermore, a message coming through strongly from all of the chapters, was the need for user-led, strengths-based, trauma-informed models of working and researching with women and families in contact with the criminal and social justice systems. All too often, the complexities of the lives of people in the 'systems' have been ignored, misunderstood or rendered irrelevant to the present. It is only in more recent years that criminal and social justice in the UK has begun to appreciate the strengths of a trauma-informed approach. Covington (2007, 2008a) and Covington and Bloom (2008b) have long argued for gender-specific, holistic models of working with women that consider and address women's lived experiences of trauma, which sadly is all too common in the histories of women who enter the criminal justice system.

Since 2015, the Ministry of Justice has sought to ensure, via the 'One Small Thing' project[1] (led by Lady Edwina Grosvenor and Dr Stephanie Covington), that prisons are 'trauma informed', and officers are 'trained' in the trauma-informed approach and practice. Alex, Kirsty and Rose (Chapter 4) reiterated the importance of a trauma-informed approach to working with women, and advanced our understanding of its application to women with sex-working histories. They, like Nicola (Chapter 2), Lucy (Chapter 9) and Michaela and Paula (Chapter 10), highlighted the importance of relationships and 'connection' between practitioners and researchers working with criminalised women and the women themselves.

Family and relationships

The English poet John Donne (1624) said 'no man [or woman] is an island' – interactions and relationships with others are an inevitable and essential feature of life. When a mother or a father enters the criminal or social justice systems, there are many relationships that will also be touched by their reach. As this collection has highlighted, children and families are particularly affected by the imprisonment of a loved one, especially when the loved one is a parent (Codd, 2008 ; Baldwin, 2015; Beresford, 2018; Masson, 2019; Booth, 2020).

Several chapters highlighted the shortcomings in criminal and social justice responses, demonstrating the repeated failure to adequately meet the needs of criminalised women and their children. Isla's chapter (Chapter 5) identified the disproportionate harm caused to women and their children even by first short periods in custody, and how the effects of those pains extend beyond the reach of prison. Alongside others in the collection, this chapter echoes previous research in highlighting the often traumatic historical experiences of women (Carlen and Worrall, 2004), thereby contributing to a robust argument to significantly reduce or abolish custodial sentences for people with dependent children (Baldwin and Epstein, 2017; Minson, 2018; Joint Committee on Human Rights, 2019).

Anna J (Chapter 7), Anna K (Chapter 8) and Lucy (Chapter 9) all also explored more deeply the significant impact of imprisonment on children and their lives. Erin's chapter (Chapter 6) highlighted the important role of family engagement services in working with imprisoned women and their families to mitigate some of the harms of maternal imprisonment and to secure the best outcomes possible. However, Nicola (Chapter 2) highlighted how even in women who are not imprisoned, simply being drawn into the criminal justice system has an impact on women and their children, and she encourages the development of creative, gender-specific, responsive means of women to explore their experiences and their relationships. This is also echoed in Zinthiya and Isla's (Chapter 3), and Alex, Kirsty and Rose's (Chapter 4) chapters.

Concluding thoughts

The themes highlighted throughout this collection, while representing diverse experiences and approaches from different perspectives, are all consistent in their call for serious action. The WFCJ network clearly has many long-standing issues to tackle and these themes act as a powerful reminder of our priorities. We hope that you, the readers, have found this an interesting and insightful collection, and that this inspires you to join us in tackling these individual, societal and structural issues. As the network continues to grow and incites greater action, we will continue to reflect on these themes as central to our mission.

Although all of the chapters have been written by women, we are all very different in our makeup, our backgrounds, our histories and our lived experiences. To a greater or lesser extent, we are all products of our histories, but we in the network – practitioners, policy makers, academics and service users – all share a responsibility and commitment to deeply examine our thoughts, feelings, values and beliefs, and to reflect on how they might interact with our work and with our actions. We must ask ourselves uncomfortable questions: are we guilty of holding any stereotypical or uninformed beliefs, even to some extent? In all likelihood, we are. Perhaps it is inevitable in a society where discrimination, racism, sexism, ableism and homophobia are sadly commonplace and deeply and insidiously influential. Nonetheless, the challenge for us *all* is to explore our flaws and our prejudices openly and honestly, to be willing to accept that we may have them, regardless of whether we are conscious of them or not.

While we are hopeful that we can work towards betterment, and shall endeavour to do so in an inclusive, collaborative and reflective manner, systemic and ongoing injustices continue to manifest in new and ever more painful ways. The tragic, unlawful killing/murder of George Floyd,[2] has proven to be a powerful reminder for us all to examine our deeply held beliefs about race; but more than that, to examine privilege more widely and to examine its legacy genuinely, candidly and transparently. Although our speakers in the seminars have been from diverse backgrounds, as is our membership, diversity can refer to many different qualities. We acknowledge that the collection could be more representative. We will candidly reflect on how we can better engage ethnic minorities communities in our network to facilitate voice, equality and representation in subsequent collections and to expand our actions beyond acknowledgement. Nonetheless, this collection challenges the reader to consider privilege beyond that related to whiteness, but also to consider privilege related to class, to status, to power, and to lived experience and gender.

We hope that this collection encourages researchers and practitioners to be willing to examine their own privileges and how this interacts with their research and practice. It is inspiring to see so many diverse people of all generations engaging with the Black Lives Matter protests, and it is the hope that these powerful advocates may also become engaged in WFCJ issues. Similarly, we hope that this text stands as a message to research participants and service users to listen to their own voices too; to challenge and question what feels uncomfortable, and to seize and recognise their power, where perhaps it has previously felt out of reach.

In working together, we seek to drive action to support and improve justice for all communities. As such, we were saddened to see the recent Ministry of Justice announcement that the current Conservative government intends to build more prisons[3], and with the addition of hundreds more cells in women's prisons.[4] This is despite decades of evidence revealing community sentences to be a more effective and less damaging response to criminalised behaviour, but also importantly a significantly more successful means of rehabilitation. Both Farmer Reviews[5] sought to encourage the strengthening of family ties for prisoners, to reduce intergenerational offending. However, research has clearly demonstrated that the most effective means of reducing intergenerational offending is to address social injustice, by addressing poverty and inequality, to rejuvenate and invest in communities, and to abolish short prison sentences for non-violent crimes, thereby reducing factors which contribute to high levels of imprisonment in the first instance, and which particularly impact on women.

Collectively the chapters herein highlight the frequency with which women are structurally, emotionally and physically challenged (Renzetti, 2013). One way or another, many of the women and families featured in the chapters of the collection, have experienced marginalisation, stigma, poverty, powerlessness, limited access to appropriate resources, trauma and abuse. Nevertheless, although perhaps not explicitly stated, but so powerfully demonstrated in this collection, is the resilience and strength of those in the face of such adversity. The women, the service users, the families, but also the practitioners and the researchers undertaking their ground-breaking and powerful work with women, reveal their strength, spirit and determination to be their best selves and/to support others to do the same.

We hope that in facilitating the voices of those researching, working within, and directly experiencing the decisions made in criminal and social justice, that the WFCJ research network can improve the likelihood of meaningful improvements to these systems. We will continue to reflect on the themes of stigma, power, needs and relationships, and evaluate our success as a network based on the changes made to them.

We want to thank our authors for their contributions which we, as editors, have enjoyed, reflected upon and learned from. However, we also want to take the opportunity to thank the participants who took part in their research. We acknowledge the participants' contribution and know without question that some of the changes we are seeking, as researchers and activists, would be impossible without them. We are eternally grateful for their bravery in contributing to these studies and others like them.

In this collection, we highlight the often awful experiences of real people – people forced to engage in the services described herein by their experiences, often because of failure. This is not failure on the part of the individuals, but instead, a collective failure of society to value or appropriately support individuals through trauma, adversity and/ or inequality. We believe that for true progress to be made in *criminal* justice, there must first be progress in *social* justice. Therefore, we end this collection, a united celebration of feminist voices, with a call to arms, a request for others to join us in challenging inequality in society, and to commit to seeking to elevate and promote the voices of all women and families negatively affected by criminal and social injustice.

Notes

1   One Small Thing is a registered charity devoted to creating efficacy and cultural change within the criminal justice system. The charity provides training for frontline staff, to enable a greater understanding of the pervasive impact of trauma. See: https://onesmallthing.org.uk/about

2   George Floyd, a black male, was arrested and died under police restraint in America. Mr Floyd's death triggered a worldwide call to actively challenge racism and to consider white privilege.

3   On 11 August 2019 and reiterated 28 June 2020: https://www.gov.uk/ government/news/10-000-extra-prison-places-to-keep-the-public-safe and https://corporatewatch.org/newprisons/

4   Recent plans to increase female estate: https://www.theguardian.com/ society/2021/jan/23/ministers-criticised-for-plans-to-create-500-new-uk-prison-places-for-women

5   Female-focused Farmer Review (June 2019). Available at: https://assets.publishing. service.gov.uk/government/uploads/system/uploads/attachment_data/file/ 809467/farmer-review-women.PDF. Accessed: 19 June 2019; male-focused Farmer Review (August 2017). Available at: https://assets.publishing.service.gov. uk/government/uploads/system/uploads/attachment_data/file/642244/farmer-review-report.pdf. Accessed: September 2017.

References

Baldwin, L. (2015) *Mothering Justice: Working with Mothers in Social and Criminal Justice Settings*, East Sussex: Waterside Press.

Baldwin, L. and Epstein, R. (2017) *Short But Not Sweet: A Study of the Impact of Short Sentences on Mothers and their Children*. Available at: https://www.dora.dmu.ac.uk/bitstream/handle/2086/14301. Accessed: 11 December 2020.

Beresford, S. (2018) *What About Me? The Impact on Children When Mothers Are Involved in the Criminal Justice System*. Available at: http://www.prisonreformtrust.org.uk/portals/0/documents/what%20about%20me.pdf. Accessed: 14 May 2019.

Booth, N. (2020) *Maternal Imprisonment and Family Life: From the Caregiver's Perspective*, Bristol: Policy Press.

Carlen, P. and Worrall, A. (2004) *Analysing Women's Imprisonment*, Devon: Willan.

Codd, H. (2008) *In the Shadow of Prison: Families, Imprisonment and Criminal Justice*, Devon: Willan.

Covington, S. S. (2007) *Women and Addiction: A Gender-Responsive Approach*, Clinical Innovator's Series, Center City, MN: Hazelden.

Covington, S. S. (2008a) 'Women and addiction: a trauma-informed approach', *Journal of Psychoactive Drugs*, 40(5): 377–85.

Covington, S. S. and Bloom, B. E. (2008b) 'Gender-responsive treatment and services in correctional settings', *Women and Therapy*, 29(3): 9–33.

Howe, A. (1994) *Punish and Critique: Towards a Feminist Analysis of Penality*, London: Routledge.

Joint Committee on Human Rights (2019) *The Right to Family Life: Children Whose Mothers are in Prison*. Available at: https://publications.parliament.uk/pa/jt201719/jtselect/jtrights/1610/report-files/161007.htm#footnote-059. Accessed: 21 May 2020.

Leverentz, A. (2014) *The Ex-Prisoner's Dilemma: How Women Negotiate Competing Narratives of Reentry and Desistance*, New Jersey: Rutgers University Press.

Masson, I. (2019) *Incarcerating Motherhood: The Enduring Harms of First Short Periods of Imprisonment on Mothers*, Abingdon: Routledge.

McNay, L. (2013) *Gender and Agency: Reconfiguring the Subject in Feminist and Social Theory*, Cambridge: Polity Press.

Minson, S. (2018) 'Direct harms and social consequences: an analysis of the impact of maternal imprisonment on dependent children in England and Wales', *Criminology and Criminal Justice*, 19(5): 1–18.

Renzetti, C. M. (2013) *Feminist Criminology*, Abingdon: Routledge.

Index